"Twenty-volume folios will never make a revolution. It's the little pocket pamphlets that are to be feared."
Voltaire

THE FIELD NOTES SERIES

On Risk
Mark Kingwell

On Property
Rinaldo Walcott

On Decline
Andrew Potter

On the Origin of the Deadliest Pandemic in 100 Years
Elaine Dewar

On Browsing
Jason Guriel

On Writing and Failure
Stephen Marche

On Class
Deborah Dundas

On Community
Casey Plett

On Book Banning
Ira Wells

On Oil
Don Gillmor

On Sports
David Macfarlane

On Treason
Patrick Lennox

PATRICK LENNOX

On Treason

Alberta Separatism, Foreign Interference, and Canada's Survival in a Revolutionary Age

BIBLIOASIS
Windsor, Ontario

FIRST EDITION
10 9 8 7 6 5 4 3 2 1

Library and Archives Canada Cataloguing in Publication
Title: On treason : Alberta separatism, foreign Interference, and Canada's survival in a revolutionary age / Patrick Lennox.
Names: Lennox, Patrick, author
Series: Field notes (Biblioasis) ; #12.
Description: Series statement: Field notes ; #12
Identifiers: Canadiana (print) 20260201197 | Canadiana (ebook) 2026020126X ISBN 9781771967709 (softcover) | ISBN 9781771967716 (EPUB)
Subjects: LCSH: Referendum—Alberta. | LCSH: Alberta—History—Autonomy and independence movements. | LCSH: Foreign interference in elections—Canada.
Classification: LCC JF497.C34 L46 2026 | DDC 328.27123—dc23

Edited by Daniel Wells
Copyedited by Jill Ainsley
Cover and text designed by Ingrid Paulson
Cover photos: eagle, ©iStockPhoto/Serjio74; flag of Alberta ©iStockPhoto/ Marvin Samuel Tolentino Pineda

Published with the generous assistance of the Canada Council for the Arts, which last year invested $153 million to bring the arts to Canadians throughout the country, and the financial support of the Government of Canada. Biblioasis also acknowledges the support of the Ontario Arts Council (OAC), an agency of the Government of Ontario, which last year funded 1,709 individual artists and 1,078 organizations in 204 communities across Ontario, for a total of $52.1 million, and the contribution of the Government of Ontario through the Ontario Book Publishing Tax Credit and Ontario Creates.

PRINTED AND BOUND IN THE UNITED STATES OF AMERICA

PATRICK LENNOX

On Treason

Alberta Separatism, Foreign Interference, and Canada's Survival in a Revolutionary Age

BIBLIOASIS

Windsor, Ontario

FIRST EDITION
10 9 8 7 6 5 4 3 2 1

Library and Archives Canada Cataloguing in Publication
Title: On treason : Alberta separatism, foreign Interference, and Canada's survival in a revolutionary age / Patrick Lennox.
Names: Lennox, Patrick, author
Series: Field notes (Biblioasis) ; #12.
Description: Series statement: Field notes ; #12
Identifiers: Canadiana (print) 20260201197 | Canadiana (ebook) 2026020126X
ISBN 9781771967709 (softcover) | ISBN 9781771967716 (EPUB)
Subjects: LCSH: Referendum—Alberta. | LCSH: Alberta—History—Autonomy and independence movements. | LCSH: Foreign interference in elections—Canada.
Classification: LCC JF497.C34 L46 2026 | DDC 328.27123—dc23

Edited by Daniel Wells
Copyedited by Jill Ainsley
Cover and text designed by Ingrid Paulson
Cover photos: eagle, ©iStockPhoto/Serjio74; flag of Alberta ©iStockPhoto/Marvin Samuel Tolentino Pineda

Canada Council for the Arts | Conseil des Arts du Canada
Ontario Arts Council | Conseil des arts de l'Ontario
Ontario
Canada
Ontario Creates | Ontario Créatif

Published with the generous assistance of the Canada Council for the Arts, which last year invested $153 million to bring the arts to Canadians throughout the country, and the financial support of the Government of Canada. Biblioasis also acknowledges the support of the Ontario Arts Council (OAC), an agency of the Government of Ontario, which last year funded 1,709 individual artists and 1,078 organizations in 204 communities across Ontario, for a total of $52.1 million, and the contribution of the Government of Ontario through the Ontario Book Publishing Tax Credit and Ontario Creates.

PRINTED AND BOUND IN THE UNITED STATES OF AMERICA

For my sons

Contents

PART 1: INTRODUCTION

1: The Paradox of Tolerance

"At one point toleration would destroy society; at another, persecution is fatal to liberty."
Lord Acton

ALBERTA WILL HOLD a referendum on October 19. The government has determined of its own volition to put ten questions to the electorate. Each question, in its own way, seeks to undermine the very idea of Canada at a moment of great national peril. The first five questions deal with matters of immigration, a matter of federal jurisdiction. The next four deal with constitutional issues, which the province of Alberta has no power to change on its own. The last is a question about whether Alberta should even be part of Canada at all. The real question, however, is why such plebiscites are happening in the first place; now, at this revolutionary moment in history.

The entire scenario is bewildering, especially to those outside of Alberta who have yet to come to terms with the nature of the government that has taken power in the province.

There is the sense that this can't possibly be happening out in the Wild West. That a vote to secede won't happen, in fact. That the status quo will prevail because it always has and that's the way it needs to be. Especially now. The impulse to survive, the impulse to unify and pull together under external threat, is unquestionably the expected one in this moment.[1] It is natural to believe that this impulse will overcome its contradiction, the impulse to fracture. It must, and therefore we can look away now, shift our focus. There remain many other pressing matters with which we must deal, and such a distraction surely cannot be our collective undoing.

There's no indication from the polls—present or historical—of even a remote possibility that a clear majority will vote in favour of Alberta leaving Canada and becoming an independent state. The courts have ruled the separatist petition question unconstitutional. They have ruled that Elections Alberta failed in its duty to consult First Nations, who would inevitably be affected by the consideration of the separatists' fractious question. And even though the provincial government has chosen to disregard the court rulings and pursue the question through an executive order, and even if by some turn of fate a majority votes in favour of separation, then surely the Clarity Act and the constitution and the rest of Canada will present such obstacles that eventually the whole enterprise of Alberta secession will collapse under its own inflated weight. Surely.

Except that logic chain is anchored in status quo concepts of the rule of law prevailing; of our constitution holding firm; of peace, order, and good government holding sway through all of this; and in the increasingly contestable belief that our democratic processes and our cognitive sovereignty are in fact our own and not subject to destabilizing, disorienting, and ultimately debilitating forms of foreign interference[2] levelled at us by the usual suspects, one ominously unusual one, and sometimes all in combination, on American platforms, guided by American algorithms, and accelerated by American artificial intelligence.[3]

Why, we ask, is such a "very dangerous bluff"[4]—as Prime Minister Carney described it—being made now?

AS I WRITE this book from my home in Edmonton, Alberta, in the weeks prior to a potentially fateful vote for the future of the country, and I ponder its implications and the motivations of those who are intent on bringing it about despite the lack of a democratic mandate to do so, despite court rulings, despite the divisiveness of the exercise, despite the relentless threats of annexation from an increasingly erratic president in Washington, DC, and despite the diverse forms of foreign interference from state-based adversaries, and even, it would seem, for-profit chancers trying to get in on an evidently profitable rage-farming exercise by stoking the flames of separatism, my mind goes to an unsettling place.

What is happening here in Alberta is an aberration. It does not resemble, in any fashion, democratic politics as normal in Canada. Something more untoward, more malign is transpiring. For the last ten years Canadians have watched these forces play out in the United States. But now these same forces have arrived here, within our own country. They are threatening to tear us asunder at the precise moment when we are most vulnerable, at the precise moment when our national unity is most paramount. This is not a coincidence.

Must we allow these forces to run unchecked through our polity? In other words, are there limits to our tolerance in a just society? These are questions as old as Western philosophy itself. Their answers define the intellectual underpinning of our liberal democracy. For decades in Canada we've assumed a laissez-faire approach in our answering of these questions. Some amongst the commentariat have therefore concluded that we are the most tolerant country in the world.[5] We are now being asked to tolerate Alberta separatism as a form of grievance. To do so would require us to make a significant error in analysis. It would require us to understand the foundations of the movement as being rooted in Western alienation that derives from a view that Confederation from the start was unfair to the Western provinces, whose voices were not well represented in the federal government; that the equalization formula that allows for all Canadians to have access to broadly comparable public services is unfair to wealthier Western provinces; that the country's climate policies have unfairly placed limits on the fossil fuels industry in an effort to limit the carbon output of the country and do our part in the global effort to turn back catastrophic climate change; and that official bilingualism creates a barrier to Western participation in the institutions of federal governance. As the University of Saskatchewan political studies professor Loleen Berdahl wrote about Western alienation, "it calls attention to how that Canada, in theory and practice, privileges central Canadian interests and worldviews over those of others and demands change."[6]

Perceptions of unfair economic treatment and a lack of respect from central Canada coalesce in a malaise that is indeed one of the defining features of Western political culture. But as this book will demonstrate, conflating this Western alienation with Alberta separatism is a dangerous mistake that sets us up to tolerate a malign, illiberal, foreign-influenced force that is intent on destroying our country. The Alberta separatist movement, whatever the separatists might otherwise claim, was not born of generationally held grievances dating back to before Alberta's entry into Confederation in 1905. It was born of 2022's Freedom Convoy and founded on conspiracy theory, xenophobia, and ahistorical notions of a free Alberta standing alone in North America without taxation or immigration and unconstrained from pursuing its future as a "faith, family, and freedom" loving nation.

As this book will demonstrate, the passive tolerance of such a movement against Canada, its principles, and its ability to remain self-determining in the present disinformation age will pose a grave danger to the country's survival. Over the last twelve years the global far right has influenced and leveraged secession referendums in Scotland, the UK (Brexit), Catalonia, Crimea, Donetsk, and Luhansk with goals ranging from undermining the trust and confidence of the electorate in their democratic processes, to fracturing democratic unions, to using democratic processes as a pretext to territorial expansion. The political, economic, and social consequences of all these referendums for their respective polities have been negative in the extreme.

Canadians have been exposed to this full spectrum of threat by an executive order made by a far-right provincial government in Alberta. Premier Danielle Smith and her United Conservative Party (UCP) government were neither formed as a (quasi) separatist party nor elected as one in either 2019 (under the leadership of Jason Kenney) or in

2023 (with Smith at the helm). They have on their own volition and will made the choice to go smash the Overton Window and subject the province and the country to a profoundly risk-laden, sham political process set to play out on the nineteenth of October.

This experiment in direct democracy remains intentionally exposed to the forces of foreign interference, which have and will unquestionably continue to pollute Canada's information ecosystem with mis- and disinformation designed to distort the democratic discourse, to discombobulate the demos, and to distract us from the one objective that must remain at the forefront of the Canadian mind: our national unity, which is paramount to our survival as an independent nation state in a revolutionary age.

The province has none of the security and intelligence architecture required to cope with the differing forms of covert and overt foreign interference that will flood the anti-democratic process the government has initiated. It has established no mechanism to warn the public of any foreign interference activity that the federal security and intelligence community or the media discovers, and it has made no commitment to conduct any form of post-mortem on the process aimed at uncovering the efforts of their global far-right brethren or any other foreign actors to tamper with its outcome.[7] This exposure of the soft underbelly of a concocted provincial plebiscite to the known malign effects of the global far-right disinformation machine is by design.

It is also by design that the premier has repeatedly cast the decision to hold this vote as a response to deeply held legitimate grievances. With this intentional muddying of Western alienation and the separatist movement, the premier has sought to lend legitimacy to an otherwise obviously nefarious group of conspiracists intent on overthrowing the federal government. As we will see in the coming chapters, the same folks from the Freedom Convoy and the Coutts blockade now have designs on breaking up Canada. These are the people leading the separatist charge and the ones being given access to democratic mechanisms within the province to do so. They are not the representatives of a distinct people under international law, with its "own social, cultural, and political attributes richly rooted in history."[8] They have no legitimate claims to having been systematically oppressed by the federal government—although they do make the claim, as offensive and absurd as that may be.[9] Their culture, if the word applies at all, is based on conspiracy theory, racism, and bigotry. According to the writer Marcello Di Cintio, they see "diversity, tolerance and equality... as social ills unsuited to the Christian nation these separatists seem to groan for."[10] Their music, their art, and their manifesto were generated not by human effort but by artificial intelligence. This is not an ideological movement; it is a slop-fuelled political technique, and its explicit aim is to crack Confederation. And yet it is their supposed sense of grievance the premier is asking us to tolerate.

She has refused to condemn the separatists who have made multiple envoys to Washington and held meetings in secure facilities with high-ranking Trump officials to plan out America's role in recognizing, first, and supporting, second, a post-secession referendum Alberta as an independent state. "I'm not going to demonize or marginalize a million of my fellow citizens when they've got legitimate grievances," Smith said after Premier David Eby's remarks at a First Ministers' meeting in Ottawa at the end of January this year in which he characterized as "treason" the travels of a handful of Alberta separatists to Washington to solicit support for their independence mission.[11]

The premier has chosen to go ahead with this vote despite the breach of Alberta's voters list and the exposure of the personal data—full legal names, addresses, polling stations, and in some cases emails and telephone numbers—of the entire voting population of the province. The list that was hijacked was the copy provided by Elections Alberta to the separatist Alberta Republican Party and its leader Cameron Davies, who had previously been on the receiving end of a series of historic sanctions from Elections Alberta for his role in conspiring to rig the contest that installed Jason Kenney as the first leader of the UCP. The breach was conducted by the Centurion Project, a group established by David Parker, the person responsible for leading an internal party coup against Premier Kenney and installing the UCP's second leader, Danielle Smith, in his stead to assist the separatist movement. This will be set out in detail in part two of this book.

But it is vital to establish here at the onset that our tolerance of this is being used to advance the ends of those who would see our destruction as a nation and as a people committed to liberal democratic principles. The twentieth-century philosopher Karl Popper identified what he called the "paradox of tolerance" in his 1945 treatise *The Open Society and Its Enemies*. Popper argued: "If we extend unlimited tolerance even to those who are intolerant, if we are not prepared to defend a tolerant society against the onslaught of the intolerant, then the tolerant will be destroyed, and tolerance with them."[12] Open societies, in other words, need to define and defend the limits of their tolerance.

By encouraging the definition of those limits Popper was trying to close the loophole in liberalism that Adolph Hitler's propagandist Joseph Goebbels had slithered through. Goebbels famously noted that "it will always remain one of the best jokes of democracy, that it gave its deadly enemies the means by which it was destroyed."[13] The Nazis ended democracy in Germany by exploiting the Trojan Horse of all open societies: their democratic tolerance. The German political scientist Karl Loewenstein understood as early as 1937 that "democracy and democratic tolerance have been used for their own destruction," and he therefore advocated for what he called militant democracy.[14]

Many open societies since have enshrined powers of defensive or militant democracy designed to allow their states to take protective measures against illiberal forces from within. Those that seek the state's destruction and the subjugation of its people to tyranny are not entitled to the full slate of its freedoms—or so goes the logic of militant democracy. You can't establish a neo-Nazi party in Germany, or deny the Holocaust in many European countries, or create a pro-Russian political party in Ukraine while the country is currently at war with Russia. But militant democracy can obviously swing too far and become illiberal in its own right. It is possible to overshoot in our defence of democratic values and have the effect—unintended or otherwise—of weakening them. Finding the correct balance becomes critical, especially in an age when democracy is under attack by populist leaders and groups who dismiss pluralism and the rule of law and seek unchecked power to advance their own interests and those of their supporters.[15]

Treason has traditionally been a line across which an open society's tolerance does not extend. If you betray the country to which you owe allegiance, if you turn it over to its enemies, your entitlements no longer stand. The democratic city states of ancient Greece had a law of ostracism that allowed them to banish tyrants and traitors.[16] It is from this law that much of the modern legislation on militant democracy is thought to derive. Loewenstein, however, is often credited with bringing the idea back into focus with his observation that the Weimar Republic had been too fundamentalist in its democracy and as a result had tragically failed to defend itself against subversive movements. As Loewenstein wrote, "a survey of the legislative defences of the Republic against the enemies of the democratic order reveals an almost tragi-comical picture of half-hearted, laggard, and thoroughly ineffective methods of dealing with the subversive technique." Driving the point home further, Loewenstein theorized that "the German Republic foundered on its own concepts of constitutional legality, which opened the way to Hitler."[17]

To prevent this from happening again, democracies must realize that they have become too precious, too enamoured with their own openness. In the face of a fascist world movement that seeks only to serve the purpose of power, democracy, according to Loewenstein, "must become militant."[18] Democracies must recognize that the fascist technique of overstatement and oversimplification on repeat aimed crudely towards the emotional (grievance) triggers of a population exploits its very openness. Fascism's goal is not to find pluralistic solutions to what ails the masses but to concentrate power. By becoming militant in the face of a war fought on an inner front, democracies have to rescue themselves, even at the risk of violating their own fundamental principles, by restricting the rights of those who seek their overthrow. "The liberal-democratic order reckons with normal times," wrote Loewenstein.

These are not normal times.

THIS BOOK IS written in defence of Canada and in defence of Canada's democracy. Its second chapter considers the fundamentals of representative democracy in this country and how the Alberta provincial government's grand experiment with direct democracy is subverting them. Chapter 3 resurfaces the ancient concept of treason and situates it within the current context of the Alberta separatist movement. Many critics have instinctively reached for the words *treason* and *traitor* in reaction to the actions of the leaders of the separatist movement. The levelling of such moral charges, however, should not be done without great intellectual care to ensure they are truly applicable. That is the aim of chapter 3: to provide us with the conceptual clarity necessary to understand the danger the separatist movement presents.

The fourth chapter begins the evidence section of the book by tracing the origins of the separatist movement to the Freedom Convoy of 2022, its weeks long occupation of the National Capital Region, and its blockades of highways and bridges across the country, which caused extensive economic harm in reaction to the public health measures put in place to deal with the fourth Omicron wave of COVID-19. Chapter 5 explores the corrupt origins of the United Conservative Party, a necessary precursor to understanding the UCP's present form, and examines how the UCP was overtaken by its own far-right and separatist elements, which led to the ouster of the committed federalist premier Jason Kenney and the installment of Danielle Smith. In chapter 6 the leaders of the separatist movement are brought into plain view, including their collaborations with the Trump administration and their conspiracist way of thinking about Canada and Alberta's place within it. Chapter 7 details the extreme influence these individuals have within the UCP by showing how the government has repeatedly legislated in their interest to hold a secession referendum despite multiple judicial rulings deeming such a vote unconstitutional and in breach of the treaty rights of First Nations. The eighth chapter concludes the evidence section of the book by examining the role of the largest data breach in Canada's history in the separatists' quest to secure enough petition signatures to trigger a vote on whether Alberta should leave Canada and become an independent state.

In the ninth chapter we situate the domestic situation in Alberta within the known international context of the last twelve years of secession votes in Europe. How the global far-right has leveraged these votes to fray and fracture democratic societies reminds us of the true danger of holding such referendums in the disinformation age. Chapter 10 brings us back to the big lie foisted upon our nation by the Smith government: that this referendum on whether to hold a more formal one on the province's place in Confederation is a genuine expression of the popular will that is in any way worth the extreme perils it places the country in at this moment in world history. We conclude in moral judgement of the separatist movement and the UCP government that has enabled them to set back our will to self-determination as an independent nation. This, it will be shown, is the definition of treason. It is the line our tolerance should not cross if we wish to survive as a democratic nation.

2: References and Referendums in a Revolutionary Age

THE MOVE TOWARDS a secession referendum in Alberta has reintroduced a set of concepts and terms that have laid dormant for a quarter of a century in Canada. We do, however, have a firm record of those words in the form of the 1998 Supreme Court of Canada judgment commonly known as the secession reference.

After Quebec narrowly voted against seceding from Canada in a referendum held in 1995, the attorney general, Allan Rock, asked three straightforward questions of the SCC. The answers his government received from the court bear tremendous weight in the current context. What is not clear is whether they will collapse under that weight when confronted with what is a very different secession movement than the one the reference considered.

The decision is concise and remarkably accessible. It was very likely intentionally written that way to ensure that all Canadians, whether legally trained or not, could read for themselves what the court decided on whether Quebec could unilaterally secede from Canada under the constitution; whether international law could provide an avenue for unilateral secession through recourse to a right of self-determination of a "people"; and, thirdly, in the event of a conflict between the Canadian constitution and international law, which of the two would take precedence.[1]

On the first question, the court decided that "the underlying principles animating the whole of the Constitution, including the principles of federalism, democracy, constitutionalism and the rule of law, and respect for minorities... must inform our overall appreciation of the constitutional rights and obligations that would come into play in the event that a clear majority of Quebecers votes on a clear question in favour of secession."[2]

Canada's democracy, according to the SCC, is "more than simple majority rule." Rather:

> Since confederation, the people of the provinces and territories have created close ties of interdependence (economic, social, political, cultural) based on shared values that include federalism, democracy, constitutionalism and the rule of law, and respect for minorities. A democratic decision of Quebecers in favour of secession would put those relationships at risk. The Constitution vouchsafes order and stability, and accordingly secession of a province "under the Constitution" could not be achieved unilaterally, that is without principled negotiation with other participants in Confederation within the existing constitutional framework.[3]

The essence of Canada's democracy is contained within this extraordinary paragraph. To be reminded of it as a rogue faction of a provincial political party that has shown increasing disregard for the democratic principles articulated above threatens our collective future is to be reminded of who Canadians are as a people. Our democracy is far more than majority rule. Indeed all political theorists, according to Queen's University professor Margaret Moore,[4] agree on this point. There is a consensus among them that democracy is more complex than that and must be assessed accordingly in terms of an agenda-setting phase, a deliberation phase, and a voting phase. Those in positions of authority—the class of political actors comprising elected representatives in cabinet positions, senior bureaucratic staff, and corporate power-brokers—can drive and distort all three of these phases by setting the agenda without concern to the proper aggregation of the electorate's interest, by truncating or manipulating deliberations, and of course by rigging voting outcomes through processes like gerrymandering, which intentionally dilutes the weight of some votes in favour of others.

Canada is a country of close ties of interdependence made possible by shared values. Our constitution privileges order and stability over any unilateral right to secede. Therefore, to secede a province must first demonstrate "a clear expression of democratic will," "free of ambiguity both in terms of the question asked and in terms of the support it achieves." The Clarity Act gives the House of Commons the authority to determine both the clarity of the question and the clarity of the majority, should one in fact emerge from a provincial population to vote in favour of secession from Canada.

As Saskatchewan attorney general John Whyte explained in his oral submission to the court: "A nation is built when the communities that comprise it make commitments to it, when they forgo choices and opportunities on behalf of a nation . . . when the communities that comprise it make compromises, when they offer each other guarantees, when they make transfers and perhaps most pointedly, when they receive from others the benefits of national solidarity. The threads of a thousand acts of accommodation are the fabric of a nation."[5] Former premier of Saskatchewan Roy Romanow followed up a few years later, writing that "this is one of the best descriptions of shared destiny" perhaps ever written. Indeed, continued Romanow, "This point of view speaks to a sovereign nation of citizens with rights and responsibilities, and with a commitment to act in the best interests of the nation as a whole. . . . Citizenship, regardless of where one lives, is at the heart of Canada and our never ending project of nation-building."[6] Between the Supreme Court justices and Whyte and Romanow, two strong Western voices, we find a version of our national soul, one dedicated to the public good through a constant search for compromise involving collective sacrifice for the betterment of us all.

On the second question, the court determined that only a "people" that has been colonized and ruled by an imperial power, subjected to domination or exploitation and "denied any meaningful exercise of its right to self-determination within the state of which it forms a part," would under international law have a right to unilateral secession.[7] The court chose not to pass judgement on whether Quebec constituted a people under international law, only that regardless of whether Quebec could be seen as a people, it was clearly enough not subject to the aforementioned forms of oppression within Canada.

Accordingly, neither the constitution nor international law afford Quebec a right of unilateral secession. The court, however, did not rule out a possibility of an unconstitutional declaration of secession that could lead to what it called a de facto secession, which could only succeed if the international community recognized it. The court reasoned that the international community would be "likely to consider the legality and legitimacy of secession having regard to, amongst other facts, the conduct of Quebec and Canada, in determining whether to grant or withhold recognition."[8]

The reasoning of the court here seems to rest on the assumption of a rules-based international system where the principle of state sovereignty prevails over any temptation to meddle in the internal affairs of other nations. The court's conclusion that there would accordingly be no conflict between domestic and international law seems not to have anticipated the current context. While certain of Canada's middle-power allies would in all likelihood follow the reasoning expected of them by the court, a growing cohort of states, including the United States and Russia and China, are very unlikely to follow that same path of restraint. The fading rules-based international order, useful fiction though it may have been, has very real implications for any secession referendum in Canada or elsewhere in the world.

As we will see in chapter 10, secession movements and referendums have become a favourite target of the global far right as it looks to turn societal cleavages into chasms in rival liberal-democratic societies. Rather than measured neutrality and respect for state sovereignty, it is more reasonable to anticipate active and aggressive efforts to meddle through overt and covert support of the secession movement and to expect direct and indirect attempts to influence referendum processes and the ultimate outcome.

The act of initiating a secession movement towards a referendum process in the age of disinformation, therefore, is as much an invitation to malign actors to meddle in the information space of the country concerned as an attempt to engage the collective will, expression, and consent of the people. To make this invitation without democratic safeguards in place to preserve the integrity of the information space is an intentionally reckless move sure to subject a society to deliberate, large-scale, and increasingly sophisticated attempts at its division from contrived and disingenuous, external forces.

The last time we held a secession referendum in this country was in 1995, more than thirty years ago. Hotmail arrived in our lives the next year, Facebook and Twitter about a decade later. The Canada-US relationship was on stable ground. China was still an emerging economy. Post-Soviet Union Russia was still on its back heels in the aftermath of the Cold War. Liberal democracy and open markets were on the rise worldwide as the international system went through a period of globalization. Francis Fukuyama had even gone out on a long intellectual limb and declared the end of history with liberalism and capitalism having forever triumphed over fascism and communism.[9] If you were ever going to hold a secession referendum, 1995 was the year to do it.

The secession reference decision assumes a status quo ante scenario, where one democratic society within Canada arrives at a democratic decision to separate from the remainder of that democratic society within the context of a rules-based international system wherein the principle of state sovereignty is upheld as the cornerstone of world order. In 1995 these assumptions were sound. In 2026, they are deeply flawed for three reasons.

First, the international system is in rupture, according to our prime minister.[10] Much of the Davos crowd agrees; it has become uncontroversial to assert that not only has history returned, but it is hurtling towards a troubling period of instability, uncertainty, and unrest. We are already there.

Second, according to Justice Marie-Josée Hogue, who oversaw a sixteen-month public inquiry into foreign interference in Canada's federal elections that heard from over 150 witnesses, the spread of mis- and disinformation in the media and on social networks, "is noxious, and it is powerful, it poses a major risk to Canadian democracy. If we do not find ways of addressing it, misinformation and disinformation have the ability to distort our discourse, change our views, and shape our society. In my view it is no exaggeration to say that at this juncture, information manipulation (whether foreign or not) poses the single biggest risk to our democracy. It is an existential threat."[11]

Third, the rule of law is under attack in Alberta by the UCP government. The province's chief justices have come to its defence,[12] as has the chief justice of the Supreme Court of Canada.[13] These justices have made extraordinary statements defending judicial independence and the rule of law against a steady rhythm of assaults by the UCP government. These assaults have involved pre-emptive use of the notwithstanding clause to deny justice to striking teachers in the province; three more uses of the notwithstanding clause to target the rights of trans children; the banning of certain books; the prohibition of pride flags in schools; an effort to silence the court on rulings related to the separatist petition (which will be discussed in some detail in chapter 8); threatening to withhold funding to support any judicial appointments in the province until the federal government gives the province more sway in determining those appointments; and passing multiple major pieces of legislation in shotgun fashion in the middle of the night to avoid legislative scrutiny in service to the separatist cause to hold a secession referendum this fall. Federal justice minister Sean Fraser has described this as a form of "democratic backsliding" designed "to cater to a unique political opportunity that may be a good fundraising email but will potentially violate constitutionally protected rights of vulnerability."[14] The Canadian Bar Association's Alberta branch wrote directly to Premier Smith, with a cc to the prime minister, to express its "grave concerns" about the government's efforts to politicize the judicial appointments process.[15]

The secession reference was then codified into law in the form of the Clarity Act in 2000. As indicated in its title, the act is about providing clarity on what it describes as "a matter of the utmost gravity"—that is "any proposal relating to the break-up of a democratic state."[16] The act acknowledges that such a matter is "of fundamental importance" to all citizens of the democratic state proposed for partition.

Accordingly, clear law regarding negotiations between the federal government and Quebec was required because secession would necessarily mean the "termination of citizenship and other rights that Canadian citizens resident in the province enjoy as full participants in Canada."[17] It would also mean the rupture of the country and in many ways the end of Canada. So having a bit of a legal roadmap for the process seemed wise.

The House of Commons would be required to consider in advance the clarity of the question the aspiring secessionist provincial government would put to its residents, and there would have to be a clear expression of the will of the population of that province on whether it should cease to be part of Canada. Alberta has not been required to adhere to this because of the "referendum on a referendum" nature of the question the executive has elected to put to the province. Accordingly, the House of Commons has also been excluded from having any opportunity to deliberate on the agenda-setting of the Smith government.

The act lives up to its name: pose a clear question, get a clear expression of the will of the people, and we can start a negotiation on breaking up the country. Otherwise, there's no unilateral right to secede emanating from international law or the constitution of Canada, as determined by the high court.

Except what if the provincial government that aspires to secede has little to no regard for the rule of law, which the Clarity Act obviously relies upon? And what if the same could be said for the key major powers in the international system? And what if one of those powers happened to be threatening Canada's annexation repeatedly not from afar but from right next door? And what if the aspiring secessionist provincial government was itself more aligned ideologically with the regime next door than with that of its own capital? And what if, to further complicate matters (as if that were necessary), humanity had been on a tempo run towards inhabiting a post-truth future for the last decade or more, where facts were arbitrary and relentlessly challenged and reconstructed in real time by demagogues and influencers and their billionaire-class backers who had seized control of the dominant medium of communication? What if our democracy was under assault by foreign actors seeking to contaminate our information spaces with rage bait and disinformation designed to divide and disorient us to the point where our collective cognitive sovereignty was being questioned?

A lot has happened in the quarter century since the Clarity Act came into force. Placing the fate of the county on a twenty-six-year-old law that could not have contemplated the current threat environment does seem a rather risky bet. The law's very existence promotes a passivity on the part of the federal government in the face of a malign, anti-democratic attempt to fracture the nation.

For all the talk of Western alienation, separatists have almost never passed a hard democratic test in Alberta. There has been only one openly separatist MLA ever elected in the province. Gordon Kesler of the Western Canada Concept Party won a by-election in 1982 in the riding of Olds-Didsbury after the incumbent, Robert C. Clark, stepped down from leading the official opposition Social Credit Party. Kesler lost his seat just six weeks later in the general election. The Western Canada Concept Party ran a full slate of candidates in that election but returned no MLAs and garnered only 11.8 percent of the popular vote. Kesler, the party's leader, folded the tent after that humiliating defeat. But forty-three years later, Kesler backed Cameron Davies in his failed by-election bid for the Olds-Didsbury seat in the provincial legislature.[18] Davies's Republican Party ran candidates in all three by-elections held in 2025 and was handily demolished in each.

Indeed, the groundswell of separatist support is in such abundance in the province that Premier Smith's government had to amend the Citizens Initiative Act, which had been in effect for less than four years, to more than cut in half the number of signatures required to trigger a referendum on secession, add 30 days to the signature collection period (90 days to 120), and eliminate any requirement for signatures from urban centres.

Separatist sentiment is so prevalent in the province, according to the premier, that it is best to hold a plebiscite on Alberta's future in confederation along with nine other questions aimed at dividing the populace and distracting the nation while Washington wages its hybrid war against us, which includes a punishing trade war intended to cripple our core industries and a relentless information war aimed at making us question our very right to exist as a sovereign nation.[19] People have lost hope in Canada—35 percent of Albertans, in fact, according to the premier—and are angry and frustrated with Ottawa.[20]

The premier has decided that a referendum on having a secession referendum must happen rather than risk letting all of this pent-up frustration fester. She has asserted as if it were the plainest of truths that direct democracy is "the ultimate form of democracy."[21] Just like her claims about the state of secessionist sentiment in the province—currently sitting below 20 percent[22]—this is also a highly contestable claim.

Plebiscites, or referendums, are easy to manipulate.[23] Consider Napoleon's referendum on whether he should be consul for life. Votes were almost 100 percent in favour. Why? Because the ballot wasn't secret, and the guillotines from Robespierre's reign of terror were still hanging around. People valued their necks, and their votes showed as much. Both Mussolini and Hitler, following the German political theorist Carl Schmitt's advice, used referendums to strengthen their own authoritarian power structures.[24] Similarly, so did Saddam Hussein. So while referendums might be symbolic of popular power, in reality they may be more akin to a "democratic chimera."[25]

Elites can reduce questions about complex matters of public policy to yes or no options and prompt the electorate to make "decisions" they themselves lack the courage to make. But the electorate aren't responsible to one another to remain up to speed on the nuances of the issues upon which they are being forced to decide. They don't, in other words, have anywhere near what might be considered perfect information. Rather, the likelihood is greater that the electorate is liable to be uninformed or disinformed and has no obligation to alter this condition through study of the consequences of their votes one way or the other. Furthermore, they have no obligation to show up to vote, either. That's the job of their elected representatives. But when those representatives delegate their duties to debate and find pluralistic solutions to those who elected them, reasoned discourse aimed at policy and law that achieves the greatest good for the greatest number devolves into emotional, fear-driven campaigns for yes or no, leave or stay.

The people who drive those debates often have no democratic mandate to do so. Enter Nigel Farage, for example, into Brexit. Or Mitch Sylvestre, Keith Wilson, or Jason Kenney into the present campaign over Alberta secession. Folks like these may be well-intentioned. But no one elected them. This presents an accountability deficit that further dilutes the integrity of direct democracy. This is especially the case with the referendum in question here. Unlike in Quebec, where electors were presented with and voted for the separatist Parti Québécois who delivered upon promised secession referendums in 1980 and 1995 under premiers Lévesque and Parizeau respectively, the UCP was neither formed as a separatist party in 2017 nor has it run as a separatist party in either of the general elections it has contested and won. As Chantal Hébert wrote in the preface to her much-lauded book on the 1995 Quebec referendum, *The Morning After*, "Quebecers decided their political fate."[26] In Alberta, by stark contrast, the premier and her quasi-separatist party are forcing our political fate and the fate of the nation upon us. And in a perverse irony, the premier has said she will champion the federalist cause in the campaign. A more disingenuous spokesperson for a united Canada would be hard to find.

And if the deliberative questions are unclear or convoluted, auxiliary challenges arise by creating a greater likelihood that resolution to whatever political problem is being considered remains elusive. If the question is unclear, how could the answer be determinative unless in the hands of an authoritarian regime unconcerned with the actual will of the people?

Nevertheless, populist governments seem to like the show of a referendum. It's a fine sop to the people—let them decide! And it creates a great opportunity to stoke division and distract from the real issues of concern to most: education, health care, a stable political jurisdiction, a functioning economy, the future of the planet.

But who are the people? In this case, almost twice the number of people signed the Forever Canada petition to prevent a secession referendum than were verified to have signed the independence petition. The First Nations of the province won two landmark court cases in support of their opposition to a secession referendum that could cause irreparable harm to their treaty rights, which were enshrined in their agreements with the Crown (i.e., Canada). The province of Alberta came into existence well after Treaties 6, 7, and 8 were signed with Canada.

So we see that "the people" that matter to the premier are not the federalists or the First Nations who comprise the vast majority of the province, but 222,597 separatists. A very small minority of Albertans, and an even more minuscule minority of Canadians, are setting the agenda and, as political philosopher Margaret Moore explained, "defining what Alberta and the rest of Canada will be talking about and grappling with over the coming months."[27]

And referendums sure aren't cheap. Elections Alberta is in the midst of a hiring drive as it seeks sixty thousand workers for the upcoming referendum. It is printing forty-five million ballots to cover the ten questions. It has been estimated that the full cost for the exercise will be between $100 and 130 million.[28] For context, the base salary of the eighty-seven MLAs in Alberta is $130,000.00. For $100 million we could pay them all to sit in the legislature and represent us for roughly a decade. If they did their jobs passably, chances are we'd get a few pieces of legislation out of those years. But it's difficult to say what if any positive results we'll get out of the ten referendum questions scheduled for the fall. Referendums are clearly not an efficient way to solve political problems.

Smith argues she would like a "mandate" to move forward and pursue "more power" on a range of divisive public policy issues targeting immigrants and refugees, voter restrictions, and constitutional changes beyond her control, such as abolishing the Senate; appointing judges;

opting out of federal health care, education, and social services programs while maintaining access to funding tied to these initiatives; and setting up a provincial veto over federal laws when provincial laws come into conflict with them.

The questions are offensive to the norms and principles at the foundation of Canadian federalism, largely because they seem to be grounded in little to no comprehension of how Canada works at a constitutional level and little to no recognition of our collective history as a people of empathy. I gather that's the point.

This is not difficult coding to read. The nine questions that seek to oppugn immigrants and Canada's constitution build to the tenth on whether Alberta should "remain a province of the country (option 1); or (option 2) whether the Government of Alberta should commence the legal process required under the Canadian constitution to hold a binding provincial referendum on whether or not Alberta should separate from Canada."[29] Planting thoughts of radical change to immigration policy and the constitution before popping the big question is what psychologists call anchoring or anchoring bias.[30] The manipulative practice is designed to influence the tenth judgment by assimilating it to the previous nine. A voter might feel strongly, for example, about immigration and the unelected Senate, carry those thoughts into the question about Alberta secession, and be influenced to vote in favour of moving down that path.

The fundamental problem with all of this is that in a representative democracy, mandates are won on the hustings. Parties campaign on platforms of ideas. If elected, they have a mandate to legislate those ideas into existence.

Separatism and xenophobia are ideas that are extremely unlikely to pass hard democratic tests in Alberta, despite Smith's trumped-up claims about how angry she thinks Albertans are with Ottawa. The current polling suggest just two in ten Albertans will vote in October in favour of holding a future secession referendum.[31]

In other words, as we have seen, they aren't electable planks in a campaign platform. The party has never campaigned on secession or on anti-immigration policies—something that in a province composed of a high percentage of immigrants (23.2 percent according to the 2021 census[32]) would be as electorally suicidal as running on Alberta independence.

A political *cordon sanitaire* surrounds these issues when presented in the context of electoral politics. But as many new fringe parties in Europe have discovered, it is easier to push for a referendum than it is to win an election. Popular topics for referendums include membership in the EU and refugee policy—some thirty-five of these proposals were put forward between the post-war period and 2017, according to the political scientist Liubomir Topaloff of Tokyo's Meiji University. This has allowed these fringe parties to break into mainstream political debates with previously thought taboo issues while simultaneously denouncing traditional politics as "corrupt" and calling for a return of power to the people.[33]

With the ten October referendum questions, Smith seems to be angling for an inversion of Canada's representative democracy. By asserting direct democracy as the ultimate and "purest and most direct"[34] expression of the people's will, she's saying representative democracy is inferior to its more direct cousin. There is, however, no constitutional right in

Canada to a referendum, as the constitution contains no provisions on the matter.[35] This has been taken as permissive of referendums. There have been just three "national" referendums in Canada's history and only seven province-wide referendums in Alberta's history. And yet the premier has decried as "anti-democratic" court rulings that have held a prospective secession referendum to be unconstitutional and requiring the consent of First Nations. As I write, the government is appealing the second of these rulings.

While it may be too strong to assert Smith is trying to flip Alberta's representative democracy on its head entirely, she is no doubt introducing a tension between competing sources of legitimacy—general elections on the one hand, and direct popular votes on the other—while undermining the essential democratic role of the courts in the process.[36] Would-be autocrats before her have used referendums to consolidate their power. Is it any wonder that Smith is doing likewise?

There is no precedent for this in the democratic world. No democratically elected sub-national government has ever gone free-range after an election and, without a mandate won at the polls, tried to engineer the breakup of a county through a direct-democratic process. The move is a betrayal of the electorate, it is a betrayal of Alberta's democratic traditions which extend back over 120 years, and it is a betrayal of Canada (of which Alberta is a provincial part) at a time of intense global uncertainty. To blithely set aside this last bit as if Alberta existed in its own sublime bubble of security is the height of irresponsibility. It significantly undermines Canada's ability to pursue its self-determination in the midst of a national security emergency.

The radical, the arbitrary, and the opportunistic are hallmarks of authoritarian regimes. The UCP is ticking all of those boxes. The question we can ask now is whether its actions, and those of the mobilizing separatists, can be judged morally as treason.

3: Tresoun | Trāditiō | Traïson | Treason

IN HER BOOK, *At a Loss for Words: Conversations in an Age of Rage*, Carol Off writes about the importance of words in the fight to defend our democracy from the forces of authoritarianism. "When we lack a way to express an idea then the idea itself may be gone. Even the range of our thoughts becomes diminished."[1] Off, a longtime broadcaster and author, understands both the power of words and the necessity of having the proper vocabulary to formulate common understanding in the midst of crises manufactured by the "flood the zone" tactics of far right, conspiratorial, populist governments intent on pushing the normative and institutional boundaries of democracy beyond their breaking points and leading us into an authoritarian future.

"We need vocabulary of weight and substance," observes Off, "words that convey our shared history but that are stripped of sentimentality. To accurately identify the causes of our anger and resentment, we need to be able to trust our language and each other; to agree on what it means and to recognize with a keen eye whose interests are served by this engineered breakdown in civil society. The political rage that has engulfed us is exhausting, rendering us almost incapable of rational conversations. But that's the intent of those who are fuelling it."[2]

Words matter. Definitions matter. Concepts matter. In the disinformation age they perhaps matter more than ever before. They are the cognitive orientation points on the map that charts our future in a rational, fact-based, rules-based world. They are the intellectual armour that defends democracy, the building blocks of progress, equality, and all human flourishing.

Authoritarianism doesn't work in facts and common conceptual foundations. It works on emotion. It works on bully tactics and intimidation and lies. It works outside of the parameters of established democratic norms and rules and conventions, actively trying to tear them down. In their stead, authoritarianism erects a world largely in the image of the ruler, a world where the meaning of words and concepts change to suit the purposes of the regime. Black becomes white. Up, down. Two plus two, five. Ignorance, strength.[3]

With impudent zeal and fervour, would-be despots move against established understanding in the fact-based world. Scientists, judges, professors, journalists, regulators, all become vilified as "elites," enemies of the people. What is meant is that these keepers of the fact-based world are obstacles to authoritarian ambitions.

AN INSTINCT TO call out the Alberta separatist movement and the leaders who are driving it has compelled a range of Canadians to reach for the ancient, potent labels used to describe a fundamental betrayal of one's country. From a unified front of First Nations chiefs to a former Conservative premier, from sitting NDP premiers to podcasters to well-spoken homeless people and many average citizens in between, has emerged a collective sense that something is fundamentally suspect with this separatist movement.

The Assembly of Treaty Chiefs has passed a unanimous resolution that calls upon the RCMP to investigate the premier and her party for the criminal offence of treason (Criminal Code of Canada, section 46): "We call for this investigation on the basis of the intentional violation of the Treaties; of calling a referendum in the face of severe risks to Canada's sovereignty and the Treaty Relationship and of failing to take action on the violation of privacy rights of millions of people. Further, Premier Smith and the UCP government have done all this with significant risks of foreign interference and influence." The resolution further notes that the RCMP committed, at the time of the treaties, to ensure the safety of First Nations and their peace and goodwill in exchange for sharing these lands.[4] The First Nations of the province have reported heightened levels of racism and hatred since the separatist petition process was first launched in January.[5] The premier has responded that the chiefs should "check themselves"[6] after their allegation of treason and has threatened to use the powers of the province's controversial critical infrastructure defence law to clamp down on any civil disobedience protests engaged in by First Nations. "I think you saw how serious we are about enforcing that law as we have many times over previous years,"[7] said the premier after First Nations chiefs suggested they would take their struggle to stop separation to the highways after the government disregarded multiple court rulings finding the referendum would violate the treaties. Treaty 8 grand chief Trevor Mercredi noted on an Instagram reel in response: "When we look at instances of civil disobedience, we should look at the UCP party themselves. They are very lawless. They seem to think they are above the law. Introducing and passing legislation that protects themselves. Talking about the nations as if we're the law-breaking people. But we have a right to protect ourselves. And if our rights are threatened then we will make sure they're protected."[8]

JASON KENNEY, a former premier of the province, has called one of the separatist leaders, Jeffrey Rath, a "treasonous kook." "He's just a blowhard desperate for media attention. Don't fall for his schtick," said Kenney on X in March 2025, after Rath made an appearance on Fox News to discuss the efforts of his "delegation" to Washington, their meetings with Trump appointees, and their desire to become part of the United States.[9] Rath concluded his interview on Fox by asking President Trump to support Alberta self-determination "and promise it to Alberta in the same way you promised it to Greenland" before laughing at the host's suggestion that "maybe you will be governor of our fifty-first state."[10]

Ryan Jespersen, a podcast host with a long-standing political talk show in the province, said of Rath's ventures to Washington that "in a lot of countries, this tomfoolery would get you strung up for treason."[11] More eloquent than both was a homeless man in a wheelchair confronted outside of Roger's Place Arena in early February—the home of the Edmonton Oilers—by a separatist making a YouTube video about his efforts to break up the country.

"Hey, God bless you, sir. I don't have anything to give ya. But yeah, hey, God bless ya. Can I ask your opinion on Alberta independence?"

"Oh, I'm against it," the homeless man replied. "It's . . . it's treason.

"You're against it?"

"It's treason. Canada's a great country. A fuckin' great country. And you know what? They gotta work things out between the provinces, for Canada. It's my home. And I would defend it to my death. We separate, and the States is gonna pick us clean. They will pick Alberta clean. They'll take the oil. They'll take everything of value. They'll take it all, [then] they'll leave us. That's the way it is down there . . . To break up Canada, it's the greatest country in the world. We are looked upon so highly by the rest of the world. To break us up, it's just ludicrous. Ludicrous."[12]

While in attendance at a First Ministers' meeting in Ottawa at the end of January, Premier David Eby addressed the press gallery in a solemn tone and expressed his view that the group of "people from Alberta, I won't call them Albertans," who had attended the White House and "asked for assistance in breaking up Canada" had crossed a line. "There's an old-fashioned word for that. And that word is treason. It is completely inappropriate to seek to weaken Canada," Eby said, by seeking assistance from a foreign power that had "not been particularly respectful of Canada's sovereignty," and concluded: "There is a line."[13]

A few days later Eby furthered his thought and called upon all Canadians to call out what he so clearly saw as treason. If we aren't willing to do that, he asked, "then what actually are we standing for as Canadians? We have to defend this country, we have to fight for this country, we have to call out people who would organize with a foreign government to destroy what we hold precious and close to our hearts. That is the definition of being Canadian in my opinion."[14] When confronted about Eby's remarks, Rath called them "stupid"[15] and called the *Financial Times* piece about his covert meetings with the Trump administration "fake news."[16]

I had been tracking Rath's ramblings about his multiple meetings in Washington with some alarm before the international media brought the story into view. I wrote a Substack that broke down the national security implications of a lengthy interview of Rath's that had been posted on YouTube on December 24, 2025. The aim of the article was to define the line between separatist movement and national security threat.[17]

Much like Eby, I concluded that while it is perfectly legal in Canada to advocate for the secession of a province from Confederation, collaborating with foreign powers to plan for an eventual break-up of the country was the line that, if crossed, constituted a threat to Canada's national security and would accordingly become the purview of Canada's Security Intelligence Service, and potentially the RCMP. I was, however, hesitant at the time to use the word *treason*. This was largely due to the Criminal Code's definition, which appears to have been imported from England's Treason Act of 1352. The "Great Statutes of Treason" is one of the oldest pieces of legislation on the statute book in the United Kingdom. The crime of high treason was codified to protect the king and his bloodline and also to protect the king's subjects from arbitrary accusation of the crime.[18] High treason was defined in narrow terms and required the element of violence or a plot of violence against the monarch, just as it does now in Canada, to be chargeable.[19] In an age of hybrid warfare, the code is woefully out of date.

It seemed more fruitful to consider whether the activity could become the purview of Canada's national security community at all. In relation to separatist movements, Canada has grappled with where the line between political movement and national security threat can be drawn in the past. The Royal Commission on Security, released in 1969, addressed the issue in the context of the Quebec secession movement.

The commission argued that separatism in Quebec, pursued legally and democratically, should be dealt with in a political rather than a security context. Evidence of anti-democratic, subversive, or seditious intentions or "any suggestion of foreign influence," however, would alter the calculation fundamentally, rendering it necessary to treat the issue as one of national security. The government, at the very least, would be required to "take adequate steps to inform itself of any such threats."[20]

What struck me in reading the report was just how simple the security environment of the day sounded compared to our present moment. Beyond international communism and Quebec separatism, the potential threats to Canada's national security then were limited.[21] The Cold War was the defining and all-encompassing feature of the security landscape. Quebec separatism was a loose thread. The federal government, according to the commission, should therefore be seen to be taking steps to prevent the infiltration of the Quebec separatist movement "by persons who are clearly committed to the dissolution of Canada, or who are involved with elements of the separatist movement in which seditious activity or foreign involvement are factors."[22] This seemed a straightforward recommendation even if it risked critics casting the government's security services as heavy handed in their treatment of Quebec separatists. Clearly, the federal government should not lay supine while KGB intelligence operatives drove support to a secession movement that, if successful, could significantly weaken a democratic rival closely allied with the United States.

ALMOST SIXTY YEARS on, the unthinkable had happened to the once "special relationship" between Canada and the United States. The prevailing dynamics of trust, open trade, deep defence and security integration, and mutual respect between the two North American neighbours had taken a radical turn. Donald Trump began musing about Canada becoming the fifty-first state before he was inaugurated for the second time in January 2024. He threatened outrageous tariffs that would violate the trade agreement he himself had signed in his first term. He trolled Prime Minister Justin Trudeau, calling him "governor" of the "great state of Canada."[23]

Trudeau came to understand the trolling as a real threat stemming from the president's desire to acquire Canada's vast stores of critical minerals, which are central to great power competition in an increasingly lawless international system.[24] Trump said he was willing to use "economic force" to "get rid of that artificially drawn line," referring to the longest undefended border in the world, and posted maps depicting North America as entirely American on his

Truth Social platform. He felt this would be "much better for national security... we basically protect Canada."[25]

In mid-April of this year the *Globe and Mail* quantified Trump's enmity towards Canada. The national newspaper tallied a "constant supply of threats, complaints, accusations, insults and taunts" from the forty-seventh president. More than 200 times over the course of the previous four months, Trump had threatened tariffs, and 69 times he'd gone further threatening annexation in some manner, either by calling us the "cherished" fifty-first state, referring to our leaders disparagingly as "governor," or claiming the "imaginary" border could simply be eliminated.[26]

Trump's rhetorical psyops have combined with targeted trade warfare designed to destabilize and cripple critical sectors of the Canadian economy. Auto manufacturing, aluminum, steel, and softwood lumber—crown jewels of the Canadian economy—are all under assault. This weaponization of the interdependence built up over decades of cooperation and partnership has put Canada as the subordinate state in the continental hierarchy in a very precarious position.[27] As the lone remaining liberal democracy in North America, Canada has become a target of Trump's increasingly authoritarian regime, which, if history is a guide, by its very nature will seek to extinguish liberalism in its entirety from the international system.[28] We have found ourselves, in other words, very much in the crosshairs of a hybrid form of warfare being conducted against us by our once greatest ally.[29] The Trump regime's rationale for this may be to access our critical minerals, abundance of fresh water, and oil and gas reserves, or it may be a desire for greater Arctic security. These are proximate material causes which are underlined by Canada's essential stature as a liberal democracy. It is our commitment to equality, to the rule of law, to multiculturalism, to science, and to the fact-based world that makes us a threat to Trump's America.

His administration has been in the process of systematically destroying the liberal world order that has held fast for the last eighty-odd years.[30] They have made a mockery of international law over and over again by extrajudicially executing alleged drug smugglers in the Caribbean Sea and the Pacific Ocean,[31] by decapitating the regime in Venezuela under cover of darkness, by launching an unprovoked war of choice on Iran that has killed thousands and choked a vital global shipping lane,[32] and by imposing a devastating blockade on Cuba that has triggered a horrific humanitarian crisis.[33]

In their own country they have operated with equal lawlessness. They have funded and recruited a masked militia operating with impunity under the banner of ICE. It has an annual budget that dwarfs other federal law-enforcement agencies at around $29 billion and mirrors Canada's entire defence budget, which was up 15 percent to $30.6 billion last fiscal year.[34] And it has been deployed as an occupying force in blue states like California and Minnesota, where it has carried out daylight executions of American citizens who would not cower in the face of authoritarian intimidation. In response to these executions, the world was told not to believe their own eyes and ears but rather to believe that the deceased had it coming. That a young mother who had just dropped her child off at school was a "domestic terrorist."[35] That a young nurse who helped veterans recover from war wounds was a "would-be assassin."[36]

The updated National Security Strategy of the United States, released in 2025, decrees that "we will reward and encourage the region's governments, political parties, and movements broadly aligned with our principles and strategy."[37] This provides a clear rationale for the administration's otherwise inexplicable willingness to meet on multiple occasions with Alberta separatists. It aims for hemispheric dominance and appears oriented only by a principle of strategic resource imperialism that entitles the Trump administration to seize assets across the hemisphere at will. The so-called Donroe Doctrine that has come to encapsulate this strategy has Canada squarely in its sights.

In response, Canada has scrambled to diversify its international trading arrangements, worked to eliminate internal barriers to trade, made generational investments in defence and security and major critical infrastructure projects, and has even put forward the country's first defence industrial strategy with the goal of creating a "sovereign defence industrial base that will supply the material required to defend the nation from direct attack."[38]

The animating force behind all of this was the "rupture in the world order" Prime Minister Carney acknowledged in his now famous speech at the World Economic Forum in Davos, Switzerland in January 2026.[39] Canada would take the sign out of the window and stop performing as though the rules-based order was still a useful fiction. It would seek a better, stronger, more just order led by middle powers who would partner genuinely with one another on the foundation of their domestic strengths and shared democratic values. The speech echoed around the world.[40] The next day Trump stepped up to the podium at Davos and took direct aim at Carney. "Canada lives because of the United States. Remember that, Mark, the next time you make your statements."[41] In the interregnum between a collapsing world order and the emergence of a new one, Canada's survival hinges on its ability to remain united and self-determining in the pursuit of its national interests and security.

Can a separatist movement working against these broader interests of the Canadian polity be considered treasonous? Treason, when alleged, carries extreme negative moral valence. The word *treason* comes from the Latin *tradition(n):* "the giving up, surrender, or betrayal of something or someone."[42] But to use the word reveals a vulnerability, an anxiety about the stability of a society and the fragility of its customs, norms, values, and collective identity. *You gave us up*. In modern usage, it is an accusation of betrayal of one's country and of providing aid to its enemies. It is an accusation with profound reverberation and rhetorical power because it means the breaking of the loyalty bonds that hold a polity together.

The academic literature on the subject of treason helps fill out the concept that so many have instinctively reached for when considering Alberta separatism and its enablers. The medieval historian Larissa Tracy has written importantly about the parameters and effects of treason:

> Ultimately, treason is the highest crime, but it can be experienced at all levels of life. It is not simply the act of providing comfort and aid to enemies in war, nor is it always an act of treachery against a king or state. Treason is the betrayal of trust; it is an insidious act that undermines the stability of families, communities, and societies; it eats away at the fibre of social relationships and causes us to question the very nature of our interactions with our rulers, with our institutions, and with each other.[43]

Here, Tracey considers both the act and the effect of the betrayal that is treason. The act can be contemplated from a moral perspective, and a legal one. The effect, however, is more pervasive and diffuse. It is more akin to the introduction of a contagion to a society than a singular criminal act with narrow implications, like an occurrence of shoplifting or an isolated murder might be. The effect of treason, according to Tracey, can be destabilizing to an entire society, which can rightly be understood as the affected victims of the act.

The Oxford political philosopher Ruairí Maguire has considered the concept of treason in the context of secession movements, asking in an article published this year in the *European Journal of Political Theory* whether all unilateral secessionists are by definition traitors.[44] I spoke at length to Maguire in preparation for writing this book because I believe him to be the one scholar who has sufficiently considered this question from the perspective of moral political philosophy.

The first thing we have to consider when contemplating treason, according to Maguire, is to whom we can apply the label *traitor*. It cannot be that all secession movements are by nature treasonous. Take, for example, the case of the South Sudanese, who were marginalized for decades, often violently, by an Arab-Muslim dominated north. The African-Christian south may have had nominal Sudanese citizenship, but they did not enjoy full "social membership" in Sudanese society.[45] Accordingly, to have demanded autonomy after decades of repression, marginalization, and civil war, and to have held through international support a referendum on independence in which the south voted almost unanimously (99 percent) for secession, cannot be considered treason. The South Sudanese owed no debt of loyalty to the north, which had been systematically oppressing them. This was plain to see.

Maguire contrasts this with a hypothetical case of unilateral secession of Alberta from Canada. In this fictional (for now) scenario, Maguire describes "a long-running political feud" between the resource-rich province and the rest of the country that is a result of perceptions of "unfairness in federal taxation and revenue-sharing arrangements, coupled with frustrations over regulations impacting the energy sector," which have contributed to a sense of Western alienation.[46] These "feelings of alienation from the rest of Canada came to a head in the mid-2020s, when Alberta unilaterally seceded."

The hypothetical case of Alberta unilaterally seceding from Canada at some point in the mid-2020s contrasts starkly with the real case of the South Sudanese doing so in 2011. Canada is a liberal democracy. Albertans do not have a distinct national identity. Most Albertans come from other countries or other provinces: 27.2 percent of the population of the province identified as racialized in the 2021 census[47] (the national average is 26.1 percent), and 23 percent are first-generation Canadians.[48] Albertans enjoy full social membership in Canada. As a result, hypothetically, a unilateral secession of the province from Canada would qualify those who carried it off as traitors. But why exactly? According to Maguire, we need to consider who or what would be the victim of such an act. It is against the people of a political community—in this case, all Canadians—that treason is committed. The people are the victims because their right to self-determination is compromised by the actions of the traitors.

What actions might be considered treasonous? Is it enough to identify a breach of the trust and expectations of those to whom loyalty is owed? It is not. We must determine the interests that treason threatens. Significant attempts to undermine the ability of people to protect or rule themselves—to self-determine—by members of that polity can be considered an act of treachery.

This is especially the case when secession is not actually about secession per se but is rather a tool to undermine or overthrow a legitimate federal government. Contrasting the historical Quebec secession referendums with the Alberta case helps us to understand what is actually happening here. In Quebec a distinct society of people, sharing a distinct language and culture, elected an explicitly secessionist provincial party to form government and hold a referendum on whether that society should set out on a path to self-determination. None of those features exist within the Alberta separatist movement, as the second part of this book demonstrates. No one in the province elected a single separatist to the provincial legislature in 2023, and yet somehow we are being asked to take seriously their AI-hallucinated vision of an independent Alberta.

There is simply no precedent in the democratic world for what we are seeing in Alberta. On its face, it is absurd. It offends, and intentionally so, the idea of Canada and its right to exist as an independent nation state. As such it is a form of psychological warfare on par with President Trump's attacks on Canada, waged from inside the country by a guerrilla faction of the global far right. And it is being enabled, if not led, by Premier Smith and her UCP government. In the midst of what is unquestionably the most serious national security crisis the country has ever faced, the notion that a nominally federalist provincial government would actively provide a conspiratorial, far-right fringe movement with an intentionally divisive and potentially disastrous secession referendum without a mandate and without any indication that a majority of the population (or anywhere near) desires it confounds democratic norms. It is a profound betrayal of Canada. To be able to use the word *treason* in a moral sense and with certainty to describe it is an important step in defence of our democracy.

We have cleared the philosophical ground. We have the words. We must now examine contextually the case of the Alberta separatist movement. This requires us to go back into the cauldron of the COVID-19 pandemic, when the movement's protagonists first politicized.

PART II: EVIDENCE

4: Trial Run

IN THE BLEAK last days of January in the year 2022, I was in a dark place. Like many Canadians, I was claustrophobic and a bit strung out after too many hours behind a surgical mask, too many COVID vaccines, and too much stress and anxiety that the pandemic had piled on to an already hectic home life with a young family, and an even more stressful job. I was working in the RCMP federal policing program and had been on assignment as the officer in charge of criminal intelligence operations in Alberta. My office was in a nondescript unmarked industrial park on the west side of Edmonton near the ring road. Despite the dull surroundings it was a lively assignment for a civilian. Multiple teams of intelligence collection officers, whose job was to cultivate human sources capable of informing on threats to Canada's national security and conduct covert surveillance operations on high level criminal targets, reported to me.

The Mounties who ran these teams were a colourful bunch who wore jeans, T-shirts, and ball caps to the office; they were tattooed and mostly bearded, and not one of them would you have pegged for a cop in a lineup. They were deadly serious, but at the same time they were almost always capable of finding a form of gallows humour in the darkness we confronted. They constantly impressed me with the exquisite kernels of intelligence they pulled from their roster of informants and with their willingness to put themselves in positions of extreme danger for the good of the country. We had a range of operations running out of our Calgary and Edmonton offices, but as that January wound up, we deprioritized the better part of our efforts and shifted gears to address an emergency situation that was about to consume the nation.

We'd started to hear bits and pieces about a trucker convoy from the Ideologically Motivated Criminal Intelligence Team in Ottawa in mid-January.[1] A convoy was planned in response to some new vaccination requirements the federal government had put in place. Unless they were fully vaccinated, cross-border truckers, who had previously been exempt, would now be required to do pre-arrival testing, quarantine if deemed symptomatic upon arrival, and to test while in Canada.[2]

A group of people whose integral role in the global supply chain deemed them essential workers did not receive this new policy well. We started to get intelligence reports from the Ontario Provincial Police's Project Hendon not long after that and invitations to daily briefs on the status of the convoy. By January 28 we could tell things were getting serious in Ottawa. The Ottawa Police Service set up a National Capital Region command centre and requested to commandeer the Cartier Drill Hall parking lot as a staging area for police.

The next day, the CBC reported that the Rideau Centre Mall was shuttered. I'd lived for a few years in the ByWard Market on George Street at the beginning of my federal public service career, so the significance of the massive mall's closure was not lost on me. I could easily envision the whole area—which includes the Supreme Court, the Senate, Parliament Hill, the National Arts Centre, the Chateau Laurier, the American Embassy, the locks of the Rideau Canal, Major's Hill Park, the National Art Gallery—thrown into organized chaos by an amorphous but still, to that point, inconceivable trucker convoy. I'm not saying I predicted the eventual circus that engulfed the parliamentary precinct, but anyone who has been to a Canada Day concert on the Hill or a Remembrance Day service at the Tomb of the Unknown Soldier might have had an inkling that the area was vulnerable to crowds and traffic congestion. Politicos also know that between those two monuments—the Hill and the Tomb—is the Prime Minister's Office, the Privy Council Office, and the Office of the National Security and Intelligence Advisor to the Prime Minister. This limestone building on the corner of Wellington and Elgin streets is the Canadian government's central node of decision-making and intelligence analysis.

And by that evening it was on television, surrounded by big rigs draped in Canadian flags and blaring their horns at full volume. Confederate flags and Nazi flags were mixed into the tapestry, which included rampant indicators of Islamophobia, a mock gallows with an effigy of the prime minister hanging in a noose, bouncy castles, barbecues, and porta-potties. Besides the Confederate flags, other indicia of American influence pervaded the protest: "Trump 2024," "Don't Tread on Me," references to First Amendment rights, and the slogan "2022 is 1776," leading the Queen's University political scientist Kim Richard Nossal to conclude presciently that "we will see a further increase in cross-border movement of Trumpism's populist, illiberal, authoritarian, and White nationalist ideas" here in Canada even before Trump was back in power.[3]

If you know how Ottawa works—and how it doesn't—this was a bad sign. You can argue whether the downtown core of the nation's capital, which contains the three central agencies—Finance, Treasury Board, and PCO as well as the Bank of Canada, Public Safety Canada, and the Department of National Defence—should constitute a form of critical infrastructure in and of itself. I argue it does, though it is not officially defined as such in the regulations of the Emergencies Act. It was nevertheless evident that the trucker convoy would be a potentially catastrophic disruption to peace, order, and good government. If the civil servants and elected decision makers can't think because they can't hear, and they can't meet for the same reason, and if they aren't secure enough in their workplace to conduct the business of the state for a protracted period of time, eventually this becomes a national emergency, because it threatens the continuity of government. That was my thinking at the time, which hasn't changed.

My concerns for Ottawa were amplified by the fact that in my own city of Edmonton that day a convoy of two hundred trucks and some nine thousand people converged on the grounds of the provincial legislature, not far from RCMP headquarters and not all that far from my home. Another convoy of around a thousand vehicles left Lethbridge to travel south along the provincial highway to a town at the Montana border called Coutts, AB.[4]

Inside the RCMP headquarters in Edmonton a flurry of activity kicked off. A gold, silver, bronze incident command was struck, staff were tasked and reassigned, fleet vehicles were commandeered from units that didn't require them urgently, and a hotel in Lethbridge was block-booked. No one was allowed to take time off; everyone was ordered to the office. It was a heightened state of readiness that would eventually see a number of my intelligence officers sent down the highway to Coutts to stand watch over the blockade, and a number more sent east to Ottawa to help manage the occupation. National Headquarters was just as spun up. Questions about whether there were any nefarious elements to the convoy were asked of the National Intelligence Coordination Centre. Who were these people? What ties did they have to known criminal actors? Where was the money coming from to fund the occupation? What foreign actors were involved? How did the far right factor in all of this?

None of the answers could be pulled from the shelf. The far right had not been a major intelligence priority in Canada since 9/11. In fact, in my experience it had barely registered as a priority at all despite the January 6 riot in Washington the year before, which really should have suggested that the US had come within a hair's breadth of losing its democracy on that day due to the American far right, and that accordingly we in Canada might be wise to consider its contours and key figures in our own county. Some of my teams had done some digging into the matter after Nazi and Confederate flags were reported in a couple of small towns in the south of the province a few months into 2021 and calls for hate crimes investigations followed.[5]

But among all the other priorities consuming the federal policing program, an amorphous far right consisting of shadowy groups that feed on a stew of hateful sentiment towards non-whites, immigrants, established authority, and Western civilization in general—the Yellow Vests, the Proud

Boys, sovereign citizens/freeman on the land, Soldiers of Odin, Atomwaffen, Diagolon, and Second Sons—never really broke through to become a top federal policing priority, nor one of Canada's overarching intelligence priorities.

The truth is we didn't know much about who the Freedom Convoy was or who was backing them. Some work had been done on Diagolon and its podcaster leader Jeremy MacKenzie, but it proved superficial. Our collection efforts had not been on the far right to that point. It was focused on other forms of criminality and threat: transnational organized crime, terrorism, foreign interference, financial crimes, border integrity. To the extent that we considered the far right at all, it was as one part of a much larger conglomerate of ideologically motivated violent extremists (IMVE). This threat category also included incels and other gender- and identity-driven forms of radicalization prone to violent manifestation.

The Freedom Convoy demonstrated how the far right could use the tools of the left—protest, occupation, and blockade—to further its own ends in ways that Canada's security and intelligence community had not foreseen. Jody Thomas, the prime minister's national security and intelligence adviser, put it directly: "The people who organized that protest, and there were several factions there, there is no doubt [they] came to overthrow the government."[6] The hard core of their leadership groups sought a coup.[7] This is not to say that all of the protesters had similar ideas.

With the benefit of a few years of hindsight, I asked Thomas, who is now retired, whether, when confronted with the demands of the convoy's leadership, she had considered that Canada was in the midst of its own January 6 moment. "We thought it could become that," she said. "We thought that the seeds were being planted for something that could be very violent and very extreme, or I did. I'm not sure everybody agreed with me. We knew it wasn't there, but we were watching for that tipping point. January 6 moved really quickly. The convoy had a slow burn, but the burn was getting hotter as each day went on."[8] Still fuming from his loss to President Joe Biden, former president Donald Trump, the man who instigated the January 6 coup attempt on the US Capitol, said the Freedom Convoy protesters were "doing more to defend American freedom than our own leaders by far. We want those great Canadian truckers to know that we are with them all the way."[9]

Why the government chose not to negotiate directly with the convoy is a question that also lingers in the ongoing debate about the use of the Emergencies Act.[10] Some senior bureaucrats were willing, but for Thomas it was clear that the starting points for both sides were too far apart to make any negotiation worthwhile. "We could never get past the, okay, agree to meet, then what?" she told me. "What do you have? We're not giving them the prime minister. That's not how this is going to work. It's like a hostage situation. We're not giving them the prime minister, so what are the things we can offer? That question never got answered."

The Freedom Convoy was not a monolith, although it manifested as such on the streets of Ottawa. It had many factions, including proponents of QAnon, Diagolon supporters, even a coven of witches showed up.[11] Participants had diverse motivations for being there. But the most vocal and organized amongst them got together and penned what they called an MOU and sent it by registered mail to the leaders of the Senate and to the governor general. It was a bewildering screed of freeman-on-the-landesque legalese.[12] They hoped it would result in the "overthrow of the COVID-19 measures" and the prime minister stepping down for "committing treason and crimes against humanity."[13]

If they had not been white people, would the police response have perhaps been different, less tolerant of the occupation in its initial hours and days? Thomas told me she asked this of the Ottawa police chief Peter Sloly in their first phone call. She said that her team had gotten a sense that if the protestors had been of different skin tones, the whole thing might have gone differently. The question didn't go over well with the police chief. "He hung up on us. He was very offended. We got him back on the phone," she said, "but he was very offended."

At Coutts, where the blockade shut down traffic at the province's key trade route and busiest Canada-US border crossing for two weeks, the situation was also dire. We had sent in undercover operators to infiltrate the core group of blockade organizers and set up unauthorized emergency wiretap warrants on some of their phones to allow us to intercept their communications.[14] (To be clear, these operations were outside my purview, and I am not sharing here any classified information that hasn't already been disclosed in the courts or reported by the media.)

A highly trained female undercover operator put herself into the nerve centre—a place now permanently closed called Smugglers Saloon. She testified about her encounters with one of four of the leaders of the blockade who were eventually charged with conspiracy to murder police officers, mischief, and possession of a pipe bomb.[15] "He said this is war and why he is willing to give his life. This is ground zero," she said. "If the RCMP comes into Coutts with force, they will be met with greater force. It was really intense."[16]

A search warrant turned up a heavy cache of weaponry brought to Coutts in preparation for a potential armed confrontation with the RCMP. Over a dozen long guns, handguns, sets of body armour (one of which bore a Diagolon patch), a machete, large quantities of ammunition, and high-capacity magazines were discovered in trailers[17] near the blockade.[18] At the rural property of the individual who was the target of the undercover operation, Anthony Olienick, pipe bombs, a shotgun, a rifle, and forty-thousand rounds of ammunition were discovered.[19]

The undercover operators, who posed as blockade volunteers, later told the court that Olienick believed he was part of a "revolution" and the Mounties were pawns of the federal government who should be hanged and that he threatened to slit their throats if they raided the blockade. He also believed Prime Minister Trudeau was the devil.[20] After Olienick's arrest, under interrogation, he denied targeting police but did note that he feared invasion by the Communist Chinese and the globalist troops of the United Nations.[21] Such thinking prevailed in the Freedom Convoy, which, according to political scientists Corey Robinson and Scott D. Wilson, "mobilized far-right anti-globalist conspiracy theories to articulate its opposition to a range of measures associated with the World Economic Forum and the 'Great Reset'"[22]—a conspiracy theory that posited public health measures as deliberately manipulated to bring about economic collapse and eventually a socialist world government, but for the benefit of a capitalist class.[23]

Federal public safety minister Marco Mendicino stated that "it could have been deadly for citizens, protesters and officers. We need to be clear-eyed about the seriousness of these incidents and, indeed, several of the individuals at Coutts have strong ties to a far-right extreme organization with leaders who are in Ottawa."[24] Mendicino here was likely referring to three members of Diagolon—Jeremy MacKenzie, Derek Harrison, and Alexander Vriend—whom the Canadian Security Intelligence Service had observed attending the Ottawa protest and reported on in a confidential report that was redacted and made available to the Public Order Emergency Commission. "This is the good guys versus the bad guys [Canadian government]. The showdown has finally fucking begun in Canada," the report quotes Mackenize saying. "You could go be part of the story now. This is the beach, get yourself out there"—an apparent reference to Juno Beach on D-Day.[25]

Meanwhile in southern Ontario, Freedom Convoy protesters aligned with those who occupied Ottawa's downtown core and at Coutts had blockaded the Ambassador Bridge connecting Windsor and Detroit for nearly a week. In Manitoba, at the Emerson border crossing, another blockade of some seventy-five vehicles—semi-trucks, farm machinery, and snowplows—had formed on February 10 and been dug in for days.[26] On February 12, the Pacific Highway was blockaded as well at a key commercial trade corridor connecting British Columbia with the state of Washington.

The Ambassador Bridge is probably the most critical piece of commercial trade infrastructure in North America. It's closure, even for a short period, did severe damage to the Canadian economy. Almost $4 billion in trade flows were halted. Motor companies began shutting down their plants. General Motors even contemplated renting an icebreaker to ship vehicle parts across the Great Lakes.[27]

Having it and three other trade points of entry blockaded simultaneously led the Canadian Border Services Agency to report to the government on February 14 that "there has been a significant operational impact that may result in a threat to Canada's economic security and prosperity."[28]

In response to the combination of the highly combustible situation at Coutts and the border blockades, the Trudeau government invoked the Emergencies Act. It was the first time a sitting government ever deemed the extraordinary powers of the act, which came into force in 1988, necessary. "This is about keeping Canadians safe, protecting people's jobs and restoring confidence in our institutions," said Prime Minister Trudeau when he announced he was invoking the act to enable police to get a handle on what had clearly evolved well beyond the parameters of any commonsense notion of lawful protest.

The Freedom Convoy had become a threat to Canadian democracy. Invoking the Emergencies Act allowed for a time-limited and proportionate use of power necessary to restore peace, order, and good government to the nation. Law enforcement did this with remarkable efficiency and in a way that peacefully defused a situation that could easily have ended in significant violence, injury, and death. But while a statutorily mandated commission of inquiry on the use of the act determined it appropriate, the federal court and the Court of Appeals disagreed, finding that the legal thresholds hadn't been met since the act does not contemplate economic security, and without that element no national emergency as defined in the act had occurred to justify the government's decision.[29] The government is, at present, appealing to the Supreme Court for a final judgment.[30]

Those who drafted the original 1988 Emergencies Act could never have imagined the effects on the Canadian social fabric of a global pandemic in the age of disinformation. The Freedom Convoy was spawned in a singular moment—the pandemic and the public health measures deemed necessary to curb its lethal effects on the population and preserve the ability of the provincial health care systems to function.

This was a profoundly disorienting period. For many it was their first foray into politics. They formulated their newly found political opinions on perspectives they found in a conspiratorial online universe. "Influencers" on Facebook, YouTube, TikTok, and X preyed on the collective paranoia that had bred. Instead of drawing on the expertise of credentialed scientists and medical doctors, these influencers, whom the Center for Countering Digital Hate identified in a report published in March 2021 called *The Disinformation Dozen*, invented conspiracy theories about the pandemic's causes, curbing mechanisms, and cures. Between them, just twelve of these committed conspiracists were responsible for 65 percent of the anti-vaccine content on social media.[31] As the COVID contagion spread across the world, the contagion of disinformation about it spread through social media channels.

If there was a common jumping off point for this conspiratorial ontology, it was a sense that the governments of the day had overshot the mark in curtailing peoples' freedoms. All conspiracy theory requires a kernel of truth to be blown up into a cloud of misinformation and disinformation, which in the case of the COVID conspiracy theories still hangs over us. Wild notions emerged, like COVID-19 was a hoax (it is directly responsible for the deaths of

7.1 million people to date worldwide), that it was spread on purpose or was a bioweapon, that liberal governments were leveraging it to pursue anti-democratic objectives, that 5G technologies were spreading it further, that vaccines would contain microchips made by Bill Gates's Microsoft and used by "globalists" to control people and determine whether they had been tested.[32] The thought leaders of the far right promulgated all of these in online spaces, on podcasts, and on radio shows.

Alex Jones, Joseph Mercola, Robert F. Kennedy, Jr., as well as Donald Trump and Danielle Smith, played roles in pushing conspiratorial narratives about the pandemic. Like Trump, Smith, during her pre-premier days as a shock talk-radio host, pushed alternative treatments to COVID-19 like ivermectin—a medicine used to rid horses of worms—and hydroxychloroquine, which she claimed would cure the disease 100 percent of the time.[33] Other journalists and her own radio station called her out on such reckless claims, and she deleted the tweets in which she made them, but after leaving Global News to concentrate on her podcast, Smith returned to pushing conspiratorial lines of thinking about the pandemic.

In her campaign to replace Jason Kenney as leader of the UCP, Smith kept at it, promising to fire the governing board of Alberta Health Services if elected. She made good on that promise after taking the reigns as premier. One fired member of that board, Tony Dagnone, wrote an open letter in response to the mass firing, which included ten others. He expressed his view that Smith held "warped" anti-science beliefs and accused her of playing "to her misguided followers who rant against science and academic medicine under the veiled guise of freedom."[34]

Many of those followers held positions of prominence in the Freedom Convoy. Far-right activists like Tamara Lich, Pat King, James Bauder, and Chris Barber were instrumental in organizing the occupations and blockades, backed by millions of crowd-funded dollars channelled through the Christian site GiveSendGo. A hack of the site revealed donor information that journalists at the *Intercept* analyzed. The list of roughly 104,000 donors had collectively contributed $9.6 million to two separate campaigns—Freedom Convoy 2022 and Adopt a Trucker. The *Intercept* surmised that the majority of the donors were American, including the tech billionaire Thomas Siebel, who donated $90,000. The Oath Keepers, an American far-right paramilitary organization that led the January 6 insurrection, were also major donors, with hundreds of their members making contributions to the Freedom Convoy.[35]

Tamara Lich also created a GoFundMe campaign on January 14, 2022, and linked it to her personal TD savings account.[36] The money poured in so fast that GoFundMe started asking questions. Lich pulled in lawyer Jeffrey Rath, who had been working with Lich and the other organizers, to provide answers.[37] Before the end of the same month, and before the end of the Freedom Convoy, Rath founded the Alberta Prosperity Society (Project), now one of the leading voices in the Alberta separatist movement.[38] Lawyer Keith Wilson, who alongside Rath is the most prominent credentialed separatist voice, chartered a plane, flew to Ottawa, and took up lodgings in the Arc Hotel in the ByWard Market to sign up new clientele.[39] He and Eva Chipiuk became the main lawyers for the Convoy. Chipiuk is, unsurprisingly, a prominent Alberta separatist who has now partnered with Rath to spearhead a class-action lawsuit "on behalf of Albertans harmed by COVID-19 vaccines."[40]

According to a submission made by the University of Alberta political science professor Jared Wesley to the Public Order Emergency Commission Inquiry, the Freedom Convoy has "deep roots in Western Canada," and its emergence "coincided with a rise in Western separatism." Wesley's analysis of the elements of both movements remains instructive even as the Freedom Convoy fades from view and the separatist movement emerges far more prominently than it ever has before. Three forces simultaneously animate this new populism: first, a sense among a small minority of Alberta's population that the rest of society is leaving them behind; second, an insular, us vs. them tribalism that turns opponents into enemies; and third, a distinct lack of deference to traditional sources of authority and institutions of democracy, which imperils the legitimacy of governments and elections. In combination, these forces and the separatist movement they have manifested create, in Wesley's words, "one of the largest threats to national unity today."[41]

VOLUMES OF PRACTITIONER testimony and policy submissions from experts across the country informed the Public Order Emergency Commission and Justice Paul Rouleau's final report. For the purposes of understanding where we might be headed with the Alberta separatist movement and the referendum in October, a few points boil to the surface.

First, the new Canadian populism, as Rouleau pointed out, comes with "increasingly hostile" rhetoric towards the institutions of our society. The proponents of this movement see the officials who represent those institutions—politicians, public health officials—as "enemies to be imprisoned or worse." Second, the convoy organizers, in Rouleau's judgement, "demonstrated a range of views that I have no difficulty characterizing as being based on misinformation. Some views were outright conspiratorial."[42] Of one organizer, he noted: "Patrick King . . . testified to his apparent belief that the Government of Canada had 'implement[ed]' the presence of Chinese soldiers in Canada."[43] And third, the myriad intelligence, planning, command, communications, and decision-making failures that characterized much of the early response to the large-scale, nationwide protest exposed in stark detail the limits of Canada's byzantine policing, intelligence, and bureaucratic systems.

Three years on from the commission, it is unclear how many of Justice Rouleau's nearly sixty recommendations to the federal government have been implemented. Have the nation's police forces and intelligence agencies developed and put in practice enhanced protocols on information sharing, intelligence gathering, and distribution (recommendation 1)? Has a concept of operations for major events of a national or interprovincial dimension been created for the single national intelligence coordinator (recommendation 2)? Have the nation's various law enforcement agencies come together to discuss protocols on how to request and offer additional resources when a police service is unable to deal with a major event in its area of responsibility (recommendation 3)? Has Canada's national security and intelligence community evolved and adapted to face the massive changes in the threat environment that the Freedom Convoy experience telegraphed? It is difficult to know. But should we find ourselves brought to the brink of another large-scale public-order emergency courtesy of the Alberta separatists, who evidently are not the types to accept quietly the outcome of a democratic process, we may soon find out.

If the Freedom Convoy was a trial run, it demonstrated the fragility of our fragmented and overstretched policing and intelligence communities and our critical infrastructure when confronted with a novel and asymmetrical threat. It also demonstrated how dark (unregulated) money from the global far right can influence and enhance the impact of domestic political actors. It revealed the toxic effects of mis- and disinformation on populist movements, which appear increasingly prone to violence and to targeting the institutions central to human progress in western civilization.

5: Origins of a Quasi-Separatist Party

"It is an easy thing for men to be deceived by the specious name of liberty."
Thomas Hobbes, *Leviathan*

"Beware, for I am fearless and therefore powerful."
Mary Shelley, *Frankenstein*

THE UNITED CONSERVATIVE Party was formed in deception and fraud. In desperation to defeat Rachel Notley's majority NDP government, the province's warring conservative factions forged a dubious political union that privileged power over any sense of principle. The storied Progressive Conservatives of Peter Lougheed and Ralph Klein merged with the fringe populist Wild Rose party in an effort to form a large enough right-wing coalition to defeat a progressive, primarily urban base of voters in Calgary and Edmonton. This political technique would fuse populism, Western alienation, and a fervent hostility to federal regulation of the fossil fuels industry into a winning coalition. The pledge to "fight back" against the threats to provincial prosperity posed by the Trudeau government's environmental policies would eventually make Jason Kenney premier in 2019.[1] But first he had to create a Frankenstein party and become its first master.

Kenney, a former federal cabinet minister under Prime Minister Stephen Harper, had taken the reigns of Alberta's Progressive Conservatives in 2017, a couple of years after it suffered an historic defeat in the 2015 provincial election. A cagey political operator, Kenney sought a shake-up in party politics that would make him premier. His read of the political map suggested that any split of votes on the right would allow progressives to set the agenda. So he proposed a merger of the two parties on the right of the political spectrum—a move that would have the effect of eliminating any option for a conservative voter still committed to pluralism by replacing that option with a populist one. The body of the former Alberta Conservative Party would take on the mind of the former Wild Rose Party.

With populism on the rise worldwide, it was an astute merger. Donald Trump had become president of the United States just a year earlier, running on an anti-elite platform that characterized the American people as victims of the establishment, the deep state, and fake news. He pledged to save the virtuous from these various enemies of the people and Make America Great Again. The same forces were observable in the United Kingdom throughout the Leave campaign, where proponents like Nigel Farage exploited in spectacular fashion an "us versus them" logic and were able to galvanize those who felt left behind by progressive changes in society and blamed the UK's membership in the European Union. Globalization, neo-liberal economic policies, and rapid technological change had led to unprecedented income inequality with the hands of a billionaire class holding a farcical amount of the world's wealth. The new United Conservative Party in Alberta was part of this emerging populist countermovement. It would draw lessons from the American populist movement and in so doing begin to mainstream far-right ideology in Canada.

Populism is a contested concept. Canadian academics Daniel Drache and Marc D. Froese describe it most succinctly as a "way of speaking about politics that sets up a moral dichotomy and creates a conflict between the 'true people,' who are honest and good, and the 'elite,' who are evil and corrupt."[2] Populism rejects pluralism, which the University of Alberta political scientist Jared Wesley defines as "the norms, institutions, and habits that make disagreement workable in a diverse democracy and federation like Canada."[3] For Drache and Froese, "populism is a worldwide phenomenon, growing, metastasizing, and reaching into every corner of modern politics."[4] Populist leaders tend to be demagogues—smooth speakers who effortlessly blend fact and fiction and offer aggrieved bases simplistic solutions to the complex problems pluralism must wrestle with more inclusively. There is a history of populism on the Prairies that reaches back a century or so. In the interwar period, it manifested as openly fascist or fascist-adjacent in the form of the Alberta Social Credit movement; after the Second World War it underwent a rebrand for obvious reasons, Froese explained to me in an interview.[5]

The creation of the United Conservative party in Alberta was, on the one hand, a manifestation of this global populist movement and, on the other, a move to return the province to its tradition of one-party dominance. Party membership on both sides of the merger voted almost unanimously for its creation in July 2017, and a leadership contest was held that October. The victor had a clear electoral path to the premiership in a province that in modern memory had elected only a single progressive government. Kenney left nothing to chance. With the former Wild Rose leader Brian Jean as his one serious rival for the top job, Kenney and his campaign team set to work on a dark-arts plan that saw the insertion of a stalking horse or "kamikaze" candidate who could dirty up Jean while Kenney stood back and took the high road. The hope was Jean would blow a gasket, as he was prone to do, allowing the release of surreptitiously recorded tapes of him screaming at the Wild Rose executive committee.[6]

That kamikaze candidate was Jeff Callaway, the former president of the Wildrose Party. Callaway's co-campaign manager was Cameron Davies. Callaway's team and Kenney's operated hand in glove throughout the leadership campaign, collaborating on "attack ads, graphics . . . preparation of various speeches that Jeff Callaway was to deliver," Davies later told *Maclean's*. "From start to finish, literally from his launch speech to his debate prep attack lines, to his final speech endorsing Jason Kenney."[7] CBC journalists corroborated Davies, obtaining a leaked cache of documents demonstrating that Kenney's crew had furnished Callaway's team with "strategic political direction, media and debate talking points, speeches, videos, and attack advertisements, all aimed at undermining Kenney's main political rival, Brian Jean."[8] The CBC's Charles Rusnell and Jennie Russell confirmed with Davies during a telephone interview that the two campaigns had even gone so far as to determine in advance when Callaway would abort his bogus run.[9]

I had a chance to review the leaked documents, which one of the journalists shared with me. To read them first-hand is to bear witness to a cynical form of collusion that, even with the distance of time, still jars the democratic conscience. There is a brazen quality to the conspiracy that gives the lie to the notion that such a political entity could represent the pure people against the corrupt elite. In one email from Cameron Davies to Matt Wolf, who played a central role in Kenney's campaign and eventually became his executive director of issues management, earning a base salary of nearly $200,000 a year, Davies scripts the themes of his phoney candidate's campaign:

> Seeds of Doubt (Aug 14—26)
> Consistency (Aug. 23—Sept. 6)
> Trust (Sept. 1 – Sept. 13)
> *Jeff Drops (Although depending on when debates are you may have other ideas?)
> *By this time we hope Jean has attacked Jeff, lost his cool in a debate or two, gone off script to the media so we can release a series of "Screamin' Jean" sound cloud files in which he is screaming at the EC.
> Temperament (Sept. 15—Oct. ??)
> Rough idea of where I see this being effective.[10]

Attached to the email was a detailed communications plan with prepared lines that Callaway was to level at Jean at each phase of the campaign, alongside mocked-up attack ads.

The only problem with the kamikaze scheme, aside from it being a grossly unethical violation of anything approaching a fair and democratic process, was that to get Callaway into the race and onto the debate stage a $60,000 entry fee had to be paid. Money leaves a trail, especially in a regulated political process. This immutable reality was particularly unfortunate for Davies, who acted as the middleman in a clumsy ploy to inject $60,000 worth of illegal contributions into Callaway's campaign account so he could pay the fee.[11]

Eventually the election commissioner issued an astounding series of fines in relation to the easily detectable scam. Davies himself was slapped with two counts of obstructing the commissioner's investigation and six counts of furnishing funds in the name of another donor. His total penalty of $27,000 was referred to Crown Debt Collection before it was eventually paid almost six years later, in April of 2025, just days before he became leader of the separatist Alberta Republican Party.[12] In the months that followed, Davies visited President Trump's Mar-a-Lago resort, met with undersecretary-level officials at the White House, and connected with the MAGA acolytes Tucker Carlson and Megyn Kelly in New York. "It's becoming more and more clear that the current Alberta government has no intention of holding a referendum. So, unfortunately I think these are conversations that need to be had as an effort to increase the pressure on the existing United Conservative Party to listen to the will of the people," Davies told the *National Post* at the time.[13]

In seeming retaliation, not only did the Kenney government sack the election commissioner, Lorne Gibson, but the entire independent office was subsumed into the broader Elections Alberta bureaucracy, a regressive move in terms of elections transparency in the province. During Gibson's seventeen-month tenure his office conducted over seventy investigations and levied over $200,000 in fines.[14] Most were in relation to the kamikaze scheme that led Kenney to become the leader of the UCP. Kenney has said he didn't know a thing about it.

I HAD JUST taken up my new role in RCMP K Division in Edmonton when the kamikaze scandal broke. The matter was referred shortly thereafter to K Division for investigation. In Alberta the RCMP is is not only the federal but also the provincial police service (only Ontario and Quebec have their own provincial police services). This, to my still Ottawa-programmed mind, created a problematic conflict of interest from the start. Most of the RCMP's employees in the province were dependent on the provincial government for their contracts. How could they be expected to carry out an objective investigation into their employer, who was also, coincidentally, threatening to end the RCMP's contract and establish its own provincial police force? The same could be asked of any provincial prosecutors who might find themselves assigned to the messy work of initiating a trial against a sitting premier: could they do it objectively without finding themselves on the horns of a dilemma that could impact their careers and livelihoods?

For five years the kamikaze investigation wound on under a veil of secrecy within the division. In 2019, a special prosecutor from the Ontario Ministry of the Attorney General was assigned to the case. But it remained under the conduct of the the same team that investigated homicides in Alberta—the Major Crimes Section. The investigation considered the kamikaze scheme along one path and a series of identity frauds allegedly used to load the vote in favour of Kenney along another. The case involved some sixty-five investigators and almost a half million dollars in overtime and travel expenses.[15] Superintendent Rick Jané stated in a press conference in K Division headquarters (which I attended out of morbid curiosity) that "we did not uncover evidence that Callaway or any other person committed a criminal offence."

Of the identity fraud that led to voter fraud, Jané noted that there were less than two hundred of these and concluded therefore that these would not have impacted the outcome of the leadership contest.[16] He was arguing, bizarrely, that because the identity frauds detected were not numerous enough to determine the outcome of the campaign, criminal charges were not merited. When athletes are caught doping, they are typically stripped of their medals or awards. Consider Lance Armstrong, the winner of seven consecutive Tour de France cycling races between 1999 and 2005. When an investigation years later found he had used performance-enhancing drugs throughout this period, he was stripped of his titles and banned for life from sports that follow the world anti-doping code. Would he have won regardless of his use of drugs? Cycling commentator Phil Liggett says he would have, "no question," he was just that good.[17] Most people who watched Armstrong in those years would agree, which makes his story all the more tragic. Kenney was caught doing the equivalent of performance-enhancing drugs and was let off the hook because his margin of victory was deemed to be greater than the extent of his cheating. Nevertheless, to reach this puzzling conclusion investigators conducted over 1,200 interviews with people linked to the kamikaze scheme and to the suspicious votes.

Jason Kenney used the moment that followed Jané's press conference to proclaim complete vindication of his leadership win. It was an odd statement given the historic raft of fines at the regulatory level the operatives associated with the Callaway campaign had racked up. Sure, his team wasn't criminally charged, but a five-year investigation of their activity isn't exactly nothing. To rewrite the story in such strident terms was classic Kenney.

By the time the RCMP finally concluded its multi-year "complex and high profile" investigation into the UCP's first leadership contest, Kenney was a distant memory in Alberta politics. In the aftermath of the Freedom Convoy, and just a couple of months after the federal Conservatives pulled out the knives on Erin O'Toole and voted to replace him, Jason Kenney faced the same fate. A far-right faction of his own party ousted him before he would have a chance to contest an election as an incumbent premier. And while this scenario has become the norm in Alberta politics, it is uncommon elsewhere for such a concentration of power within a single party to determine the political leadership and fate of a jurisdiction.

In 1953, the political scientist C.B. Macpherson observed that Alberta's economy and society was so dominated by agriculture that petit bourgeois farmers had reduced the politics of the province to a single issue: maximizing the profits of the producers. They thus turned over pursuit of that profit at the political level to a single party—at that time the Alberta Social Credit Party, which held power for thirty-six consecutive years between 1935 and 1971.[18] Macpherson dubbed this form of one-party rule a "quasi-party system" and identified it as "the emergence of authoritarian populism in response to the crisis-prone character of the Canadian state in the 1930s."[19] When agriculture gave way to oil as the dominant industry in the province, the Progressive Conservatives replaced the Socreds and governed for forty-four consecutive years from 1971 to 2015. The quasi-party system persisted.

Understanding the origins of the UCP—a political party born in the fraud and deception of the electorate it sought to govern—is essential to understanding the political entity that the UCP has become. It was never a party based on a coherent ideology. To go back to Karl Loewenstein's very applicable analysis of world fascism in the interwar period, it has "no metaphysical justification which could be derived from absolute values only."[20] It was formed to take power and for the sake of power alone. It is therefore more aptly understood as a political technique that aims to hold power in the province by any means necessary.

IN THE MONTHS that followed the blockade at Coutts, a movement galvanized that saw large crowds huddled together on Highway 4 in the dead of an Alberta winter. Made up of Christian nationalists, separatists, climate-change deniers, globalist conspiracy theorists, fossil fuels evangelists, great replacement theorists, and COVID denialists, Take Back Alberta was looking to send Kenney and his big blue Dodge pickup truck back to Ontario, where he was born.[21] Kenney's cardinal sin—according to these freedom-loving folks—was that he caved to science and modern medicine and declared a public health emergency when the fourth wave of COVID-19 rocked the province.

In September 2021, Kenney reinstated a range of public health measures designed to flatten the contagion curve threatening to send very sick Albertans to the ICUs. Back in the endless days of June, Kenney had proclaimed Alberta "Open for summer" in time for the Calgary Stampede, beating every other province in its lifting of pandemic restrictions. By the time August rolled around, infections were at a thousand a day, while the UCP sold merch proclaiming "Best Summer Ever 2021."

Alberta's infection rate was quadruple the national average. Frustration with the UCP playing frat-boy politics with peoples' lives and the integrity of the health care system was as hot as a COVID fever. Pushback on social media to the rising death toll was met with bully tactics from the UCP communications staff, who in a coordinated and relentless fashion shouted over "lockdown lobbyists" who dared speak a critical word of Kenney's premature policy.[22] The attacks on average citizens were cruel and degrading. They broke norms on the Canadian political scene that paved the way to a brazen hyper-partisanship that, in the words of journalist Charles Rusnell, "sought to denigrate, demonize and dehumanize political opponents."[23]

With the morbidity numbers soaring, Kenney was forced to face the uncomfortable truth of objective reality. He made the call to put public health measures back in place as the school year began. This blasphemy in the eyes of the radicalized UCP base set in motion a movement that continues to dominate Alberta politics.

Take Back Alberta was formed by David Parker, the home-schooled son of a rural Alberta preacher, who has built a career as a right-wing political organizer and operative dating back to his teens. He was Stephen Harper's regional adviser for the Prairies. As regional organizer for Central Alberta, he helped Jason Kenney capture the UCP leadership. He has done tours with Tucker Carlson and Megyn Kelly in the United States. He has, in other words, developed next-level populist political organizing skills that have arguably transformed Alberta's political landscape.

His tactics, as we shall see, however, often demonstrably push the boundaries of what is legal at regulatory, if not criminal, levels.

Parker had camped out at Coutts with a view towards recruiting comrades-in-arms for a personal war he was about to wage against sitting premier Jason Kenney and set his sights on the blockade's most prominent ringleader: Marco Van Huigenbos. Van Huigenbos served a 120-day prison sentence for mischief over $5000 for his leadership role in the hijacking of the province's central highway.[24] With Parker as chief executive officer and Van Huigenbos, a convicted criminal, as chief financial officer, Take Back Alberta registered with Elections Alberta as a third-party political advertiser.

It had a four-phase plan. Phase 1, execute a coup against Kenney. Phase 2, replace him with Danielle Smith. Phase 3, replace the UCP board with TBC members. Phase 4, mobilize TBA resources to defeat the NDP in the 2023 general election.[25]

Take Back Alberta executed each phase with stunning precision.

Throughout phase 1, Take Back Alberta, with Parker at the mic, held hundreds of town halls across the province to drum up support. At a rally in early May 2023, Parker preached apocalyptically about what he described as a "war between pro-humans and anti-humans" and told his audience, "You can vote your way into socialism, you almost always need to shoot your way out."[26] He has also said such things as: "We are slaughtering our children in the womb. We are living in an anti-human society that literally teaches our children that they are a disease on this planet." "In light of all that," said Parker, "we need to stop the NDP."[27]

Parker's message was compelling enough to sweep Kenney into the dustbin of Alberta's political history by the middle of the month. Making matters worse, Kenney had seen the TBA posse coming for him months before. He was surreptitiously recorded in March saying of TBA: "The lunatics are trying to take over the asylum, and I won't let them."[28] These were some of Kenney's most famous last words as premier.

Phase 2 of the TBA plan was to install their preferred candidate, the "faith, family, and freedom" friendly Danielle Smith into the premier's chair. This alliteration was courtesy of Roy Beyer, TBA's regional captain for Calgary and a former pastor turned sanctioned securities fraudster and Freedom Convoy director,[29] who was looking ahead to the 2023 provincial election as "a spiritual battle for our nation."[30] According to Beyer, "God celebrates that there's nations in the world. And that's a beautiful thing. The globalists have the opposite view. They're going to eliminate nationhood and turn it into this grand scheme of a global government."[31]

Beyer's statement is anchored in globalist conspiracy theory, which is what the scholar Jacob McLean describes as a "master frame" or a catch-all term that covers "any conspiracy that follows the basic logic that an alliance of powerful elites, liberals, left-wingers, and dangerous (sometimes ethnic) Others are plotting to overthrow national governments and replace them with a single, totalitarian, socialistic or communistic regime that aims to govern the whole world."[32] I spoke to McLean about his doctoral dissertation, "Carbon Convoys: Extractive Populism and the Canadian Far Right," which he completed last year at York University. He explained that the globalist conspiracy has deep roots in Alberta dating back to the Social Credit years of the 1930s. Alberta's first populist premier, William "Bible Bill" Aberhart, who founded the Alberta Social Credit Party in 1935, held deeply conspiratorial views, mainly about a cabal of mysterious Jews who sought world dominance.[33]

In the present moment, the globalist conspiracy theory encompasses an array of outlandish notions that have become pervasive worldwide. Depending on where the conspiracist is situated geographically, different strands of thought can make up their conspiratorial tapestry. Alberta's globalist conspiracy theorists tend to understand the world through a fervour for the fossil fuel industry, which the provincial economy significantly depends upon. Accordingly, they vilify climate science and the very notion of climate change. If climate change can be dismissed out of hand as the construct of an evil global elite in the United Nations or the World Economic Forum, the transition towards renewable energy sources can be cast in similar terms. This has had the effect of preventing rational governments concerned with the sustainability of the global economy and the future of the planet from taking the policy actions required to stave off the climate catastrophe. Scientists working for the fossil fuels industry discovered climate change in the late 1970s and early 1980s. They understood that it posed an existential threat to their industry, since rational governments concerned for the health and well-being of their citizenry would naturally have to incentivize a transition to renewable energy sources as a means of ensuring the survival not just of their own people but of the human race. They chose instead to cover up their findings and find ways of discrediting those of other scientists.[34]

McLean and his colleagues at the Observatory of Populism in Canada argue that the fossil fuels industry has "mobilized around the idea that the oil and gas industry is under attack by elites and environmentalists and therefore requires 'the people' to defend it as an expression of the popular will and common good."[35] They understand the globalist conspiracy theory master frame and its pervasive influence within the strand of far-right populism in Alberta as linked to the interests of the fossil fuels industry. And they have traced this line of thinking throughout the Alberta separatist movement, which they see as a continuation of far-right mobilizations in the province that began with Yellow Vest Canada in 2018.

In a section of his dissertation titled "'Legitimate' Economic Grievances or 'Hate'?," McLean shows how some media outlets covered the Yellow Vest rallies, which attracted numerous designated far-right hate groups including the Soldiers of Odin (an Islamophobic hate group), the Proud Boys, and neo-Nazi elements, using the analytical lens of grievance politics that justified the demonstrations in terms of legitimate concerns about the carbon tax and the future of the oil and gas industry.[36] Others, like Tyler Dawson, who dug a bit deeper, discovered Yellow Vest online forums contained "more fringe and extreme views: there are fantasies about the assassination of Prime Minister Trudeau, adherence to conspiracy theories and undisguised racism, all of which pose something of a challenge for those attempting to further relatively mainstream views."[37]

McLean sees the separatist movement as a logical outgrowth of the protest cycle that began with the Yellow Vest Canada movement. He argues that the fossil fuels industry has subsidized and energized these protest cycles in an effort to capture the one modality of political influence that remained for the left: street protests and mass movement. The Take Back Alberta movement is similarly a guerrilla unit for fossil capital. As we will see, this makes Danielle Smith the fossil fuel industry's puppet premier, given TBA's role in getting her into power.

AS A FELLOW traveller in the far-right conspiracy theory and a fervent oil-and-gas advocate and former registered lobbyist for the sector,[38] Danielle Smith quickly became TBA's favoured candidate in the leadership contest that kicked off while Kenney remained lame-ducked in the premier's office. Smith was the only candidate in the UCP leadership contest to campaign openly on an anti-public health measures, anti-vaccine, and anti-cooperative federalism platform. In a leadership debate hosted by Ezra Levant, Smith said she was willing to use the separatist Alberta Prosperity Project as her "or else" in attempting to get "as much autonomy as we can" from Ottawa.[39]

In line with this she proposed a Sovereignty Act that would give Alberta the power to ignore and violate the constitution at the province's discretion. Smith's proposal was so radical that it caused Jason Kenney to break neutrality and weigh in on the leadership race, calling Smith's proposal for an Alberta Sovereignty Act "a risky, dangerous, half-baked plan that would shred the rule of law and pave the path for Alberta to become a banana republic."[40]

Smith's sops to Take Back Alberta and the far right of the party were clear and intentional. She understood that of the UCP's new membership, David Parker's organization had signed up a significant percentage and that a new and flagrantly separatist flank of the party was taking shape in the form of the Alberta Prosperity Project, led by the likes of Jeffrey Rath, Dennis Modry, and Mitch Sylvestre. TBA claimed to have thirty thousand members. The Alberta Prosperity Project claimed to have even more. To win over these folks and emerge the victor, Smith turned her back on Canada and became downright hostile towards it.[41] Was this just political cosplay, or was Smith actually saying that she too was a separatist?

SMITH WAS SWORN in a few days later, on October 11. "God Save the King" and Canada's national anthem were played. Chief Billy Morin of Enoch Cree First Nation blessed the ceremony. Reverend Susan Oliver of Edmonton's Anglican Christ Church followed with prayers for a wider circle of inclusion and a confession that we have not always treasured the gifts of this good land and the diversity of its own people. She prayed for Smith to be given the gift to discern what is right. Lieutenant-Governor Lakhani administered the oath of executive council. Like all first ministers before her, Smith solemnly swore allegiance to the Crown and affirmed a commitment to maintain cabinet confidentiality.

Her first order of business was to pass a version of the Sovereignty Act she had campaigned on, which gave her government the power to disregard federal laws at its own discretion, thus setting the legislature as the arbiter of the constitutionality of federal law. In a radical revision of constitutional democracy, the Alberta Sovereignty within a United Canada Act allows the provincial cabinet to decide whether it is in or out on specific aspects of federalism, including federal regulations and even the enforcement of the criminal code by provincial entities. The dean of the University of Calgary's School of Law at the time called the legislation an "unconstitutional gambit" and accused the premier of "engaging in a game of political chicken."[42] After the controversial legislation was introduced, Prime Minister Trudeau said: "We know that the exceptional powers that the premier is choosing to give the Alberta government in bypassing the legislature is causing a lot of eyebrows to raise in Alberta, and we're going to see how this plays out. I'm not going to take anything off the table, but I'm also not looking for a fight."[43] Trudeau's leadership had begun to take on water, but his appeasement set the tone for the prevailing dynamic between Ottawa and Alberta that followed even after he left the prime minister's office. Smith would continue with her shakedown approach to federalism and in so doing destabilize the cooperative foundation of the nation. She would try to remake Canada in transactional terms, extorting the rest of the country in the interests of the fossil fuels industry.

Speaking at the bill's third reading just after midnight during an evening sitting of the legislature that had begun on December 7, the NDP MLA from Lethbridge-West, Shannon Phillips, asserted that the Sovereignty Act was written not by the Smith government but by the political science professor and committed separatist Barry Cooper of the University of Calgary. Phillips used her five minutes to explain the bill's origins in a document called "Free Alberta Strategy" written by Cooper—whom she said made "Rudy Giuliani look like a legal scholar"—the premier's chief of staff, Rob Anderson, as well as a constitutional lawyer named Derek From. The Sovereignty Act, in Cooper's view, was intended to be unconstitutional. "Indeed, that is the whole point," he wrote in an op-ed in the *National Post* in June 2022. The idea was to fundamentally destabilize Canadian federalism and rewrite the rules as "the last stop before independence."[44] Shannon Phillips said: "I don't think that Albertans or Canadians, but certainly Albertans, expect that we politicize the basic traffic signals of our democracy. We just don't. These stabilizing principles are what give us the good life . . . They're what give us equality, dignity of the person, individual liberty. They are what govern our property rights transactions, trade, and commerce. They are what govern scientific advances, development of knowledge, dissemination of knowledge, widespread literacy, even."[45] It was getting late, but Phillips was on to the fact that the Sovereignty Act had the potential to fundamentally transform both Alberta's and Canada's democracy.

The premier, who would not win a seat in the legislature until a few months later, rose to deny Cooper's involvement and lash out at the federal NDP and its coalition with the Federal Liberals. "I find it so remarkable that they've been talking about investment like capital flight, saying that it has been—they're projecting that there would be unprecedented capital flight," Smith said. "Well, that would be hard to beat because there was unprecedented capital flight when they brought through the climate leadership plan. That was once again partnering with our enemies who want to shut down our industry to try in some flawed way to get appeasement from Ottawa. I don't know why it is they felt that they needed to suck up to Ottawa. It's not like Ottawa is a national government. The way our country works is that we are a federation of sovereign, independent jurisdictions. They are of those signatories to the Constitution, and the rest of us are signatories to the Constitution, and have a right to exercise our sovereign powers in our own area of jurisdiction."

In Smith's version of Canadian federalism, the provinces get promoted to sovereign entities that have formed a political union with Ottawa, whose role seems to be only that of a bogeyman holding back the fossil fuel sector from realizing its full potential. It is a dangerously revisionist interpretation of the nation, one that is a very long distance from the Supreme Court of Canada's secession reference's conception ("close ties of interdependence based on shared values"), or John Whyte's "thousand acts of accommodation," or Roy Romanow's notion of the responsibility of citizenship and Canadians' "never-ending project of nation-building." Smith's version must be understood as a grave threat to Canada's continuance.

The premier went on to detail her issues with Liberal climate policies, which she blamed for a string of setbacks for the oil and gas and coal industries in the province. "One of the things that occurred, of course, was that Northern Gateway ended up getting cancelled, cheered along by the members opposite. They never supported Northern Gateway, which would have done so much to help advance our economy. Energy East, once again, also got shut down with no support from the opposition," she argued. "Koch Oil announced that they had two oil sands projects that they walked away from because of the uncertainty being created by the climate leadership plan."[46]

The courts shut down Northern Gateway because the federal government failed to consult First Nations about the pipeline project that would run through their ancestral territories. Its cancellation had nothing to do with the Liberal climate plan.[47] TransCanada killed the Energy East pipeline because commodity prices tanked, and it was no longer profitable. The energy company wrote off a $1 billion charge to cancel the project in 2017.[48] The Koch projects were cancelled in part due to the Notley government's climate policies and also because of what the company referred to as the "regulatory uncertainty around the Climate Leadership Program, at its potential impacts on the project, from carbon tax to the emissions cap."[49] Neither fact nor Canadian federalism would stand in Smith's way as she pushed forward with the intentionally unconstitutional Sovereignty Act. Using the interests of Koch Industries as the primary factual justification for the bill was a haunting harbinger of the direction in which Smith would take both her province and the country.

Koch Industries is one of the largest, most powerful private companies in the world. The two brothers that founded it bought large swaths of bitumen-rich land in Alberta in the 1960s. By the 1980s they had leases on some "sixty thousand acres in northern Alberta," according to the journalist Geoff Dembicki.[50] They were among the first to begin to develop the Alberta oil sands. And they also were among the first to understand that the development of the oil sands at scale would lead to a warming climate. That is why they have spent billions building a political machine capable of casting doubt on climate science that includes one of the "largest corporate lobbying offices" in the United States, according to an opinion piece published in the *New York Times*, and a "constellation of Koch-funded think-tanks and university centers. They all convey a consistent message: that government programs can only cause more harm than good and that market forces alone must shape human society."[51]

For his part, Barry Cooper seems to understand the gravity of this at both the philosophical and practical levels. In an interview he gave to BC journalist Stuart McNish,

Cooper explained his understanding of the implications of pursuing the path to independence he would eventually set out in the Free Alberta Strategy and that the UCP under Smith would begin implementing as soon as she took power. "Of course it is treasonous, of course it is illegal, and of course it is going to be very unpleasant, and we're going to have, as the American colonists had, help from abroad. They relied upon the French; we are going to have to rely upon the Americans. It's not a legal issue. It's entirely political, and it will depend on whether or not Saskatchewan and Alberta have leaders who are willing to understand the very serious implications, which means, among other things, getting the Americans on board."[52]

I also had the opportunity to speak with Cooper in February of this year for a related project. I had met him many years previous when I was a postdoctoral fellow at the University of Calgary's Centre for Military, Security and Strategic Studies. I'd found him engaging, with a quick, wry sense of humour and a lively intelligence. The academic work of his that I'd read dealt with the RCMP having lost its policing ethos and Canada's need for a foreign intelligence service. I'd found his work to be of high academic standard, both incisive and illuminating. Cooper is a cherubic, affable sort. He presents his ideas in a reasoned, impassioned manner that masks their radical nature. As the philosopher king of Alberta independence, he's formidable. He's like Steve Bannon in the United States but without the social media megaphone, and he's not to be taken lightly.

In our interview he said he hadn't spoken with the premier or her chief of staff in three or four years and wasn't sure what their strategic plans were in terms of independence. I asked him whether the sovereignty referendum path the government seemed to be on had been initiated in a democratic way. "The government of Alberta," Cooper explained, "was certainly not elected to establish Alberta as an independent country. So they have no reason to be sovereigntists." But the tack it was taking was "prudent" as far as Cooper was concerned because there was a fairly high level of support for independence, "somewhere around 30 or 40 percent." Nevertheless, he said, "I have no idea what her thinking about this is because it's a very fraught game. The premier of British Columbia is not entirely wrong when he talked about treason. Certainly, metaphorically, it looks that way. Whether it is treason in law I think is absurd. But metaphorically it looks that way, particularly to people in British Columbia because they are terrified at what would happen to their economy if Alberta became independent. They'd be dependent on us, and they sure as hell don't like that."[53]

Cooper understands the betrayal at the moral core of Alberta secessionism. His antagonism towards the Laurentian elites out East and British Columbians on the other side of the Rockies seems to justify it in his mind. But he is not advocating for Alberta to eventually become an authoritarian regime, either. He recognizes the UCP doesn't have a mandate to operate as a separatist party.

Indeed, during the spring election campaign, Smith's UCP failed to even utter the words *separatism* or *referendum*. It ran a straight and narrow campaign on issues that matter to Albertans: tax cuts, safe streets, mental health supports, education and career training, investing in tourism, improving health care for women and children, a guarantee to maintain public health care, and even a new arena for the Calgary Flames. During the campaign, the UCP did not make a promise to Albertans about holding a referendum on the province exiting Confederation. That outcome was not written into its platform; it was not part of the pitch on the doorsteps. There was no advertising to the effect that "a vote for the UCP is a vote for a referendum on Alberta leaving Canada" or anything remotely of the sort. The almost 60 percent of the electorate who turned out to vote returned a reduced eleven-seat majority for the UCP without ever hearing of its plan to vote on the province's place in Confederation.

We would only find out later that Take Back Alberta played an outsized role in the campaign. In February 2025, Elections Alberta issued a sweeping series of fines against TBA, the third-party advertiser, for its circumvention of election advertising spending limits ($22,500), for accepting contributions from outside the province and outside Canada ($13,500), for failing to deposit contributions into appropriate advertising accounts ($27,000), for failure to report gross income from any fundraising events ($9000), for failure to obtain a loan from a financial institution ($9000), and for failure to pay expenses from the appropriate advertising account ($13,500). The significance of TBA racking up over $100,000 in fines for serious electoral offences seemed to barely register with the electorate. Parker declared the rulings "ridiculous" and politically motivated "lawfare."[54] But money matters in Canadian politics because, unlike in the United States, there isn't much of it to go around. Donation limits are set intentionally low, and donations are tightly regulated to keep the playing field as level as possible. When those limits are blown through and those regulations ignored, a campaign can be influenced without voters realizing it until long after the votes are counted.

TBA's chief financial officer, Marco Van Huigenbos, was personally fined $1,900 for knowingly making false statements on election financing reports filed with the chief electoral officer. Director and CEO David Parker was fined a total of $6,500 for four counts of making false statements to the chief electoral officer and an additional $1,000 for exceeding the aggregate contribution limit of $30,000. The fines are extraordinary for Canadian politics. They indicate that TBA flagrantly violated a significant number of the regulations that Elections Alberta oversees and did so with little to no regard for the fairness or transparency that are fundamental norms of Canadian electoral politics. It is difficult to find a record of any electoral violations even approaching the same severity and scale in modern Canadian history. The only case that comes close is the robocalls voter suppression scandal that saw one Conservative Party of Canada staffer sentenced to nine months in prison for his role in making spoof calls to voters and directing them to the wrong polling stations in close ridings in the 2011 federal election.

People like Parker and Davies are to democracy what biker gangs are to public safety: dangerous individuals who know exactly what they are doing to undermine Canada's political integrity. They must accordingly be taken as serious threats, or they will continue to find ways to destabilize our polity. It is evident that Elections Alberta understood TBA's brazen breaches of its regulations as a grave threat, which is why it issued such a sweeping series of fines against the far-right organization. As we will see in chapter 8, the fines did nothing to stop these nefarious actors from conspiring to commit the largest data breach in Canadian history, exposing the personal information of every single voting-age Albertan. This kind of activity will continue to corrode the foundations of our democracy unless it is effectively sanctioned and prosecuted.

Parker has refused to pay the fines and instead articulated the view that he ought to be given an award by the regulator for his contributions to democracy in the province. The fines have been referred to Crown Debt Collection. When asked about the case by Postmedia, Parker expressed an intent to "further damage" Elections Alberta.[55] Professor Duane Bratt of Mount Royal University noted that the fines were some of the largest ever issued by Elections Alberta and expressed his opinion that Parker did not seem to think rules or laws applied to him.[56] This is a commonly held view amongst the far right because, as Marc Froese says,

> When you are an anti-liberal, it's rules for you but not for me. The rule of law is made to bind and constrain those people who are enemies, those people who need to be constrained by law. Black people, immigrants, people who are too poor to have a stake in society. Those people need to be bound by law, but those of us who are living in a free society as free men in the traditions of our fathers, we don't need to be bound by law. We have tradition, we have honour. We don't need law to bind us. And that's exactly how they view themselves. That is what makes them anti-liberal because they don't view the rule of law as a thing that binds everybody. That's a liberal concept that is rooted in the equality of the individual. They fundamentally don't believe in the equality of the individual.[57]

Not captured by the Elections Alberta fines were well-substantiated reports that TBA had trained scrutineers to infiltrate campaigns and act as "security" on election day. Only registered candidates can sign up scrutineers to represent them at polling stations to ensure fairness and transparency. Third-party advertisers have no legitimate role in that essential feature of a free and fair vote. TBA members who conducted the webinar training, like Benita Pedersen and Roy Beyer, pushed conspiracy theories imported from the United States about vote tabulators and finding ways to "minimize the cheating" by getting TBA members inside polling stations.[58]

Could TBA's illegal actions have affected the outcome of the historically close provincial election? Few have asked the question.[59] It would require an inquiry on the scale of the Hogue Commission to determine the answer. What is clear, however, is that Kenney's UCP Frankenstein has become a quasi-separatist monster, and it is the one in control. Indeed, support for separation in the province has remained flat for eight years, according to a leading Alberta pollster, Janet Brown. It hovers around a quarter of the province who say they would vote to separate if given the opportunity, according to Brown, who tracks the sentiment higher than other pollsters. But among UCP voters, that number is now a majority, with 57 percent of UCP supporters saying they would vote to separate.[60]

6: The Betrayal of Canada

ON MAY 29, 2023, after the UCP won its slim majority over Rachel Notley's New Democrats, Albertans expected that the UCP would continue to run the province like an oil and gas lobbying firm. Few would have anticipated a steady drumbeat of legislation not only designed to bring about a referendum on secession but with the dice loaded in favour of the secessionists.

The latter was the direct result of the unexpected victory of Mark Carney's Liberal Party in the federal election on April 28, 2025. Canadians re-elected a strong minority government, much to the dismay of Conservatives across the country who expected to reduce the reds to a handful of seats before Carney rescued the party from certain electoral annihilation over four of the most extraordinary months in Canadian political history.

At the tail end of Justin Trudeau's time in office, Pierre Poilievre's Conservatives had a 20-point lead over the Liberals in many opinion polls. Such a margin would have translated into a rout so devastating that some speculated the Liberals would lose official party status in the House of Commons. But Trump's trade war against Canada, and his threats to make us the fifty-first American state, rekindled a sense of nationalism that had laid dormant for decades. Carney was the perfect candidate to harness this renewed spirit of independence in the face of increasingly real and menacing threats from Washington. Poilievre, by contrast, didn't seem up to the task of leading Canada on a new course. More than that, he seemed too ideologically aligned with the Trump regime to mount an effective defence against its attacks on Canadian sovereignty.

In the lead-up to the federal campaign, Premier Smith went on Breitbart News, Steven Bannon's far-right American news agency, to explain the implications of the tariff war and the fifty-first state threat for the forthcoming election. "I would hope that we could put things on pause, is what I've told administration officials," she said. "'Let's just put things on pause so we can get through an election. Let's have the best person at the table make the argument for how they would deal with that,' and I think that's Pierre Poilievre."[1] The comment grabbed attention because it seemed to suggest that the premier attempted to conspire with Trump officials to influence the election. Smith reasoned that if Trump's threats could be set aside while her populist friend campaigned in the next federal election, everything would be just grand.

Smith attended Trump's inauguration in Washington in January and leveraged her connections with the *Dragon's Den* billionaire Kevin O'Leary to get an audience with the president at Mar-a-Lago. Smith was the only Canadian premier in attendance at the president's inauguration, and she had refused to sign a joint statement with fellow provincial leaders and the prime minister regarding Canada's planned response to Trump's tariff threats. The country's premiers had gathered a few days before the inauguration in Ottawa to craft a unified response to the havoc Trump's administration was set to wreak on Canada's economy. Smith was the only premier to attend virtually. Images of the meeting show her glowering from the screen at the room of leaders who bore the responsibility of defending the nation against the incoming presidential administration's looming threats.[2]

Toward the end of the month, Smith continued her courtship of the American far right and appeared at a $1,500 per head private fundraiser for PragerU in south Florida hosted by Ben Shapiro. Despite the name, PragerU is a long way from being a university. Rather, it is a fracking-funded far-right propaganda mill that produces Judeo-Christian "edutainment" content aimed at indoctrinating babies, toddlers, children, and adults with anti-science beliefs and climate-change denialism. Its founder, Dennis Prager, is infamous for arguing throughout the 1980s and 1990s that gay rights were a threat to western civilization. His PragerU has moved on now to fossil fuels advocacy and alerting its audience to the dangers of "radical Islam."[3]

Up on stage at PragerU HQ, Smith gleefully discussed with Shapiro "the massive conservative movement that's happening in Canada" and "the obstacles that need to be removed," in Shapiro's words, "for the United States to have actual solid allies running in Canada than to have some of the schmucks that have been running Canada over the past few years." Smith responded by saying, "I think the president recognizes especially the importance of oil and gas. We already ship about 4.3 million barrels a day of oil to the

United States. We'll keep it coming." Shapiro had previously called Canada "a silly country" that he felt "will greet us as liberators."[4] Albertans paid out nearly $20,000 in government travel expenses for Smith's contribution to PragerU's war chest.[5]

But as it turned out, Trump unexpectedly took to Carney and took umbrage with Poilievre because he was "not positive about me." Trump said Poilievre's "biggest problem is he's not a MAGA guy."[6]

The day after the federal election, Smith's UCP, in reactionary fashion, introduced Bill 54. The bill was transparently designed to pave the way for a referendum on secession by lowering the thresholds necessary for a citizen-led petition to trigger one.

Equally troubling is the hard-to-shake sense that Bill 54 was a continuation of the betrayal of Canada that Smith began in January, when she refused to show up to the First Ministers' meeting in Ottawa in person and to sign the premiers' statement on the Canada-US relationship. That statement concluded: "First Ministers agreed that Canada is a proud and sovereign nation, committed to upholding its values and responsibilities on the global stage. As a strong, independent county, we make decisions that reflect the best interests of our citizens, while actively contributing to global peace and stability. We stand firm in our resolve to protect our borders, support our communities, and collaborate with international partners to address common challenges." It was an extraordinary statement to have to make. In italics below the final paragraph, it hauntingly noted: "*The Government of Alberta did not approve the joint statement between the Government of Canada and the Council of the Federation.*"[7]

For her part, Smith seemed solely concerned with how the fortunes of the fossil fuels giants would fare in the trade war. Rather than stand united with her fellow First Ministers, she posted on social media her rationale for not signing the joint statement, writing in part: "federal government officials continue to publicly and privately float the idea of cutting off energy supply to the U.S. and imposing export tariffs on Alberta energy and other products to the United States. Until these threats cease, Alberta will not be able to fully support the federal government's plan in dealing with the threatened tariffs. Alberta will simply not agree to export tariffs on our energy."[8]

With callousness she turned her back on her fellow premiers and the prime minister and headed for Washington.

THE SEPARATIST MOVEMENT that had coalesced around Coutts and David Parker's Take Back Alberta had its marching orders from the premier: go get the reduced number of signatures required to trigger a secession referendum, and do it as soon as possible. Rather than live under another term of Liberal rule, Smith's UCP was willing to overthrow the duly elected government by pulling Alberta out of Canada.

Parker, however, found himself in the penalty box with the Conservative establishment after an ill-advised ad hominem rant on X against some of its central figures. By making insinuations about the integrity of the Poilievre marriage, Parker, ever the norm breaker, went too far. The premier called his comments "inappropriate and hurtful" and told him to seek help and delete his X account.[9] With Parker going through a punitive phase, the Alberta Prosperity Project moved to the forefront of a decentralized movement. The

Alberta separatists, like the Yellow Vests and the Freedom Convoy, are not a homogenous entity ideologically, nor are they organized hierarchically. Like much of the far right they enjoy relative autonomy to organize at the local level. Parker is philosophically committed to this approach. Once a self-labelled "Stephen Harper storm trooper," Parker has also described his personal political philosophy as decentralist. "I believe in localism. I believe we need to take power away from institutions," he told Donna Kennedy-Glans, a writer and former Alberta cabinet minister, in an interview for a profile in the *National Post*.[10]

Also formed in the COVID crucible, the Alberta Prosperity Project is a collection of separatists organized as an "educational initiative" to focus on galvanizing support for Alberta's independence by expounding a "retrotopian" vision of an idealized past Albertan nation that never existed but is promised as the ultimate exclusionary community and triggers hope for a new golden age. This technique is standard fare for far right political groups seeking power.[11] In this new/old independent version of itself, Alberta would be free to become the nation it has always dreamed of being—faith, family, freedom, farms, oil rigs, rifles and boots by the door, horses in the barn, women in the kitchen, rugged men in their trucks, immigrants deported, and taxes eliminated. To quote the AI-generated "Alberta Anthem," which is loaded with this imagery: "We ride sovereign steel/through fire and frost/We ain't the last/We're the line they lost."[12]

Assuming the mantle of all Albertans, spokesmen for the APP, like the organization's CEO Jeffrey Rath and Dennis Modry, would sell merch and preach angrily at town halls and on alternative media about the grievances of their fellow citizens without ever being elected to do anything of the sort by anyone other than themselves. APP corporate statements for its first year of operation in 2022 demonstrate that it received $1million in donations, generated over $100,000 in event income, raised over $233,000 in membership sales (that's roughly 11,667 one-time, $20 memberships), over $55,000 in event sponsorships, and almost $88,000 in merchandise sales. APP's gross profit line was $1,473,602.00.[13] To put these figures into context, consider that the Alberta NDP raised $7.2 million in donations during the same period in what was a record fundraising year for the opposition party. The UCP raised only $4.4 million in donations.[14] Every cent of donations to both the NDP and UCP was closely accounted for and traceable back to the donor. In contrast, all we know about the APP's finances are the line items. We don't know where the million dollars in seed money came from; we just know that it entered the APP's coffers in 2022.

Jeffrey Rath, APP's CEO and also its lawyer, is a cowboy-hat wearing firebrand prone to long-winded and aggressive rambling during live television interviews. Without a hint of irony, he describes himself as a career Indigenous-rights lawyer who has been practising in the province since 1991. The vast majority of practising lawyers go their entire careers without receiving a single citation from their professional conduct board, but Rath's conduct has come under Alberta Law Society scrutiny on a number of occasions. Last summer, the society reprimanded Rath and ordered him to pay $10,000 in costs after admitting to two citations involving his work for Thunderchild First Nation, although no notice to the profession was deemed necessary nor was a referral to the attorney general.[15]

Early in 2026, on a separate matter, a Law Society hearing examined claims Rath had breached professional conduct rules when he repeatedly contacted the CEO of Alberta Health Services and threatened murder, war crimes, and crimes against humanity charges against provincial and federal government officials, including Prime Minister Trudeau, for approving COVID vaccines. On these complaints, he skated. More recently, at the end of May, Rath received three more citations under the Legal Profession Act for abusive communications, abusing a tribunal process by bringing proceedings out of malice or with intent to injure the other party, and for not cooperating with a lawyer who replaced him on a file.[16] Those are just the Law Society citations.

In 2021, the Alberta Court of Queen's Bench reviewed Rath & Co.'s contingency fee agreement with the Tallcree First Nation for its $57.5 million "Cows and Ploughs" settlement with the federal government. Rath & Co. represented Tallcree First Nation in the later stages of the negotiated settlement for a 20 percent contingency fee. This entitled the firm to an $11.5 million payout, a sum the court ultimately determined to be too high for the largely administrative work the firm conducted. "Most of the work product found in the record are actually simple emails created and signed" by a paralegal with the firm, according to the judge.[17] The court found that rather than $11.5 million, Rath's firm, a six-lawyer operation run out of Rath's ranch near Bragg Creek at the time, was entitled to only $3 million, a still rather handsome payout, all things considered.

Rath represented to the Tallcree First nation that he had close connections to the Trudeau government. But it wasn't Rath's connections, real or imagined, that resulted in the settlement. The previous Harper government had taken a hard line negotiating the claims, whereas the Trudeau government took a different approach in alignment with its broader policy of renewal and restitution of the government's relationship with First Nations. For not honouring the agricultural promises made in the numbered treaties—to provide promised ploughs, seeds for crops, livestock such as cows and bulls, and other farming necessities, which left a newly settled population without the means to self-sufficiency—the Trudeau government expedited the settlement of nearly $2 billion in claims, aiming to advance the United Nations Declaration on the Rights of Indigenous Peoples and rebuild trust with Indigenous communities.[18]

In another "Cows and Ploughs" claim, Rath & Co. represented Sturgeon Lake Cree First Nation—a Treaty 8 nation situated in Peace County in Northern Alberta. Again on contingency, Rath raked in $28.6 million for his role in a settlement with a total value of $142 million. The Alberta Court of Appeal found the contingency fee to be unenforceable.

The settlement was a *fait accompli*. It was the Trudeau government's stated policy to settle the historic claims. To pocket a large percentage of that settlement was highly unethical, considering virtually no actual legal effort was required that could have amounted to such an extraordinary fee. Say, for example, that Rath's hourly rate was $1,000, he would have to have put in 28,600 hours to account for the bill he presented Sturgeon, which is the equivalent of 715 40-hour work weeks. The court unsurprisingly found Rath was not entitled to the entire contingency fee. Rath has yet to repay any of the money and has delayed a hearing to determine just how much he must pay back. The chief of Sturgeon Lake Cree, Sheldon

Sunshine, said in a Facebook post to the First Nation: "Too often we see lawyers and law firms making millions off the backs of vulnerable nations that have already suffered at the hands of the Crown. This has to stop."[19]

Rath is a conveyor of conspiratorial thinking who traced his own involvement in the separatist movement to the COVID pandemic.[20] Over the last decade, this kind of conspiratorial thinking, which finds causation in hidden malevolent groups secretly plotting calamitous social outcomes, has become prevalent among those politically attracted to the far right. As an example, in a widely watched interview with CTV's Vassy Kapelos outside of a Calgary courthouse, Rath went on a number of conspiratorial tangents as he swirled around Kapelos's questioning of the APP's trips to Washington to meet with members of the Trump administration, which the *Financial Times* had reported days earlier.[21] After citing his academic credentials, Rath rhetorically asked Kapelos whether she thought "communist Ottawa is leveraging communist China against Alberta?" He continued, "I mean come on. I mean, you know, we live in the world of realpolitik." Kapelos asked whether Rath minded being a pawn in that game. He responded, again on behalf of the province, "We're not a pawn. We're actually more like a, you know, a rook or a queen moving forward on the chessboard in the direction we want to move freely on the board. You know, the pawns are the provincial premiers like Danielle Smith that are being manipulated by Carney and Eby and Communist China to do their globalist bidding."[22]

Rath and his separatist brethren are predisposed to interpret political circumstances through an us-versus-them lens, with "us" being the monolithic Alberta that exists only in their own minds but for which they speak and act and "them" being a collusive cabal of global liberal elites responsible for imposing the policies at the core of their grievances. "Do you think the three of us could get a meeting with Tim Hodgson to talk about the need for a pipeline to the Pacific Northwest so that David Eby can't continue to hold us hostage? Of course not, because they want us to be held hostage," argued Rath, referring to his claim of having had three high-level meetings with the Trump administration.[23] Rath, who, again, is not an elected official or provincial deputy minister and does not appear to hold a position in the oil and gas sector, would have no business meeting with the federal minister of industry to discuss the issue of a pipeline to anywhere. The notion that his lack of status with the minister of industry is due to a desire to hold him and those he purports to speak for hostage is equally conspiratorial and bizarre.

Dennis Modry is Rath's highest-profile partner in the Alberta Prosperity Project, and he attended the Washington meetings with Rath. Modry is a former heart surgeon whose license to practise was suspended by Alberta Health Services in 2013 over serious concerns about his professionalism and skill.[24] Modry appealed the suspension to the Supreme Court of Canada, alleging AHS conspired against him, but his license was never reinstated.

In a recent unrelated civil case, a BC Supreme Court judge ruled that Modry had misappropriated funds from family members diagnosed with dementia over whom he had power of attorney. Modry wrote cheques to himself from the savings and chequing accounts of his ailing relatives and claimed to have invested the money in a condominium project he was developing that later went into foreclosure. Modry's affidavit swears that he lost his home, his condo development project, and his retirement savings, as well as all the money he took from his relatives.[25] The court ordered Modry to pay back $1.3 million with interest in March 2025, but as of a year later, despite the court order, he has not.[26]

During the pandemic, Modry published an open letter to Premier Jason Kenney on Western Standard, a far-right propaganda outlet that has been pushing Alberta separatism. The letter argued for an end to most of the public health measures intended to curb the spread of the deadly disease. It alluded to "gathering evidence on the use of Ivermectin to prevent COVID-19" and demanded that "contract tracing and snitching should cease immediately."[27]

The premier took the time to write back, noting that while he appreciated debate on pandemic policy, "it must be based on facts."[28] The College of Physicians and Surgeons of Alberta was forced to weigh in, clarifying that while Modry's letter suggested he was a practising physician, "it's important to note he is not licensed to practise medicine in Alberta." The college further clarified that "Dr. Modry's specialization was in surgery, he does not have expertise in public health."[29]

Modry has played an outsized role in the separatist movement in Alberta. He claims to have attended all three meetings the APP has had in Washington with Trump officials. In an NBC news article dated February 12, 2026, he's quoted as saying: "For those of us who are very much in support of Alberta becoming a sovereign country, it's heartening to us at each of the three meetings that we've had with the U.S. administration to be informed that the entire U.S. administration is supportive of Alberta becoming a sovereign country."[30]

It's tempting to dismiss Modry's sweeping claims as delusions of grandeur made by an aged conspiracy theorist who has sadly lost his way. Unfortunately, White House officials didn't deny the meetings took place, though they sought to "tamp down the seriousness of the discussions," according to NBC News. The meetings were at the staff level and not, as Rath suggested, at the principal level with people with direct access to the president, according to an unnamed senior State Department official. Modry claimed the meetings covered the gamut of issues prerequisite to Alberta becoming an independent country.

Rath had previously disclosed a voluminous amount of information about the APP's three meetings, the last of which, according to Rath, was conducted in a secure compartmented information facility (SCIF), which is traditionally used for the storage, discussion, and transmission of highly sensitive classified information. Rath had just returned from the meeting when he joined David Parker's wife, Rachel Parker on her YouTube channel prior to Christmas 2025. In that interview, Rath disclosed a long list of damning details that suggested strongly that he had been involved in planning meetings to leverage American power to shatter his own country. "We've now moved on from the first meeting, which was introductory, to the second meeting, which was more, OK, let's get our heads around how this is going to look and how it's going to work, to the third meeting, where we're now working at a very high policy level to discuss communications plans and so on," Rath said. "People will see the communications plan as it rolls out. There's definitely a communications plan in place, and we're being continually reassured with all of our meetings that there's very robust support for a free and independent Alberta in Washington, DC."[31]

The third meeting was, according to Rath, a lengthy one in a secure facility shielded from the signals intelligence or eavesdropping capabilities of US adversaries. They were "at it for several hours, going through all the ways in which the United States government could support Alberta independence when the timing was right," he said. "They are very enthusiastic about Alberta becoming an independent country. The one thing we all fervently believe and have in common is that the government in Ottawa and the landlocking of Alberta's resources is being done by Ottawa at the behest of the communist Chinese and the Americans see it in their national interest both under the Monroe Doctrine . . . and their new national security strategy to support Alberta independence and freeing the third largest oil field in the world from control by the communist Chinese." He later declared: "The people that we're meeting with go directly from our meetings to the Oval Office."

I'm not sure what compelled me to click the Rachel Parker video in my YouTube feed one evening in early January of this year. Perhaps it was the headline "Trump's INSANE PLAN for Alberta Independence." I had a visceral reaction as soon as Rath began to bloviate about his latest contact with Washington. I suspected that what I was hearing was criminal and knew instantly how wrong it was. The term *useful idiot* leapt to mind. It was certain to me that any self-respecting American whom Rath met with in Washington would be fundamentally aware that if they themselves had shown up in the capital of a superpower adversary to meet with government officials to plot the breakup of the United States, they ought not return home unless they fancied spending the rest of their lives in a dark hole. So what, in agreeing to meet with Rath and his cadre on multiple occasions, were these nameless Americans hoping to achieve?

Rath told Rachel Parker a fourth meeting was planned for January in Washington and that he was "basically in contact with them weekly now either by email or other forms of communication."[32] He said the same thing to Rebel News in November 2025.[33] Rath's claims about a mythologized "Ottawa" that is run by the "communist Chinese" who in turn control "the third-largest oil field in the world" (i.e. Alberta), repeated at every opportunity, have begun to sound more like a psyop than an organic grievance, conspiratorial as they are.[34]

The foundation for this psyop, if such a term can be applied to such a flimsy screed, is a document the APP published in July 2025, *The Value of Freedom*.[35] Rath claims it was developed by professionals—"economists, actuaries, bankers, business people, etcetera, using a very sophisticated AI model to show people that a free and independent Alberta would be far more successful and far more wealthy and far more prosperous than an Alberta that remained in Canada."[36] No names and no academic studies are cited in *The Value of Freedom*. It would appear that this document, which is subtitled "A Draft Fully Costed Fiscal Plan for an Independent Alberta," was generated largely through the use of AI. Indeed, as Tyler Dawson has reflected, "the promises in the document are practically unbelievable—spending on all sorts of services, coupled with deep tax cuts given to the Alberta population, is hard to reconcile with a balanced budget."[37] But of course that isn't the point. The point is to provide simple solutions to complex challenges, which is what gives populism its mass appeal. For example, the document's "immigration and deportation plan" allows for immigration to the future country of Alberta on a points system that privileges "like-minded Canadian brothers and sisters" who "fit easily into the Albertan culture" and "have at least a fighting chance of being able to drive acceptably on snow and ice."[38]

Unsurprisingly, in the case of *The Value of Freedom* we find an AI hallucination wielded as "evidence" that not only could Alberta separate, but it would be substantially better off if it did. I guess we should take ChatGPT's word for it, eh? The impact of this AI-produced disinformation, propounded by a domestic actor, is amplified when it appears as if that actor is backed by the most powerful state on the planet. For those unhappy with their lot in life, blaming a federal government thousands of kilometres away provides an easy scapegoat. The APP has given them false hope that their lives will vastly improve if they vote to separate from Canada in October. But the sad reality is that a group of far-right conspiracy theorists engaged in a profound betrayal of Canada when our national unity is most paramount is selling them a bill of goods.

Many, it would appear, have bought in to the separatist movement with a form of religious zeal. For his part, David Parker clearly sees himself as something of a prophet from the prairie. He says that his wife has described him as having a "messianic complex." He doesn't disagree with her. He speaks with an evangelical cadence that seems acquired from growing up listening to his father in the pulpit of Haynes Community Church. His rhetoric, though, is more crusader than pastor. He sees himself as a martyr, and he seems to encourage others to follow him down a similar path. This makes him a Christian nationalist who believes in the fusion of Christian identity and political power. And this, according to Marc Froese, is important context because it situates Parker and the separatist movement within the broader North American Christian nationalist project. The majority of the Republican Party in the United States, according to Froese, and a plurality of the Conservative Party in Canada are part of this movement, which makes it far less fringe than meets the eye.[39]

It is this messianic, crusader dimension to the separatist movement that should be of significant concern from a national security perspective, especially as it connects to a transcontinental Christian nationalism ascendant in the White House and in full display in the US-Israel war against Iran. The US secretary of war, Pete Hegseth, has pursued the illegal war of choice on Iran with a chilling bloodlust and tried to couch it in Christian crusader terms, praying for "overwhelming violence of action against those who deserve no mercy."[40] This so troubled Pope Leo that on Palm Sunday he reminded Catholics that "this is our God: Jesus, King of Peace, who rejects war, whom no one can use to justify war. He does not listen to those who wage war, but rejects them, saying: 'Even though you make many prayers, I will not listen: your hands are full of blood' (Is 1:15)."[41]

Christian nationalists in the United States see the world through a revolutionary lens. Within the western hemisphere, they seek dominance and control over scarce natural resources, including water, oil, and critical minerals. They show no regard for international law when pursuing their interests. The decapitation of the Maduro regime in Venezuela, the assassinations at sea of alleged drug smugglers, and strikes on seven countries so far this term have blown out of the water the obligation to respect state sovereignty, the prohibition on the use of force, and the principle of non-intervention.[42] Thomas Homer-Dixon and Adam Gordon constructed a scenario that sees a referendum on Alberta independence (even if it is a referendum once removed from a binding referendum under Canadian law) produce an outcome where 30 percent or more vote to separate. But Trump declares the result "fake" and asserts that actual support for separation is much higher—"well over" 50 percent. From there, Homer-Dixon and Gordon theorize that the separatists will appeal to the United States for assistance, claiming all manner of oppression. In response, "The U.S. moves troops to the northern Montana border and tells the rest of Canada that Alberta must be allowed to join America as the '51st state'."[43]

This scenario appeared in an opinion piece they wrote early this year for the *Globe and Mail*. They lacked the space to consider the transcontinental Christian nationalist movement that could add a layer of motivation and justification for US intervention in the fall. Nor could they note that their scenario wasn't far-fetched at all—at least as far as recent history in Europe is concerned. Vladimir Putin's Russia had done much the same after referendums in the Crimea and the Donbas, as chapter 9 shows. Nevertheless, their piece was a clear warning that we need to game out how we'll respond to such an action by the United States in the uncertain aftermath of Alberta's referendum. "Ensuring electoral process integrity is clearly job one," Homer-Dixon and Gordon concluded. But as we will see in the following chapters, the UCP approach has been the opposite. It has intentionally brought this referendum into a uniquely exposed provincial jurisdiction with little to no capacity to defend its integrity from the forces of foreign interference—Russian, American, Chinese or otherwise. In so doing, it is daring the federal government to intervene to defend its national interests.

7: Constitutional Crash Out

"We are all treaty people."
Chief Desmond Bull, Louis Bull Tribe[1]

THE ALBERTA PROSPERITY Project never registered in any way with Elections Alberta, so it was not able to lead the petition charge. For this, a new vehicle was required. Stay Free Alberta was born of this necessity, and Mitch Sylvestre was chosen to lead the collection of the reduced number of signatures required to trigger a secession referendum. Sylvestre, like so many others associated with the Alberta separatist movement, got into politics during the COVID pandemic. He partnered with David Parker, became Take Back Alberta's regional captain for Northern Alberta and quickly proved a fundraising force within the UCP. He is the owner of a gun and sporting goods store in Bonnyville, Alberta, a town of nearly 6,500 that is roughly a two-and-half-hour drive east of Edmonton, adjacent to the Athabasca and Cold Lake tar sands.

Sylvestre has been radicalized by far-right conspiracy theories to the point that he believes the king of England seeks to assassinate him because he's uncovered and exposed the theft of billions of Canadian dollars that Liberal prime ministers Trudeau and Carney shipped to the king.[2] *Toronto Star* journalist Richard Warnica, who grew up in rural Alberta, spent an extended period following Sylvestre during his Stay Free Alberta petition signature-gathering tour. He recorded hours of Sylvestre's stump speeches and then spent weeks meticulously fact-checking them. So laced with conspiracist thinking were Sylvestre's speeches that Warnica called them "packed with near ceaseless errors of fact and interpretation." At its core, Sylvestre's pitch for an independent Alberta is "dangerously detached from reality," Warnica wrote. He described Sylvestre as "perhaps the most important person in Canadian politics right now."[3]

Indeed, Sylvestre's name topped the separatists' petition and was on the court docket for one of the most significant democracy cases in Canadian history, heard over the course of three days in November 2025 and an additional day in early December by Justice Colin C.J. Feasby of the Alberta Court of King's Bench. Alberta's chief electoral officer, who was statutorily obligated to ensure that any referendum process set in motion under the province's Citizen Initiative Act would not result in unconstitutional outcomes or violations of treaties, asked the court if the question the separatists wanted to put to a referendum contravened either the Charter of Rights and Freedoms or treaty rights.

Sylvestre was represented by lawyers Jeffrey Rath and Eva Chipiuk. Like Rath, Chipiuk is a holdover from the Freedom Convoy, having represented some of its protagonists in the Public Order Emergency Commission hearings, during which she cross-examined Prime Minister Trudeau.

She has since become an outspoken advocate for Alberta independence.

A number of First Nations, including the Athabasca Chipewyan, Samson Cree, Mikisew Cree, Blackfoot Confederacy, and Sturgeon Lake Cree Nation, asked Justice Feasby if they could provide interventions in the case, given the potential impacts of a secession referendum on their communities, which he granted.

Tensions had been building over the previous summer and fall between First Nations and the Alberta government. The First Nations chiefs were among the first to understand what Bill 54 was telegraphing to the nation. Within hours, they began to mount a resistance to the spectre of separation the bill foreshadowed. The federal government failed to follow the chiefs' lead or support them in any way, leaving them to fight for national unity alone. A delegation of chiefs from Treaties 6, 7, and 8 headed for Ottawa on a mission to bring the federal government into the battle it should have led from the start. I spoke to Chief Desmond Bull of Louis Bull First Nation, who attended the meeting with the prime minister in December. He told me that the chiefs asked the prime minister, "What are you doing about this separation issue?" Bull's biggest concern, he told me, was that "it is us as Indigenous people on the front line. We are the ones doing the fighting. We are the only ones holding this governing body [the provincial government] accountable to the rule of law." A delegation of chiefs that Bull was part of also met with King Charles, and they let him know how the separation issue was impacting "not only treaties but the Canadian constitution."[4]

On April 30, the chiefs of the Sturgeon Cree and Mikisew Cree First Nations collaborated on a strongly worded letter to the premier with the subject line "Cease and Desist—Separatist Threats." Chief Sheldon Sunshine and Chief Billy-Joe Tuccaro wrote:

> You are attempting to manufacture a national unity crisis—by enabling a referendum on separatism and a fanatical cell of individuals—at the exact moment when Canadians need to unite against Donald Trump's America.
>
> The Province is on Treaty lands.
>
> Please be advised that your irresponsible statements and actions are in breach of Treaties 6 7, and 8. We demand that you immediately stand down from this conduct.
>
> Our Treaties are sacred covenants and are to last forever. Alberta did not exist when our ancestors agreed to share the land with the Crown. The province has no authority to supersede or interfere with our Treaties, even indirectly by passing the buck to a "citizen" referendum.[5]

The chiefs were explicit: there would be no legal right for an "independent" Alberta to occupy treaty lands. Any provincial secession referendum would accordingly be entirely illegitimate and non-binding. In their eyes the whole thing was a non-starter that would not be tolerated.[6] They wrote a letter on the same day to Prime Minister Carney, congratulating him on his election and requesting that he "get the province of Alberta in line."[7] Neither the prime minister nor his office ever responded to that letter.

On May 1, the Blackfoot Confederacy chiefs representing Siksika, Kainai, Piikani, and Aamskapi Piikani formally rejected Bill 54, asserting that it "threatens the constitutional and legal order by disregarding Nation-to-Crown agreements that define our relationship with the state. It undermines the authority of the Blackfoot Treaty, signed in 1877 at Blackfoot Crossing, which predates Alberta's entry into Confederation by nearly three decades."[8] The letter signed by the chiefs Ouray Crowfoot, Travis Plaited Hair, and Troy Knowlton concluded by stating: "The Blackfoot Treaty is not a document of the past. It is a sacred, enduring commitment meant to build relationships 'as long as the sun shines, the grass grows, and the rivers flow'."

On May 2, more Treaty 7 chiefs weighed in. Representing Tsuu'tina, Bearspaw, Chiniki, and Goodstoney Nations, Roy Whitney, Darcy Dixon, Aaron Young, and Clifford Poucette concluded their own letter with the following: "First Nations will not separate. Any efforts to separate will be met with our full opposition."[9] Piikani First Nation also issued a public statement that concluded with a reminder that "we are here, we will aggressively protect our historic Treaty rights and our inherent rights, and we will require that the Crown's obligations to First Nations be honoured and fulfilled."[10]

A law professor from the University of Calgary named Robert Hamilton surmised that far from being merely rhetorical arguments, the letters from the chiefs were chock full of powerful constitutional arguments bound to have an enduring impact on the separatist discussion the Smith government had unleashed. Of the demand that Prime Minister Carney get the province in line, Hamilton noted that the Crown has constitutional obligations flowing from s.91 (24) of the constitution, which grants Parliament exclusive authority over "Indians, and Lands reserved for Indians."[11] "If provinces do not uphold treaty rights, the federal Crown has an obligation to take steps to ensure those rights are protected," he wrote. He also noted the effect of the United Nations Declaration on the Rights of Indigenous Peoples, concluding that the inherent right of Indigenous peoples to self-determination and to the recognition, observance, and enforcement of treaties covered in articles 3 and 37 respectively imposed a further obligation on the part of the federal government to take all necessary measures to ensure Canada's laws were consistent with these inherent rights and treaties.

Hamilton did not conclude that the First Nations were an irreconcilable impediment to separation; rather, he confirmed that for separation to go ahead, their consent would be required. In the absence of that consent, the federal government would be obligated to ensure its treaty promises were not violated.[12] It would, in other words, have to get the province of Alberta in line, as the Sturgeon and Mikisew chiefs had respectfully requested. It is worth considering briefly at a practical level what getting the province in line might mean. In the event of an illegal or unilateral declaration of independence on the part of the province, it would mean the rule of law had broken down and the First Nations were engaged in a form of civil warfare with provincial authorities. This would force the federal government to make a decision on whether to intervene on behalf of the First Nations, as obligated by the treaties and the constitution, and directly intervene on behalf of the vast majority who had become subject to the tyranny of the minority.

The letters from the chiefs made no impact on the provincial government. On May 5 the premier gave an address during which she demanded the elimination of key pillars of the federal government's efforts to curb climate change, including the rescinding of the Impact Assessment Act, net-zero policies, the oil and gas emissions cap, and the ban on tankers off the BC coast. She demanded more pipelines to the Pacific and Atlantic Oceans. She demanded changes to federal equalization and accused the federal government of "hostility" towards her province, raising the spectre of a separation referendum in 2026 if these demands were not met.

With a measles outbreak exploding in the province and a historic teachers' strike looming, the speaker of the Legislative Assembly, Nathan Cooper, resigned his position as the MLA for Olds-Didsbury (the only riding in Alberta's provincial history to elect a declared separatist in 1982). Cooper was appointed to the role of the province's official representative in Washington as Trump's trade war raged and his annexation threats continued to punctuate the Canada-US relationship.

The Republican Party of Alberta launched in the same week with a speech from its leader, Cameron Davies, at the Cochrane RancheHouse. Davies outlined his five-step vision for a "stronger, independent Alberta."[13] The RPA later added a page to its website that included a list of sitting MLAs it said who supported independence.[14] Nathan Cooper—even though he had resigned by that time—was among those listed, as were eighteen UCP MLAs.[15] His inclusion on the RPA's list doesn't make Cooper, a credentialed Canadian diplomat, a separatist sympathizer, but he has not denied that he is one, nor has he demanded his name and image be removed from the RPA's separatist sympathizers list, as two previously listed MLAs have done, where his name and image remain in support of Alberta independence.[16]

An old adage about diplomacy says "an ambassador is an honest man sent to lie abroad for the good of his country." In Cooper's case the saying might need a rewrite. It is not unreasonable to conclude that Albertans are paying a pretty penny to have a person who doesn't have the best interests of the country in mind sit in the Canadian embassy in Washington.[17] Cooper is a former WestJet lead flight attendant and Carstairs town councillor whose only experience with foreign relations was as a Rotary exchange student in Australia in 1997.[18] When he took up his position in Washington, he replaced James Rajotte, whom Jason Kenney had appointed on May 1, 2020. Rajotte, a former member of Parliament, chaired the House of Commons Finance Committee during the 2008 global financial crisis and is said to have built a network of useful connections in Washington during his fifteen-year run in Ottawa. Rajotte was paid a salary of approximately $250,000.[19] It is not known what Cooper makes, but it is likely more than that, despite having no discernable qualifications for the job other than his staunch partisanship and (perhaps) sympathies for Alberta separatism.

"The [Canadian] embassy is pretty good to us," Cooper told Donna Kennedy-Glans, "and I think we're pretty fair with the embassy. On most things we're 'Team Canada.'" But "there are some issues, around energy and resource development, where we have a different view of the world." Cooper said he was not agitating for Alberta independence, but "if there's no pipeline with hydrocarbons in it, be it gas or oil, in the approved list of [nation-building] projects, that will have significant impact on how Albertans feel about national unity."[20]

IN FOLLOW UP to their letters to the premier and the prime minister, the chiefs of the Treaty 6, 7, and 8 First Nations gathered for an emergency meeting in Edmonton. At the press conference that followed, the chiefs stood shoulder to shoulder in their headdresses as each in turn denounced Bill 54 and the premier's separation threats. Chief Troy Knowlton said: "The rhetoric and insanity of separation here in Alberta has united First Nations. . . . We're not going anywhere." When it came to his turn to address the room, Chief Billy-Joe Tuccaro held the printed pages of Bill 54 in his hand. He first thanked the premier for bringing the First Nations together "as treaty people to stand and oppose this. Yesterday you made four demands to the Prime Minister of Canada. That was a no-no because you gave him a time limit to 2026 to get their things in order. But you will not do what you want without the approval of the treaty people. You talk about a reset with Canada. You must reset with the Indigenous peoples of Turtle Island. Bill 54, this is what we think of you." He concluded his fiery speech by tossing the pages of the bill into the air and calling them "garbage" as they fluttered to the floor in front of the podium.

An immovable force had set itself against separation. The tectonic tremors were felt across the country in mid-November as the Sylvestre case played out before Justice Feasby. Observers of the hearing, me included, could see a good probability that the judge would answer the questions before him in the affirmative: namely, Alberta's independence would contravene both the Charter and treaty rights. Such a ruling would scupper the petition and put the independence movement in limbo. So the government instantly began drafting a legislative work around. The Citizen Initiative Act did not originally give citizens the power to propose taking away Charter or treaty rights. This was wise, since giving a small minority of the population the power to trigger a vote on whether, for example, disabled people should be entitled to attend public schools or women should be able to vote would damage the principle of equality enshrined in Section 15 of the Canadian Charter of Rights and Freedoms. A similar logic applies to violating the sanctity of treaty rights.

The UCP, however, was so hell-bent on the idea of advancing a secession referendum that it jettisoned those guardrails entirely. In so doing it carried out a dangerously destabilizing assault on the rule of law and continued to pursue it over the following months, thus threatening to supersede Canada's constitutional government with a form of emotional government characteristic of dictatorships. To carry this off it would need the assistance of lawyers willing to abdicate their responsibility for protecting the rule of law. Indeed, "it is hard to subvert a rule of law state without lawyers," as Timothy Snyder explained in *On Tyranny*.[21]

On December 4, with the hearing set to enter its final day, government lawyer Nicholas Trofimuk wrote directly to Justice Feasby to inform him that legislation was in train that would affect the case before him. Bill 14, the Justice Statutes Amendment Act, 2025, had been introduced that afternoon and would run over the constitution and the treaties in the government's zeal to hold a secession referendum in the fall. Accordingly, Trofimuk implied that rather than allow the hearing to run its natural course, Feasby should end it and bury any decision he had intended to issue. "I am writing to advise the Court of a Bill that was just tabled in the Legislative Assembly which will affect this Action once it comes into force," the letter read. "Accordingly, once this legislation takes legal effect, this Action will be discontinued."[22]

Trofimuk was professionally obligated as a government lawyer to understand that in signing his name to this letter he was helping the government push the province into the realm of the arbitrary and authoritarian. Government lawyers play a unique role in the legal profession. They are, according to the University of Ottawa legal scholar Adam M. Dodek, "custodians of the rule of law." Accordingly, they have an even higher ethical duty than their private sector counterparts.[23] Trofimuk was acutely aware of this, having argued a case on behalf of the government of Alberta in 2025 on the oath of allegiance that all new lawyers swear to support the rule of law and constitutional government.[24] Trofimuk had become an instrument of a rogue provincial regime that was transparently working to break apart the country.

The legislation, however, had just been introduced and required time to move through the requisite readings to become law. This immutable parliamentary obstacle provided the judge with a narrow timeframe in which to issue his decision regardless of Trofimuk's letter. Feasby did so with verve the next day. In a section of his decision titled "Is this Proceeding Anti-Democratic," he wrote a pair of sentences that neatly contextualize the revolutionary moment we find ourselves in: "Courts play an essential role in interpreting the laws passed by Parliament and the provincial legislatures. Attacking courts as anti-democratic may be politically convenient but it is corrosive of the rule of law and, indeed, of democracy." In clear and forceful terms, Feasby warned of the threat to Canada's democracy that the Smith government's flagrant undermining of the rule of law in the province posed. "Alberta's argument is not just wrong," Feasby continued "it is dishonourable. The Justice Minister cannot stand in the Legislative Assembly in May citing CIA s 2(4) as a protection for Treaty rights and then send his lawyers into Court in November to make a technical argument that CIA s 2 (4) is not protection for Treaty rights."[25]

Feasby's decision included an epilogue that explained how the government had tried to make an end run around the legal process he had presided over and in so doing "silence the Court." He recognized that while the government certainly had authority to run amok and again change the law that was at the crux the case, to do so was "contrary to the rule of law." From paragraph 252:

> The rule of law plays a critical role with respect to the democratic process where stability of the governing legal regime enhances legitimacy and public confidence in the outcomes of elections and referendums. Changing legislation to circumvent a valid legal process commenced by the independent officer of the Legislative Assembly responsible for administering democratic processes is the antithesis of the stable, predictable, and ordered society that rule of law contemplates, and democracy demands.[26]

He went on to explain his reasoning for issuing the decision despite the fact that the government was choosing to legislate pre-emptively to end the proceeding and thus "disrespect the administration of justice." Contrary to the pending passage of Bill 14, Feasby wrote, "this case cannot be discontinued, and the Court cannot be silenced because the case has been decided. These reasons are delivered despite the anticipated change to the law because reason giving *is* democratic. This case concerned a matter of importance to the public . . . The public is entitled to the fruits of this process that has been conducted largely at their expense so that if they are asked to vote on Alberta independence, they have a tool that may help them make sense of the legal dimensions of the secession of Alberta from Canada."[27]

In a final nod to the First Nations of Canada, Feasby included a map of the historic treaties as an appendix to his decision. The map is a strong visual reminder of the foundations of the country that date back over two hundred years and that the Smith government is actively calling into question in its efforts to bring about a referendum on Alberta separatism.[28]

SMITH TOOK UP the matter on her radio talk show the following weekend and opined that referendums were never meant to have a "pile of gatekeepers" holding them back. Justice minister Mickey Amery said the new legislation would provide a "reset" and ensure the courts couldn't delay direct democracy. This was the chance the independence movement had been waiting for, and Amery encouraged them to prove their case.[29]

Alberta's three chief justices jointly issued extremely rare public statement about what had transpired. Evidently compelled by the UCP's abuse of the role of the courts, the justices took it upon themselves to lay out for the public the basics of "a properly functioning democracy" with "three separate branches of government that exercise their power and authority independently according to the Constitution." Continuing to expound Alberta's grade 8 social studies curriculum, the justices explained that "[t]he independence of each branch ensures there are checks and balances across the system. It is the foundation of a healthy democracy. Public trust and confidence in our institutions—and all three branches of government—depend on it. It is equally important that each branch respect and support the independence of the others."[30]

The chief justices may have been compelled to make their statement by what had most recently occurred in the Sylvestre case and the introduction of Bill 14. But the case was just the most recent of a series of flagrant UCP attacks on the justice system and the rule of law. The government had resorted to the nuclear option of using the notwithstanding clause to block challenges to its unconstitutional legislative agenda targeting trans youth. It had again used the constitutional override mechanism to defeat a province-wide organized labour action that public school teachers began in the fall as they tried to draw attention to the crises undermining the education system.

The trend lines were hardening, and they were pointing to a government intent on incrementally dislodging the cornerstone of the rule of law from Alberta's democracy and collapsing the province into a far-right, illiberal jurisdiction.

8: The Centurion Plunder

> Such then is the general nature of political revolutions. They are produced either by violence, or by fraud, or by the union of both; for, sometimes, what is begun by fraud is ended by force.
>
> Aristotle, 350 B.C.

A FORM OF what felt like controlled chaos took over in the province of Alberta in 2026. Each day seemed to bring with it another scandal, another controversial piece of legislation, another assault on charter rights, or treaty rights, or the rule of law, or the health care system, or the education system, or the legal profession writ large. It was overwhelming, and purposefully so. The UCP was flooding the zone in a way previously unseen in Canadian politics. And while all of this was happening, the separatists began collecting the 177,732 signatures required to trigger a constitutional referendum on the question: do you agree that the Province of Alberta should cease to be a part of Canada to become an independent state? If the separatists, led by their official proponent Mitch Sylvestre, could collect the equivalent of just 10 percent of the total number of votes cast in the 2023 provincial election by May 2, they would be able to force the first secession referendum in the province's history and just the third in Canada's history.

Separatist leaders like Jeffrey Rath set the bar high as the signature-collecting campaign kicked off in the dead of an Alberta winter. Rath said he expected the movement's sixty-six thousand volunteers would gather a million signatures.[1] The numbers were ludicrous on their face, but few asked questions as the separatists carried on their fringe crusade. Early reporting out of the separatist camp was that they were off to a flying start. Grainy phone videos showing long lines of mainly middle-aged white people waiting in the cold to sign a petition sheet began surfacing on social media. Local news started to report from events in a variety of mostly rural areas throughout the province. People waiting to sign the petition articulated grievances with red tape, taxes, and immigrants making life difficult for themselves and said they wanted a better life for their children. Others claimed Canada was broke and broken and that Alberta would do better alone.

Rath continued to rattle on about how much better off Albertans would be after leaving Canada, since they would no longer have to pay federal income tax and would no longer be subject to federal regulation of "our oil and gas industry."[2] He made grandiose claims about phantom polls showing support for separation at over 40 percent. He invoked images of hundreds of thousands of Albertans lined up in the cold to sign the petition and millions who would vote for a tax-free future where seniors had doubled pensions and those who were in the province on a work permit would be deported "back to Ottawa to have Ottawa sort them out."[3] The newly independent nation, he vowed, would be the wealthiest per capita in the entire world.[4]

IT WAS A giant load of horse shit, but few of Rath's interviewers were able to marshal much of a challenge to his rambling barrage of half-truths. In fairness, it's a natural response to cow to the loudest voice in the room. This happens so routinely in White House press briefings that it has become the norm. In Canada, however, the technique is still foreign. Journalists here default to their training when confronted with it: stay neutral and allow both sides of an issue to come out. But both-siding it with these folks is a dangerous game. As we've seen in Trump's America, appeasement has its consequences. Journalists quickly go from being trusted sources of the information we need to function in a democratic society to "enemies of the people" pushing "fake news." The general population's trust and confidence in journalism erodes, creating a power vacuum where a vital system of accountability once stood. As the recently deceased Spanish journalist Carlos Hernández de Miguel wrote in his last message to humanity before his death: "Objectivity is not the same as neutrality. If there's an aggressor and a victim, a liar and an honest person, a corrupt individual and an honourable one, then your task is to describe all that clearly and forcefully."[5] In our current context it requires knowing the constitution chapter and verse in order to push back, and it means knowing how the equalization formula works to do the same. It means calling out conspiracy in real time and cutting off the flow of lies before they spread like a contagion. I'm not saying it's an easy gig. But when you platform people who want to take apart your country, you better damn well be prepared to defend it.

An example of this misplaced neutrality and unwillingness to defend the foundations of our nation in the face of a separatist bully can be seen in an interview CTV news conducted with Jeffrey Rath in early February of this year. The anchor asked Rath about his talks with US officials and his efforts to secure a $500 billion line of credit to fund his new nation if he wins support for independence in a referendum as though he were asking about the condition of the horses on Rath's ranch. Rath's reply:

> Well, first of all, let's be really clear, I mean, Alberta can completely fund itself without any help from the United States. We've already done a feasibility study on that. It's called *The Value of Freedom: A Draft Fiscal Plan for an Independent Alberta*. We send $70 billion a year to Ottawa and we get $10 billion in questionable federal services including national defence, which we know isn't really defence at all. So we can completely fund ourselves as a free and independent country. The only thing we're doing is conducting a feasibility study on putting in place a credit line to ease us through the transition of cutting off all federal tax dollars going to Ottawa from Alberta and keeping all of the money here. I mean, we're very serious people. We're treating this as a very serious project. We're doing our due diligence on behalf of the citizens of Alberta. We are looking forward to the day where we leave Canada and we will be paying no more federal income tax, no more GST, no more carbon

tax, and that Alberta will be the lowest-tax, lowest-regulated jurisdiction in North America.[6]

The anchor elected not to push back against any of this nonsense. With the benefit of not being live on air, I will. Provinces do not contribute financially to the equalization program. Canadian citizens pay taxes. There's a nuance here that gets lost when hucksters like Rath encourage us to think in tribalistic terms and not as contributing members of Canadian society. In 2024–2025 the total amount of equalization payments to all the provinces combined was $25.3 billion.[7] But in Rath's world, Alberta cuts a $70 billion dollar cheque to Ottawa each year. Where this figure comes from is anyone's guess. Now, as a province rich in oil and gas resources, the per capita income of Albertans is well above the national average. In fact, it is usually the highest, making Alberta the wealthiest province in the country. This usually means the province isn't eligible to receive equalization payments, because it doesn't need them to ensure its citizens' public services are comparable to those accessible in the rest of Canada, which is the intent of the program. It's one of the metaphorical threads of a thousand acts of accommodation that are the fabric of our nation. The highly respected former premier of Alberta Peter Lougheed saw equalization as "a crucial aspect of Canadian confederation" and "one of the most equitable methods of maintaining the economic well-being of Canadians."[8] But again, not in Rath's world, where it's acceptable to ridicule the Canadian armed forces, which defend the nation in its entirety, and not on some province-by-province basis as Rath suggests. It's worth reiterating that these self-described "serious people" doing their "due diligence" on Artificial Intelligence on behalf of Albertans were not elected, ever, by anyone to do anything of the sort. Obviously, if Alberta leaves confederation, it won't pay federal income tax or GST. But a jurisdiction without taxes or regulations is either a libertarian fantasyland or an anarchy. And by the way, the Carney government eliminated the consumer portion of the federal carbon tax as its first order of business in spring 2025, and the federal government provided the highly profitable oil and gas industry with over $10 billion in subsidies that year alone. All of this gets a pass by the CTV journalist. He just moves on to the next question, leaving the mainstream audience to sort through the shrapnel.

RATH, HOWEVER, HAS recently found himself, like his pal Dennis Modry, on the wrong side of the law—and for a practising lawyer, that's a very uncomfortable place to be, much more so than for a de-credentialed doctor. A judge has issued a Mareva injunction to freeze Rath's assets after it came to light that he, as the sole trustee, withdrew millions from the Tallcree First Nation minors' trust fund. Until he was removed by court order in June, Rath was the sole trustee of that fund after the Trudeau government settled with Tallcree on the "cows and ploughs" claim (as discussed in chapter 6) in 2017. Despite filing no evidence in response to the injunction and his counsel consenting to the terms of the court order, Rath later told CBC News that the allegations were "false."[9] A Mareva injunction is an extremely rare instrument in Canadian law. It has likely never been used against a lawyer, but the judge found a strong prima facie case to grant the order out of concern that Rath would displace the assets prior to the court's final judgment. From Justice J.J. Gill's Court of King's Bench decision on July 15th:

> [. . .] there is a strong prima facie case that the respondents [Rath and Co.] have made improper payments out of the trust, particularly in relation to the approximately 8.5 million payment to Rath PC in November 2025. There is also a strong prima facie case against Mr. Rath personally of assisting in a breach of fiduciary duty. There is also a real risk that the respondents have actively been taking steps and will continue to take steps to frustrate the process of locating the missing money. The steps taken previously include the timing of an approximately 4.6 million payment in fees to Rath PC. The changing of the trusts auditors, the failing to provide financial statements on time which would have disclosed the other payments, and of the course, the fact that the 8.5 million payment was made in direct contravention of the orders of Justice Lee and the Court of Appeal.[10]

Justice John Gill, who on July 15 extended the initial Mareva order, also considered evidence from Sturgeon Lake Cree Nation, leading him to say, "This raises a concern about a pattern of behaviour by the respondents and potential intermingling of trust assets."[11] His assets have been frozen and placed in an investigative receivership, which means that a court appointed receiver will take control of all Rath's electronic records, bookkeeping software, and bank accounts with a mandate to investigate and trace the whereabouts of the trust funds.[12]

OUT OF THE mainstream on the Rebel News and the Western Standard websites, neutrality turns to open advocacy for Alberta independence. Separatist mouthpieces receive weekly talk shows to air their grievances and spew their racism.[13] Journalist Charles Rusnell recently revealed that the Alberta government provided a sole-source contract to Western Standard worth $60,000 for "content" in July 2025.[14] The funding runs through to 2027. Public funding for this outlet can only be understood when the UCP itself is understood as a quasi-separatist party.

AS THE WINTER dragged on, rumours started to circulate that the separatists were struggling to reach their numbers. Images of ramshackle and abandoned signature-collection sites alongside provincial highways and in empty school parking lots circulated on social media, suggesting momentum had begun to wane. The separatists had resorted to collecting the signatures of snowbirds wintering in Arizona and Mexico.[15] Mitch Sylvestre even admitted to difficulties meeting identification requirements during signature collection in late March.[16] But almost as soon as those doubts began to set in, they were quashed. Sylvestre told a group meeting just three days later, on March 30, that they had reached the minimum threshold of signatures.[17] It was a bizarre turnaround that led people to question what had changed.

On March 24 Jeffrey Rath promoted something called the Centurion Project on X, which he billed as a "super canvasser" for his independence movement. Eventually some 568 individual Albertan canvassers would go the site he linked to and find out how to get a thousand signatures each in the next forty days. Included with Rath's post was an AI-generated image of a young white woman in a flowing white gown riding a horse in the Rocky Mountains, barefoot, while bearing an Alberta flag. What the heck was the Centurion Project and how could it possibly generate signatures so fast? We would find out a month later.

On March 31, Jen Gerson, an Alberta journalist, sent a profoundly troubling complaint to Elections Alberta, alleging that a David Parker–led group called the Centurion Project might have illegally acquired a copy of the voters' list and loaded it onto an American-made app with the intention to use the protected data to influence the separatists' petition and the eventual referendum.[18] Gerson had received a tip from a source about the Centurions having access to the list, but rather than break the story herself she responsibly chose to report the matter to the authorities, hoping they would be able to contain the breach before too many more bad actors got their hands on the data.

Ten years ago, if we were watching carefully enough, we saw how a data-driven campaign had mobilized the vote in favour of the United Kingdom leaving the EU. Cambridge Analytica, as we will see in chapter 9, leveraged Facebook data to micro-target messaging at specific segments of the British population over social media. Much of the messages we would now characterize as mis- or disinformation designed to stir up discord and grievance sentiments, paint a post-Brexit UK as a land transformed with more health care and fewer immigrants, and encourage the persuadable to get out and vote to leave.

No one ever suggested that the UK voter roll was stolen or had any part to play in how the disinformation campaign was carried out. If the full legal names, addresses, polling locations, emails, and in some cases phone numbers of potential voters were ever in the wrong hands in the Brexit campaign, it is news to me. But that is exactly what Gerson was reporting to Elections Alberta: the separatists had access to the voters list and thus had a massive data advantage in support of their cause. A threat was posed to the resilience of Alberta's democracy, which had clearly been made vulnerable to manipulation by anti-democratic actors.

But rather than instantly launch a full investigation and alert the public to a potential data breach that would affect every voting-age Albertan, some 2.9 million people, Elections Alberta questioned its own authority to initiate an investigation. An Elections Alberta representative called Gerson and seemed at first to take the complaint seriously, but on April 10 the journalist received a letter informing her that the agency was not able to discount the possibility that the data had come from a source other than the official voters' list. Thanks, Elections Alberta concluded, but the case of what may or may not be the largest data breach in Canadian history is now closed.

It was an odd letter, and Gerson posted it online for all to read a few weeks later, after the story broke that Elections Alberta and the RCMP were now all of a sudden investigating the matter. Why now, and why not a month before when Gerson sent her original complaint? The reason Elections Alberta gave referred the public back to Bill 54—the legislation that had passed the previous spring, legislation that had set in motion all this activity towards a referendum.

As noted, Bill 54 made it more than twice as easy to trigger a secession referendum in the province while also making it very difficult for Elections Alberta to look into any malfeasance surrounding such a referendum or any other process under its purview. The chief electoral officer, Gordon McClure, sounded warnings at the time the bill was introduced. He made it known that none of the significant investigations his office had conducted over the previous five years—the ones into Cameron Davies and the kamikaze scheme, into Take Back Alberta and the 2023 election that got the UCP back into power with the slimmest margin of victory in the province's history—would have happened under the new thresholds the legislation required to commence an investigation. He added that none of the other provinces had limited the investigative powers of their democratic guardians in such a way.[19] The UCP had intentionally kneecapped the agency responsible for the province's democratic resilience.

By May 2026, Elections Alberta had been aware of the possibility that the voters list had been compromised for at least a month. But Bill 54 had set the threshold for launching an investigation at "reasonable grounds to believe an offence has occurred," a threshold the agency interpreted to be similar to the amount of evidence police would need to arrest someone in a criminal matter.[20] So instead of taking action, Elections Alberta said thanks but no thanks to Gerson and her complaint. Eventually, it was compelled to look into the matter after Gerson passed the information to Carrie Tait of the *Globe and Mail* and the Centurion Project moved out of the online space into the real world.[21]

THE CENTURION PROJECT had its official in-person launch at the Edmonton Oilfield Technical Society on April 29, an event it billed on FreedomCalendar.net as "Operation Secure Independence."[22] Four prominent voices of the separatist movement were featured: Daryl Mark, Jason Lavigne, Marty "Up North" Belanger, and David Parker himself. A long-bearded Parker wore a battered brown thermal vest over a faded blue T-shirt as he used his time at the mic to explain messianically that the separatist movement wouldn't achieve its aims through traditional means. Holding events, knocking on doors, making phone calls, talking to people earnestly face to face was a passé form of campaigning.[23] Parker had seen the future in the United States while touring with Tucker Carlson, the far-right alt-media personality who was advocating for Canada's "liberation" by the United States and whom Danielle Smith had glowingly introduced at an event in Edmonton in January 2024.[24]

The Centurion Project was Parker's master plan to bring next-level populist campaign tactics to Canada. There is a reason the Trump administration is suing thirty states for their voter rolls. It's because it knows that in the disinformation age data drives democratic outcomes. The states individually administer the election of the president. This is the electoral college, which is foundational to the American republic. Trump wants to subvert that. Parker evidently decided that rather than pursue the Alberta voters' list by establishing an official political party and running candidates in a general election, he'd just get it another way. Luckily, his pal Cameron Davies had a copy of the list, without which Parker's plan was a pipedream.

Davies is a dual citizen. He holds both Canadian and American passports and served in the US Marine Corps. He took over the Buffalo Party—originally founded in 2022 as a conservative party calling for more autonomy from the federal government—and rebranded it the Republican Party of Alberta, a full-on separatist outfit, in February 2025. This was immediately after paying off the Elections Alberta fines he'd racked up helping Jason Kenney secure the leadership of the UCP in 2017, which the regulator had to refer Crown Debt Collection. When asked in an interview with *Canadian Affairs* to name the significant policy differences between his party and the UCP, Davies replied, "Corruption, that'd be a big difference," without a hint of irony.[25]

When Elections Alberta raided the Centurion Project's event, multiple Edmonton Police cruisers and officers in tow, it was armed with a court injunction ordering the Centurions and the Republican Party of Alberta to immediately cease and desist the operation of the database and the app that were central to the scheme that Parker and Davies planned to inflict on Alberta's democracy.

The voters' list is a democracy in its most essential form. It comprises the full complement of people eligible to elect a representative government. Parker, with the help of Davies, hijacked this list and loaded it onto an American platform called 10xVotes so that his Centurions could use it to identify low-engagement voters who might be convinced to support Alberta separatism. Elections Alberta confirmed that the specific copy of the voters' list discovered on the Centurion Project's app was in fact the one entrusted to the Republican Party of Alberta. The oversight agency seeds each list with security identifiers that allow it to determine the source of any breach. In a rare news release intended to prevent a panic over the breach, Elections Alberta stated: "This is extremely sensitive data, and there are many safeguards to ensure it is only provided to the entities and individuals entitled under law to receive it and used only as expressly permitted in the Act." Nevertheless, the regulatory penalties for inappropriate use of the list of electors consist of a fine of up to $10,000 and/or imprisonment up to a year, if convicted.[26]

Parker claimed to have acquired the voters' list online for $45,000. He then partnered with a far-right Michigan-based firm with links to the US ambassador to Canada, Pete Hoekstra, to harvest the data towards a successful separatist petition.[27] The owners of 10xVotes—Drew Born and Drew Wierda—had created an app that allowed users to identify ten low-turnout voters in their networks and then encourage them to vote for Republican candidates.[28] Parker claimed the Republican Party's use of the app was instrumental in delivering Michigan to Trump in 2024, when he flipped the swing state and defeated Kamala Harris by 1.42 percent.[29] Hoekstra actively promoted the use of the 10xVotes app at Trump rallies across the state as a way to use real-time data about the voting status of users' friends and family to, as he put it, "swamp the vote."[30]

Other far-right influencers, like Alex Jones, Steve Bannon, and Tucker Carlson, have also endorsed the use of the app to get out the vote for Republican candidates. In a speech 10xVotes posted on its YouTube channel, Carlson suggested that the app uses the voter rolls in the United States: "I've never done anything like this, but I'm going to do it now," Carlson told his audience. "There's actually a website in the state of Michigan where you can find people who probably would vote for the candidate you're voting for but don't vote. And you can look them up. The voter rolls are right there. It's called 10xVotes. And you can go on there and just contact people you know and be like, hey, by the way, we don't deserve this. These people are horrible."[31] This would be illegal in Canada and may also be in the United States. The voters' list is not something that should be in the hands of private entities attempting to influence the vote outside of the regulated process. The co-founder of 10xVotes, Drew Born, himself has advocated for Montana to annex Alberta and Saskatchewan, writing a tweet in which he tagged the ambassador to Canada and the president.[32]

The implications of the largest data breach in Canadian history will continue to reveal themselves over the coming months and years. In the immediate term, the most significant of these is the fact that the personal data of almost three million people in Alberta was exposed. Teachers, doctors, politicians, lawyers, judges, police officers, journalists, professors, and countless others now have to walk around with the chilling knowledge that their addresses are discoverable by the global far right. I can say from my own experience that, as a writer, this is a profoundly unsettling new reality in which to operate.

The UCP government, however, seemed astonishingly unconcerned by the breach. Rather than assure the populace and vow to try to resecure the voters' list, the government cast blame on the opposition for delaying notice to the government of the breach, even after it was revealed that members of the UCP had actually attended a Centurion Project virtual training session on April 16.[33]

The opposition NDP had acquired a recording of the meeting that appeared to show UCP president Rob Smith (no relation to the premier) and director of stakeholder relations Arundeep Sandhu in attendance. On May 6, Naheed Nenshi, the leader of the provincial NDP, made a dramatic announcement about the UCP's failure to report Centurion's plunder of the voters' list. Nenshi argued that the premier's top staff and most senior party officials knew about the data breach and did nothing. This itself, he explained, was an offence under the Elections Act.[34] To the allegation that Rob Smith was present at the meeting, the UCP blasted back: "Naheed Nenshi is using a common name to drag our president through the mud. Rob Smith was never at that meeting, nor has he been at any Centurion meeting. It is a flat-out lie."[35] A statement from the UCP caucus admitted that staff were in attendance at the meeting while claiming that they had no reason to believe they were shown anything unlawful.[36] The presence of Arundeep Sandhu at the meeting makes the denial that Rob Smith was there considerably less plausible, but the UCP was in damage control and were willing to sacrifice Sandu to deny Smith's presence. Lashing out at the NDP for not reporting it to the government was a further deflection, likely intended as rage bait for the separatist UCP base than to persuade a more mainstream audience still horrified by the revelation of their data being in the far-right wind. It was the kind of gaslighting that in a different era would have been so transparent that it would never have been attempted, a performative attempt to play the blame game with Nenshi and sidestep any responsibility for the breach or its containment, as if Danielle Smith and her UCP were just observers of the separatist movement and not its direct enablers.

Nenshi reported the Centurion Project's unauthorized possession and use of the voters' list to the RCMP, and the Mounties, the privacy commissioner, and Elections Alberta launched investigations. Based on precedent, the likelihood of any of these culminating before the referendum is low. Thirty-eight of the province's university professors in the fields of law and political science called for a public inquiry in an open letter, writing: "Even the perception that voters' personal information is being used for unauthorized purposes is enough to erode public confidence. In a political environment already marked by polarization and declining trust, such doubts can have lasting consequences: discouraging participation, deepening cynicism, and weakening the legitimacy of election and referendum outcomes."[37]

I asked Marcus Kolga about the implications of the largest data breach in Canadian history for the referendum. Kolga is currently under sanction from both Russia and China for his efforts to promote democracy and combat disinformation. In 2020 he founded DisinfoWatch, which has since become a leading foreign disinformation monitoring and debunking platform in Canada. It recently published a major study on foreign interference and the threat it poses to Canada's cognitive sovereignty in the case of the Alberta referendum.[38] Kolga sees the breach as having potentially grave consequences for the outcome of the referendum. "You've left the front door unlocked to the homes and minds of every Albertan who is entitled to vote," he told me. This kind of precise, comprehensive, and current data set is of significant value to our state-based adversaries. Referring to the Russian military and security intelligence agencies, Kolga said he'd "bet the farm on the fact that the GRU or the FSB already has the list through someone at the Russian embassy. There's no doubt they have it; it's just a question of how they are going to use it."[39] Having been involved in national security investigations involving Russian operatives and proxies, I agree with Kolga.

The Russians are a determined and resourceful adversary, as we will see in the next chapter, and they would not have missed the opportunity to acquire information made readily available to anyone with an email address. The same week the Centurion Project news was breaking, a consortium of journalists from six different outlets—including the *Guardian*, *Der Spiegel*, and *Le Monde*—revealed that Russia's prestigious Bauman Moscow State Technical University had developed a "special training" faculty known simply as Department 4. Department 4 prepares Russian military intelligence officers for careers in the GRU, a unit responsible for the hacking of Western parliaments, extraterritorial poisonings of dissidents, and electoral interference across Europe and the United States. To pass courses students need to master hundreds of hours of in-class work on the theory of hacking, disinformation, and information warfare and demonstrate their skills through "practical penetration tests."[40] None of these skills would have been required to access the Alberta voters list. It was out there for the taking for anyone willing to sign up to the Centurion Project.

The project's breach of the voters' list is a major compromise of the political integrity and resilience of the province. It throws into question future democratic processes, and unless and until something is done to clear that air, Alberta will continue on a path of democratic backsliding into an illiberal jurisdiction. This is why the thirty-eight university professors called for a public inquiry. They see it as necessary for the re-establishment of public trust in our democracy.

JUST DAYS AFTER the Centurion Project event was interrupted, on May 4, Mitch Sylvestre and a convoy of trucks delivered to Elections Alberta what he claimed were the signatures of three hundred thousand supporters, with the intent of triggering a secession referendum in the fall.

It's worth noting again that the First Nations would

come to the defence of the nation with a successful court action challenging Elections Alberta's verification of the signatures. In early January, as we have seen, a number of First Nations filed applications for judicial review of the decision of the chief electoral officer to allow Sylvestre's petition to go ahead in the first place. Their lawyers successfully argued for an injunction, with Justice Shaina Leonard finding that irreparable harm to the treaty relationship would result from the certification of the signatures when the petition closed on May 2, 2026. She blocked the chief electoral officer from certifying the signatures until she had a chance to make a ruling on the complex case put before her over three days, involving arguments about the duty to consult First Nations, the readiness of the province to conduct a referendum in the present age, the impact of foreign interference on the process, and the harms that First Nations would endure as a result of racist attacks inflicted upon them by white supremacist supporters of separatism.

On May 13, Justice Leonard ruled that the decision of the chief electoral officer to issue the petition to Sylvestre was in error because it should have been understood that in doing so, the Crown was setting into motion a sequence that could adversely affect treaty rights. Accordingly, the Alberta government had a duty to consult with First Nations that it had not fulfilled. Leonard thus rendered the collected signatures effectively null and void—temporarily, at least. In early July, a Court of Appeal judge ruled the signature verification process should take place.[41] And on July 24, Elections Alberta made it known that they had used random statistical sampling to conclude that of 286,593 signatures the separatists had submitted on their petition sheets, 222,597 were verified. None of the signatures submitted were found to be the seeded names used by Elections Alberta to safeguard the voters list which was acquired by the Centurion Project from the Republican Party of Alberta. Accordingly, roughly 7.5 percent of the electors in the province signed the separatist signature sheets. This number amounted to more than the 10 percent of the total votes cast in the 2023 provincial election that was required under Smith's version of the Citizens Initiative Act.[42] Under Kenney's version, the separatists petition would have failed by a very large margin. In fact, it would have missed its target by over 120,000 signatures even with the extra 30 days provided by the new legislation and the removal of the requirement to collect signatures in two-thirds of the ridings in the province. Rath's response was to declare victory and to lash out at the premier, saying "if she doesn't put our question on the ballot, she will have proven herself to be a liar and she has to resign."[43]

Following Justice Leonard's decision, Premier Danielle Smith—who is obviously not a constitutional lawyer—was quick to cast it as "anti-democratic" and an "error in law"[44] on her provincially funded radio show in mid-May. Smith vowed to appeal. When she opened the lines to callers, Sean from Edmonton blasted the premier: "You're wasting our tax money pandering to the very people in our province who hate this country, who want to kick me out of my country, and appealing this decision that correctly says that separation would be unconstitutional." Even Wayne Nelson, the host of the show, questioned Smith's vow to appeal. "By doing so, are you defending democracy, or are you pandering to the ultra-right wing of your party to avoid the same fate that befell Jason Kenney and Ralph Klein?" he asked. Nelson told Smith that her critics were accusing her of showing her "true colours."[45] Smith, ever the happy chaos agent, took it all in stride. She then went to work to immediately circumvent the decision. By adding a tenth question to her already unprecedented nine referendum questions scheduled for October 19, the premier demonstrated once again her deep commitment to the separatist cause and to finding a way to divide Albertans from Albertans and the country from itself.

Meanwhile, the federal government remained mired in the paradox of tolerance, not looking for a fight, despite polls showing a clear majority of Albertans opposed separatism. When, if ever, would the federal government step into the fray to defend the nation? The next day the chiefs of Sturgeon Lake Cree Nation and Mikisew Cree First Nation wrote to the prime minister:

> We wrote to you just over a year ago on April 30, 2025, to request that you get the province of Alberta in line over the separatist threats. We have yet to receive a response. Instead, since then, Canada has accommodated the Premier's demands while she manufactures a separatist referendum, all without First Nation consultation or consent. This provincial government has no respect for the Treaty relationship. Our treaties depend on a stable society, independent Courts, democracy (in the true sense of the word) and the rule of law, all of which the Premier is set on destroying in favour of a minority of Albertans (less than 30 percent). Today, rather than respond to our calls, it appears that you are in Alberta to announce more appeasement of the separatist Premier Danielle Smith.

They went on to explain that while the uncertainty of a separatism referendum hung over their heads they would not participate in consultation processes related to the major projects the federal government was hoping to kick-start through the memorandum of understanding it had signed with Alberta. They called on the prime minister to withhold support for investments and major projects until the premier rejected the referendum. "Respect for Treaty, stability, and certainty must come first," they wrote. "We are confident many Albertans will stand with you in supporting a united Canada founded on honourable Treaty relationships."[46]

The next week, the UCP government convened a sham committee meeting in an effort to legitimize the announcement the premier was going to make in a televised address. The day before the scheduled announcement, the Select Special Citizen Initiative Proposal Review Committee was actively debating whether an alternative "Forever Canada" question should be put to the electorate in a referendum, when at 3 pm a press release notified all that a referendum would be called the next day. The committee had yet to vote on the motion that the press release pertained to, giving the lie to the proceeding and making a farce of the democratic process to which it was supposed to be contributing. One member of the committee, NDP MLA Christina Gray, said, "Oftentimes, it feels like the politics of the UCP is a stage play to exercise their power to do what they want—but I very seriously raise this point of privilege now, because it has been never more apparent than the fact this committee is still meeting and debating this motion as the press release from you the chair has already gone out."[47] The TV slot had been bought and paid for. The decision was already made. Heck, the pre-recorded video was probably being edited while the NDP MLAs served as props in Smith's ultimate sham democratic process.

The next evening, Smith appeared on television to announce that although she herself would vote to remain in Canada, there would be a referendum on whether to hold a referendum on Alberta's continuation as a Canadian province. She then propounded her interpretation of the "last decade under the Trudeau-Singh government in Ottawa" and its "anti-Alberta agenda" that had been "catastrophic" to the "unity, energy, and economic future of our nation." She asked Albertans to join her and her UCP to vote in favour of Alberta remaining in Canada, despite the federal government's attempts to "move towards a more centralized American-style system, with Ottawa to take over many provincial areas of jurisdiction using all manner of legislative, judicial, and financial leverage."

"I categorically reject Ottawa's attempts to do so," she said, "and call on all provincial leaders and MPs to undo the extensive damage that centralization of power in Ottawa has done to our country economically and with respect to national unity." What she was referring to as "destroying the unity, energy, and economic future of our nation" was primarily, of course, federal climate policies.

The speech was a masterpiece of political manipulation and gaslighting. The premier even went so far as to invoke images of Canadians fighting together to defeat the forces of what she called "communism and terrorism" in the Second World War. "The world would be a much darker place if not for Canada," she said.[48] On the last point most would agree, but on the preceding point a few eyebrows might have raised. Canada and Canada's armed forces fought the forces of *fascism* throughout the Second World War, not "communism and terrorism." And it was at this moment in her address when I, after being bombarded by a number of blatant mistruths cast as the plainest of facts, began to feel physically ill. The media did not pick up on her rewrite of Canadian history and of the Second World War. They gave the premier almost a complete fact-checking pass on this historic speech. But this particular lie carries great significance, because it is the forces and techniques of fascism that are at work behind the anti-democratic referendum the premier announced on May 21.

It would be another week before an Order-in-Council surfaced bearing Smith's signature and making it plain for everyone to see that Smith was all along driving the move towards a separatist referendum question; it was not, as she'd repeatedly claimed, the result of any group of apparently aggrieved citizens, nor did it come from the hands of the legislature, where in a constitutional democracy such momentous decisions should be discussed and debated. Smith on her own, through a maximal use of executive power that the UCP created for itself, would call the referendum. The referendum call had been premeditated. It was a decision arrived at a full year earlier, and not in response to Justice Leonard's decision just a week prior. The decision dated back to the election of the Carney government in 2025.

Much of the evidence to support this argument has already been set down in this and the preceding chapters. But the most compelling piece of evidence is contained in provisions of Bill 54 that address amendments to the province's 1992 Referendum Act, which have not yet been discussed. The Referendum Act passed in the heady days of the Charlottetown Accord. It was designed to ensure the legislature's involvement in considering and voting on any constitutional amendments after a referendum. With the passage of the UCP's Bill 54 into law as the Election Statutes Amendment Act, 2025, those provisions were repealed. Section 3 of the original Referendum Act required that any constitutional referendum question or questions to be put to the electors at referendum be determined by a resolution of the Legislative Assembly on the motion of a member of the Executive Council.[49] Bill 54 eliminated the requirement for the legislature's approval and allowed for the implementation of a successful referendum without a vote in the legislature. This means that Smith's cabinet can call a referendum and implement its results without once debating the question or the implications of such a vote in the legislature. If anyone outside the cabinet understood the significance of this at the time the 150-page legislation passed, they didn't speak up about it. The Legislative Assembly was cut out of the process to ensure that no dissenting MLAs could raise concerns. Instead, just a single-page Trumpian executive order would decree a referendum would be held.

This was not a decision of the people; it was the decision of the premier. Her true colours as both a separatist and an authoritarian shine through. Finance minister Nate Horner and the minister of hospital and surgical health services, Matt Jones, announced they would leave cabinet and not run in the 2027 provincial election in seeming response to the decision, although neither denounced the referendum publicly.[50] In using her executive authority to add a tenth and existentially divisive question to the previously scheduled October referendum, Smith warned we must "guard against the trap of using division and demonization tactics against our fellow Albertans with whom we disagree on this matter." But this is the trap that she herself has set. This is the peril in which she has placed our democratic society. And as we will see in the following chapter, this peril is in no way theoretical.

PART III: COMING TO JUDGMENT

9: The Donbas of the Prairies

"But is it perhaps childish or morbid to terrify oneself with visions of a totalitarian future? Before writing off the totalitarian world as a nightmare that can't come true, just remember that in 1925 the world of today would have seemed a nightmare that couldn't come true. Against that shifting phantasmagoric world in which black may be white tomorrow and yesterday's weather can be changed by decree, there are in reality only two safeguards. One is that however much you deny truth, the truth goes on existing, as it were, behind your back, and you consequently can't violate it in ways that impair military efficiency. The other is that so long as some parts of the earth remain unconquered, the liberal tradition can be kept alive. Let Fascism or possibly even a combination of several Fascisms, conquer the whole world, and those two conditions no longer exist."

George Orwell, "Looking Back on the Spanish War," 1942

IN CANADA, *Foreign interference* is defined as deliberate forms of covert activity undertaken by foreign states or their proxies to advance the interests of those countries to the detriment of our own. Such acts of foreign interference in Canada's democratic processes and our democratic society are the purview of Canada's security and intelligence community, which has the power, by virtue of the CSIS Act and the RCMP Act, to deter, disrupt, and ultimately dismantle such efforts. But Canada also recognizes that non-transparent forms of foreign influence can corrode our democracy and undermine our sovereignty. At the regulatory level, the government has announced the creation of a foreign interference commissioner to preside over the 2024 Foreign Influence Transparency and Accountability Act, which came into force on August 4.

Canada's understanding of foreign interference has evolved significantly over the last decade. In 2016, the concept was not widely appreciated; now it is understood that Canada is a target for these threats specifically because of who we are. As an active promoter of democracy, the rule of law, and human rights around the world, as a G7 nation, as a NATO partner, as a home to a diverse multicultural society, and as a world leader in innovation and research, Canada stands in stark contrast to the world's authoritarian regimes.[1] Authoritarianism is by its nature expansionist. It seeks to extinguish the light of liberalism from the world so that the people it rules over have no example of what it is to be free. The number of countries currently moving towards a form of authoritarianism is more than twice that moving towards democracy.[2]

It almost goes without saying that one of those countries moving towards authoritarianism is the United States. In

2025, a survey of more than five hundred US-based political scientists found that the United States was moving swiftly from liberal democracy towards a form of authoritarianism.[3] The next year that survey, Bright Line Watch, partnered with the Safeguarding Democracy Project at UCLA School of Law to conduct a study that included legal experts, political scientists, and the public. The study found that federal judges, lawyers, and law professors perceived a "significant erosion of the rule of law since Trump returned to office, including politicized law enforcement, a dysfunctional separation of powers, and executive-branch overreach. Legal experts generally view the erosion of the rule of law as more severe than the public currently perceives it to be."[4]

Indeed, the move from democracy to its opposite can happen at a relentless pace. The Harvard political scientist Steven Levitsky and his colleague Lucan Way developed the concept of "competitive authoritarianism" to capture what they saw as a sort of purgatory on the path to full dictatorship.[5] When they first started thinking about competitive authoritarianism in the early 2000s, they "never imagined" they would "apply it to the United States."[6] But with each passing news cycle, the shining city on a hill seems to disappear deeper and deeper into the darkness of authoritarianism. The domestic policy manifestations of this are as plentiful as they are profound; the foreign policy manifestations equally so. And while the ongoing illegal war on Iran seems the most flagrant of these at the moment, the US national security strategy would suggest that it is in fact an Israel-induced side hustle to the Trump administration's full-time gig of domination over the western hemisphere. The "Donroe Doctrine" calls for supremacy over the region and the region's energy resources. "The future will be determined by our ability to protect commerce, territory, and resources that are core to our national security," Trump said the morning after the US decapitated the Maduro regime in Venezuela in a stunning illegal military operation in the middle of the night. "These are the iron laws that have always determined global power. And we're gonna keep it that way."[7] In an op-ed published in the *Globe and Mail* shortly after the White House published its national security strategy, Canada's former ambassador to NATO Kerry Buck wrote, "Those who thought the age of imperialism ended more than a century ago might have just been proven wrong."[8]

WHAT HAPPENS WHEN a nation is subjected to a secession referendum and has an imperialist authoritarian superpower on its doorstep? To answer this, we turn to the history of secessionist referendums in Europe in the last twelve years and examine the dangers of conducting such direct-democratic events in the age of disinformation and expansionist far-right super powers. Referendums in Scotland, the United Kingdom, Catalonia, Crimea, Donetsk, and Luhansk led to a spectrum of severe consequences, ranging from social division and distrust of political institutions at the low end to economic stagnation and mass disillusionment in the middle and outright annexation as the worst-case scenario. Some of these effects were felt immediately, others in the mid to long term. But in every single case, the beneficiaries of these votes are clearly not the people voting. The people suffer; the people are set back, often severely. The grand experiment about to take place in Alberta in October could undermine the right of all Canadians to self-determination. It could be the start of decades of economic decline. It could be the entry point the Trump administration is looking for to fulfil its aims of hemispheric dominance. But most assuredly it impedes our ability to move forward as a nation united in the face of an existential threat to our sovereignty.

REFERENDUMS IN THE disinformation age are uniquely prone to foreign interference. Their binary nature makes them susceptible to emotional and tribalistic forms of argumentation that thrive in social media channels where fact and truth are optional. The fallout from European secession referendums over the past twelve years provides a chilling set of cautionary tales that shows clearly that the global far-right views secession referendums as a way to destabilize and weaken western democracies by contaminating their information ecosystems with vast amounts of disinformation, dividing their populaces, and undermining their collective faith in institutions.

Russia launched a disinformation campaign targeting Scotland's independence referendum in 2014 because it understood that a leave vote would weaken the United Kingdom and NATO.[9] Russia's state-controlled news agency ran 210 stories about the Scottish referendum in the last six months of the campaign. Many of the stories contained dubious claims supporting the leave vote and were widely shared on social media in Scotland.[10]

The Scots voted to remain, but that didn't stop Russia from casting doubt on the outcome of the referendum. Russia's state-backed propagandists (both human and bot) showed up in droves on Twitter and posted fake videos on YouTube and Facebook claiming the vote was rigged and fanning disappointment among leave voters.[11] As the historian Timothy Snyder argued: "It would have been a victory for Russia had Scotland left the United Kingdom; but it was also a victory for Russia if the inhabitants of the United Kingdom came to distrust their institutions."[12]

Indeed, the seeds of distrust and division were successfully sown. And now a decade later we can perhaps see some of the results of this Russian interference. A 2025 study by the Scottish Centre for Social Research shows a clear decline in trust in the Scottish government with only 47 percent of respondents to annual survey saying they trust the government, down from 61 percent in 2019. Support amongst Scottish survey respondents for independence, furthermore, has risen from 27 percent since before the 2014 referendum to 47 percent.[13] How much of this is attributable to Russian foreign interference in the devolution campaign and its aftermath is anyone's guess. It's highly unlikely that public inquiries or studies by social scientists could make precise causal calculations about a phenomenon conducted surreptitiously and designed to have diffuse effects on large population segments. But this, it seems, is how you corrode social fabrics. This was the first post-Soviet Russian interference operation, but it appears to have revealed a successful method of degrading democracy in the disinformation age.

The Scottish independence referendum provided a trial run for far-right interference in the Brexit vote two years later, when Russia aimed a firehose of digital propaganda at the United Kingdom in an effort to influence the leave vote. It did this through the proxy of the Internet Research Agency, which Yevgeny Prigozhin funded in 2013 in an effort to assist Vladimir Putin with his desire "to destroy the utility of the internet as a democratic space."[14] Putin had claimed the internet was a "CIA project" from which Russians needed protecting. With Prigozhin's backing, the IRA hired young St.

Petersburg University grads to work in its troll factory for double the wages of average Russians. The IRA's mission was to create discord and division in nations not aligned with Russia's geopolitics and corrode confidence in democratic institutions and processes. Its main technique was to take existing social cleavages and widen them even further using disinformation spread on social media channels through extensive bot networks.[15] Like any good bureaucratic department, the IRA had performance metrics: conflict, violence, protest, and democratic decay.

Unbeknownst to Britons, IRA troll-farm accounts flooded British Twitter during the Brexit campaign, accounting for a third of the discussion of the referendum. British electors entrusted with making a fateful choice about the future of their country engaged with and shared Russian bot-driven disinformation and propaganda material. The Russians, therefore, had some influence on the Brexit referendum with which they unquestionably took deliberate covert actions to interfere. The British government and its intelligence agencies made no serious effort to figure out the extent, largely because they did not want to know.[16] They avoided looking for evidence, and then said they had not found any. Stewart Hosie, a member of the parliamentary Intelligence Security Committee and Scottish MP was scathing in his condemnation. Speaking on his committee's findings four years after the Brexit referendum he said:

> The committee found it astonishing that no one in government had sought beforehand to protect the referendum from such attempts or investigate afterwards what attempts there may have been. The UK government should have recognized the threat back

in 2014 in relation to the Scottish referendum, but it didn't understand the threat until after the hack and leak operation against the Democratic National Committee in the United States. And because it was too slow to recognize the threat it didn't take action to protect the UK in 2016.[17]

This was in stark contrast to their American counterparts, who scrupulously endeavoured to understand the impact of Russian involvement in the 2016 presidential election through a comprehensive investigation launched a few months after Trump's inauguration.

But it was perhaps the clandestine and nefarious mass-influence campaign carried out by Cambridge Analytica and the Canadian data mining firm Aggregate IQ on behalf of American tech billionaire Robert Mercer that proved even more distorting of the overall Brexit vote than the Russian interference operations. Through Cambridge Analytica and AggregateIQ, Mercer, one of the original libertarian tech tycoons, together with Steve Bannon, his dark arts philosopher king buddy, ran a massive and deeply cynical psyop on the British public that is believed to have tipped the scale in favor of the leave campaign.[18]

The experiment was, in the words of one of its chief architects, a "grossly unethical"[19] one that toyed with the psychology of a nation by using its Facebook data against it without its consent or even its knowledge. With the Facebook data it surreptitiously acquired, Cambridge Analytica constructed weapons-grade psychographics of millions of users and used them to target those users with propaganda calibrated to their specific psychological profiles. AI and

Facebook enabled this to happen at a pace and a scale that blew the doors off British democracy.

The effects of this have been devastating. As *Atlantic* writer Idrees Kahloon wrote recently, "One generation ago, Britain was a major global power; today, it is a middling one, gripped by sclerosis."[20] The National Bureau of Economic Research calculated in November 2025 that Brexit had reduced the UK's GDP 6 to 8 percent, with impact accumulating steadily over time. Investment was reduced roughly 12 percent, employment and productivity by between 3 and 4 percent.[21] These are the potential consequences of gambling with direct democracy in the disinformation age.

The same actors that broke Britain out of the EU—the Russian and American billionaire-backed ones—upped their game a few months later and deployed the same tools and techniques in the 2016 US presidential election. This time, however, the victim launched an investigation that culminated in criminal charges and a public exposure of the crimes. On July 13, 2018, after a lengthy and complex investigation led by special prosecutor Robert Mueller, the US Department of Justice indicted twelve Russian intelligence officers for hacking offences related to the election of President Trump. Mueller's investigation found they had been part of a major conspiracy to spearfish the computers of American citizens, including members of the Clinton campaign and the Democratic National Committee, steal thousands of documents, and then release them on WikiLeaks and DCLeaks. This was a tried and true Russian espionage technique called *kompromat*—spreading damaging information to undermine and discredit their enemies—updated to the digital age. The leaked emails damaged the Clinton campaign in a number of ways: they showed Hillary Clinton had collected and categorized opposition research on Trump, that her campaign was plotting ways to discredit Bernie Sanders in his run as an independent in the presidential race, and that Clinton was paid a quarter million a pop to make numerous private speeches to Wall Street that when made public suggested that she was a duplicitous individual who could not be trusted to work in the interests of the American public.[22]

The FBI investigation produced a total of thirty-seven indictments, seven guilty pleas, and compelling evidence that President Trump himself had obstructed justice on multiple occasions. Trump associates were found to have repeatedly lied to investigators about their contacts with Russian agents during the campaign. Trump had, of course, infamously encouraged the hacking of Hiliary Clinton's campaign: "Russia, if you're listening," he said, "I hope you're able to find the thirty thousand emails that are missing. I think you will probably be rewarded mightily by our press."[23] Clinton had questioned at the time whether this collusion with Russia constituted treason. Just a few days after the indictments, on July 16, Trump and Vladimir Putin held a press conference in Helsinki at which Putin admitted to wanting Trump to win but sidestepped queries about ordering influence operations to achieve that outcome.[24] In responding to the same questions, Trump directly contradicted the findings of his own intelligence community's assessment, which in 2017 found that Russia's influence operations showed a significant escalation over its previous attempts to undermine the US-led liberal democratic order. The intelligence community also concluded that Putin had directly ordered the operations with the intent of undermining the American public's trust and confidence in their democratic processes and skewering Clinton's chances.[25]

Mueller's *Report on the Investigation Into Russian Interference in the 2016 Election* called that country's interference "sweeping and systemic."[26] Social media became a theatre for an "information warfare" campaign that "favored" Trump.[27] The hacking of Clinton's campaign and the release of stolen materials through Russian-created entities and Wikileaks were sophisticated tactics in an overarching scheme to deliver the election to Trump.[28] Mueller also found that Russia had targeted databases related to administering elections in many states, gaining access to the information of millions of registered voters.[29]

IN 2017, SEPARATISTS in Catalonia, Spain—one of the country's seventeen autonomous communities that has a distinct culture, and history and language, and were once a conquered people—staged an unofficial secession referendum, setting off a crisis in the country. Catalonia's autonomous government was dissolved, and the separatist leaders either fled or were arrested for rebellion and sedition. Spain, like the United States, is constitutionally indissoluble—meaning, unlike in Canada, advocating for the secession of one part of the country is illegal. Accordingly, federal authorities stepped in to quell a movement that, it turned out, received significant assistance from Russia.[30]

Large-scale propaganda campaigns intended to destabilize Spain came from Russian and Venezuela.[31] The Russian targeting of the Catalonian separatist movement dated back to 2014. It was part of a broader FSB ploy to leverage separatist movements worldwide to create chaos in and ultimately shatter western-allied nation states.[32] Led by Alexander Ionov, the Russian state-funded Anti-Globalization Movement was established in Moscow in an effort to build a worldwide community of practice among separatist leaders. To that end, Ionov organized a series of congresses and on multiple occasions invited to Moscow separatists from Northern Ireland, Scotland, the Basque Country, Catalonia, Texas, California, Puerto Rico, and Italy to "consolidate efforts" and establish lines of "future cooperation."[33] In 2022, a US grand jury indicted him for activity related to Russian interference in the 2016 presidential election, where he was alleged to be an associate of Yevgeny Prigozhin, the founder of the IRA.[34]

To assist the Catalonian separatists, Russian agents with a direct line to Putin met with separatist leaders and offered support. A $500 billion bank certificate to pay off the new country's debt and ten thousand troops were offered to aid the attempt to make the region an independent state. In exchange the Russians wanted the separatists to agree to turn Catalonia into the "Switzerland of cryptocurrency" by passing laws favourable to setting up large crypto coin-mining factories, similar to AI data centres.[35]

RUSSIA IS CLEARLY a big supporter of independence movements in rival countries, but pursuing secession in any part of the Russian federation is a crime carrying serious penal colony time.[36] Far-right governments are rarely troubled by paradox or hypocrisy. This is particularly evident in Russia's treatment of Ukraine.

The Kremlin vocally supported Catalonian and Crimean separation from what it cast as oppressive parent states—Spain and Ukraine—and would frequently take pains to compare the two as political equivalents. Putin himself made the comparison in a speech in Sochi at a 2017 conference hyped as the Slav Davos, titled "Creative Destruction: Will a New World Order Emerge from the Current Conflicts?" Putin's remarks about Catalonia could well have been made about the present moment in Alberta: "The situation in Spain clearly shows how fragile stability can be even in a prosperous and established state. Who could have expected, even just recently, that the discussion of the status of Catalonia, which has a long history, would result in an acute political crisis?"[37] Russia had clearly marked separatist movements as the loose threads in the status quo international system, threads Russia could pull on to see how far that system would unravel.

Russia had annexed Crimea three years earlier after an imposed secession referendum in breach of Ukrainian legislation that was boycotted by many Crimeans loyal to Kyiv, and was further deemed illegal and illegitimate by the European Union. The Russian defence minister, Sergei Shoigu, later characterized the operation as "a classic example of hybrid warfare," completed "without firing a shot."[38] The groundwork for this flawlessly executed instance of "new generation" warfare was laid over the course of years. Corrupt government officials and military personnel were bought off, and large-scale disinformation campaigns were launched to stoke discontent within the Crimean public. Undercover chaos agents were also sent in at crucial moments to amplify chaos, panic, and disorder.

Russia repeated this same play in the Donbas region of Ukraine, staging sham secession referendums with the assistance of separatists inside the oblasts of Donetsk and Luhansk. The quasi-democratic instruments were used to legitimize secessionists' claims on territory and for Putin to present his territorial expansion as a manifestation of popular will.[39] A guerrilla form of geopolitics played out as Russia deployed unmarked troops, dubbed "little green men," to further its asymmetric expansion under a veil of persistent denial and disinformation. The hybrid Russian war on Ukraine transitioned into total war early in 2022, and it continues to this day.

IT IS THROUGH the lens of these case studies that the Alberta separatist movement must be seen and understood. We must not underestimate the power of foreign interference and disinformation to transform political jurisdictions. Through the vector of Alberta separatism, Canada is vulnerable to a form of hybrid warfare that could see the global far right pull us apart. It should therefore not come as a surprise that the movement seems to find support in Washington, that separatist leaders have claimed the United States will recognize an independent Alberta following a vote, and that separatist leaders and senior Trump officials have discussed a $500 billion dollar line of credit collateralized against Alberta's oil and gas reserves in covert meeting facilities in the American capital.[40]

This is the kind of collateral that separatist leaders believe will provide the wherewithal to unilaterally declare independence as soon as they deem Ottawa is not "acting in good faith" after a successful independence referendum scenario. In Jeffrey Rath's words: "If we have a five hundred billion dollar line of credit, Ottawa either behaves itself at the negotiating table and behaves appropriately or Alberta could literally issue a unilateral declaration of independence outside of the scope of the Canadian constitution."[41] Here, Rath implies that Alberta—by which he presumably means himself and his APP colleagues—could arbitrarily decide on behalf of all Albertans that the federal government is not following the Clarity Act and unilaterally withdraw the province from Confederation, so long as they have the backing of $500 billion from the US Treasury. If the United States backs Alberta independence financially, it is safe to assume it would also provide formal recognition of state sovereignty.

It should not be surprising that Russia's troll farms have taken aim at Alberta and created pro-separatist websites and TikTok and YouTube channels that aim to spread narratives about state recognition of Alberta following a successful secession vote.[42] Websites like "albertaseparatist.com" are disguised as organic content and designed to mimic well-known outlets in the province, but they are the handiwork of Storm-1516, a Russian disinformation network described by Bloomberg as the "Kremlin's most potent weapon" in the disinformation war.[43] Storm-1516 has largely focused on Ukraine, but France's service for vigilance and protection against digital interference recently investigated seventy-seven of their information operations and concluded that the group represents "a significant threat to the digital public debate, both in France and in all European countries."[44] Chris Kremidas-Courtney, a senior adviser to the European Policy Centre, a non-profit think tank in Brussels, recently wrote that the presence of Storm-1516 "reveals a sobering truth: we are under sustained cognitive attack by state actors operating at an unprecedented level of sophistication. This is not just the latest Russian disinformation campaign, it's a full-spectrum influence operation designed to corrode trust, hijack reality, and ultimately reshape public sentiment across Europe and North America."[45] When I interviewed him, Marcus Kolga told me that Storm-1516 have "demonstrated that they are very effective at injecting various different narratives into the information space. What Russian intelligence is very good at is developing the content but also exploiting western influencers to basically launder these narratives and further amplify them."

The goal of the Alberta separatists is to secede from Canada. Their leaders have made absurd arguments asserting that Alberta is in a situation comparable to that of Kosovo after Slobodan Milošević's genocidal campaign against ethnic Albanians in the Serbian province in 1998 and 1999.[46] They have no intention of following a rule of law pathway towards independence as set out in the Clarity Act. Rather, they plan to unilaterally declare independence and invite countries like the United States and Russia to recognize Alberta's statehood.

One of the lawyers supporting the Alberta separatists is Keith Wilson. Wilson is based in St. Albert, a suburb of Edmonton and one of the wealthiest municipalities in the province. He has developed an argument for Alberta independence based on the Carney government's recognition of Palestinian statehood last year. According to Wilson, "One of the things that could well happen after the referendum is the United States will recognize Alberta as an independent country. And in fact there have been ongoing meetings between the Alberta Prosperity Project and representatives and the State Department in the US, where they continue to dialogue on the situation in Alberta and it's clear that the US government is prepared to recognize Alberta independence."[47]

Wilson drew from paragraph 155 of the Supreme Court's secession reference to make this argument, which, as I argued in chapter 2, is based upon assumptions of a status quo international system that no longer hold. Storm-1516 has tried to push this narrative on the separatists' behalf through the creation of fake news articles, disguised as organic content, aimed at normalizing the idea of unilateral secession. And while these articles appear to have gained little traction and the disinformation- and conspiracy-laden albertaseparatist.com site has been disabled, the presence of Storm-1516 in our information ecosystem should serve as a very real warning of the present danger, as we have seen in the examples from Europe's recent past.

Storm-1516, like its predecessor, the Internet Research Agency, has produced extraordinary volumes of what the United Kingdom classifies as foreign information manipulation and interference material. The disinformation attributed to the shadowy agency has outperformed content produced by Russian state-backed media outlets like Sputnik and RT.[48]

In addition to the Russia-linked strands of disinformation targeting Alberta separatism, a large network of (apparently) for-profit slopagandists has emerged on YouTube to push distortion and division for click-based revenue. Twenty YouTube accounts drawing some forty million views used AI-generated scripts and paid actors to generate organic-looking content to push skewed messages about Alberta and Canada.[49] The Canadian Digital Media Research Network identified these messages' two main aims: normalize both the idea of secession and the prospect of US annexation.[50] The CBC and Radio-Canada investigated the origins of the network and traced it to three individuals located in the Netherlands. They hired actors based in Alberta and the United States to masquerade as influencers pushing pro-separation narratives.[51] The specific effort to promote the idea of US annexation is curious coming from Dutch chancers looking to rage-farm Alberta. My instinct is to see this as a foreign interference operation rather than a for-profit venture.[52] But hunting those connections is no longer within my remit.

The annexation or, as Tucker Carlson puts it, the "liberation" of Canada has been the focus of a more overt influence campaign originating south of the border. Steve Bannon has argued that Trump understands Canada as being to the United States what Ukraine is to Russia, in the sense that in so far as Arctic security is concerned, Canada sits between the US and Russia and China pursuing their interests in the north.[53] Bannon's view is that the battle for control of the Arctic is the new great game of the twenty-first century. Canada has been thrust into the middle of that and become the main prize.[54] Accordingly, Canada, which Bannon now views as "hostile" to the United States and "25% foreign born," is a vital national security interest for the United States. Indeed, Canada has become a "lynchpin" in the US national security strategy of hemispheric dominance.[55] By this logic, Alberta is the Donbas of the Prairies.

Or at least it could be if the referendum is conducted without democratic safeguards to protect it from this type of foreign interference. Any secession referendum is a provincial political process. This gives the province jurisdiction over protecting the outcome from the designs of malicious foreign actors intent on loading the proverbial dice in favour of their own preferred result—a successful leave vote. It should go without saying that Alberta has no experience running a referendum process on a question of such consequence. It has neither an independent provincial intelligence service nor a provincial cybersecurity capacity to speak of. It doesn't have the capability to trace foreign funds or dark money that enter the process. It has no independent non-partisan task force to monitor the referendum and advise Albertans of foreign interference occurring in real or next-to-real time. The only thing the province claims to have done to safeguard the process is to ask people to renew their driver's licences so they can get citizenship markers added. That belies a misunderstanding of the foreign interference threat vector that is either wilfully ignorant or intentionally aimed to abet external influence over the process.

Elections Alberta is the department responsible for ensuring the integrity of the referendum. Its organizational chart demonstrates the lack of capacity to head off foreign interference from extremely capable state-based adversaries. Just eight contract investigator positions exist. It is not known how many of those positions are currently filled. This past December, $6.7 million was added to Elections Alberta's baseline funding level to help handle recall petitions, but the *Globe and Mail* reported that the agency's compliance and enforcement budget remains unchanged from last year: $695,000. A recent Elections Alberta investigation into the losing side of a non-binding referendum on support for a coal mine in Crowsnest Pass took eight months to complete.[56]

Expecting Elections Alberta to conduct complex, transnational investigations into foreign interference and disinformation campaigns when it likely lacks connections to or support from federal security and intelligence bodies, is fanciful. Undertaking a democratic process as consequential as a secessionist referendum without the safeguards in place to defend the integrity of the outcome is, accordingly, profoundly dangerous.

Can we expect the organizations that comprise the national security community to become engaged? Let's start with the Canadian Security Intelligence Service, or CSIS. Director Dan Rogers was asked about the issue back in November 2025, after his first address on the state of our national security. He responded that the CSIS Act restricts the agency from looking at a category of activities that could be described as "lawful advocacy or protests or any sort of political debate." That's the right answer and quotes the act almost verbatim. Pushed further, later in the day, on the CBC's *Power and Politics*, Rogers eventually conceded, "We definitely have to be attentive to the possibility of information operations or interference." He also noted that any time foreign adversaries seek to divide Canadians and amplify certain narratives is a concern for his agency. "We have to position ourselves to be able to identify those intentions and actions by foreign states and that's what we do as part of the Security and Intelligence Threats to Elections Task Force," he said.[57]

Watching Rogers's appearances that day, I got the impression that he hadn't expected to be questioned quite so thoroughly on the topic of Alberta separatism. Amid the dark milieu he deals with daily, it's hard to imagine that he or the intelligence service he leads has much time to consider hypothetical threats on the somewhat distant horizon coming from Alberta, of all places. It's fair to say that the more recent international media coverage of the Alberta Prosperity Project and its trips to Washington to solicit the Trump administration's assistance in breaking up the country will have altered his calculus. But it bears repeating that, as of

November 2025, CSIS was likely looking at a plethora of other national security threats and hadn't turned its collective mind to the rather "provincial" threat of the Alberta Prosperity Project.

Moving on to the Royal Canadian Mounted Police, my former agency. Federal policing investigations on average take several years—4.3 to be exact, according to the 2022 federal policing report.[58] Even if the RCMP were to take on a novel, complex, and politically fraught investigation in a province in which it also provides police services, it wouldn't happen in time to have any meaningful impact on the integrity of the referendum process. In other words, the damage would be done long before any charges were laid.

That being said, the federal government has recently furnished the justice system with new laws that could factor in a referendum process potentially rife with foreign interference. Now punishable with life imprisonment is the following offence, per the newly enacted Foreign Interference and Security of Information Act:

> 20.4 (1) Every person commits an indictable offence who, at the direction of, or in association with, a foreign entity, engages in surreptitious or deceptive conduct with the intent to influence a political or governmental process, educational governance, the performance of a duty in relation to such a process or such governance or the exercise of a democratic right in Canada.[59]

What constitutes surreptitious or deceptive conduct is key. Connecting that conduct to the *mens rea* of intentionally influencing a political process is also critical. To be clear, I'm neither a lawyer nor a criminal investigator, but let's reason through a scenario drawn from the public record in lay terms.

An evidentiary line is traced from members of the Trump administration and its far-right entourage to a leader of the Alberta Prosperity Project. Investigation reveals that leader is perpetrating disinformation on social media about the "Chinese Communist control of Ottawa" as a rationale for separatism, disinformation constructed by someone in the State Department or elsewhere in the Trump administration. It is then shown that the Trump administration or others in its orbit instructed the APP leader to promulgate that particular thread of disinformation. The global network of far-right bots and so-called influencers are enlisted to amplify that disinformation in a clear attempt to influence the provincial referendum. If this could be demonstrated to an evidentiary standard, well, perhaps someone could find themselves locked up for life. And playing fast and loose with foreign powers and falsehoods while holding the rest of the country hostage would prove to have severe consequences.

Global Affairs Canada has a shop dedicated to reporting on state-sponsored disinformation aimed at influencing democratic processes. Whether GAC would be willing to report on American-funded and -generated disinformation, much of which emanates directly from the White House, is an open question. My guess is that Global Affairs will hesitate to involve itself not just out of fear of upsetting a potential new Canada–United States trade deal but also out of fear of inflaming the separatist movement further. I wouldn't rule GAC out completely, but if it plays a role at all, it will be a rather minor one. It doesn't have enforcement powers, so all it could hypothetically do is provide warning of the disinformation, sunlight being the best disinfectant.

Lastly let's consider the new kid on the block: the foreign influence transparency commissioner, who will administer and enforce the Foreign Influence Transparency and Accountability Act, a 2024 law requiring anyone working on behalf of foreign governments to register those activities publicly. It's an attempt to bring hidden influence into the open. I watched, with some interest, Anton Boegman's appearance at the Standing Committee on House Affairs in support of his nomination for the commissioner role. In my early assessment, he's well-suited to the position, but he's got his work cut out for him, as he acknowledged. Part of his job will be to build the registry with what sounded like few positions and a budget of just $25 million over the next ten years. With an annual budget of roughly $2.5 million to cover salary and overhead, he'll be lucky to field a staff of twenty full-time equivalents, but he is expected to do so by August 4, according to a recent Order-in-Council. From that date, people and entities working on behalf of foreign states in Canada will be mandated by law to report ongoing arrangements to the foreign influence commissioner within sixty days.[60] This means that the deadline to report would be on October 3, which is just over two weeks before the Alberta referendum.

If Boegman's office is just a registry, it will be the paper tiger of all paper tigers. My read of the new act and its regulations law, though, is that if required registrants fail to register a "description of the arrangement" they have with a foreign principal, monetary penalties of up to a million dollars could be issued. The registry itself is to have a public-facing element as well, which will allow Canadians to see, in theory, what foreign actors have relations with the Alberta Prosperity Project and any other entities aiming to factor in the referendum. At his confirmation hearing, Boegman was asked by Alberta senator Paula Simons whether his office could have a bearing on the Alberta secession referendum. He confirmed that the new law he would preside over would indeed cover provincial processes such as referendums.[61]

Boegman could have an important role to play in defending the integrity of an Alberta secession referendum from foreign meddling. It will be a race against time and against the inertia of the federal bureaucracy. Let's make no mistake here: none of Canada's present-day adversaries have an interest in helping preserve our national unity.[62] A divided Canada is a weakened Canada. In a post-rules-based world order, in a post-truth era that is rapidly trending authoritarian, willingly exposing the nation to this sort of direct-democratic experiment is either pure folly or treasonous. It is the antithesis of responsible government.

Alberta has no capacity to insulate the referendum the provincial government is orchestrating from malicious foreign interference and disinformation. As such, it is clear that United Conservative Party has intentionally left the barn door open and invited the wolves in among the chickens. We will see how far the UCP goes in reaching out to the federal government's security and intelligence community for assistance in preserving the integrity of their grand experiment in direct democracy. We will also see how willing and able the federal security and intelligence community is to deal with such a novel threat amid the myriad other priorities it must manage.

This is the situation in which we find ourselves as summer turns to fall and the referendum looms in Alberta.

10: Surviving the Big Lie

> "Nothing so sharpens one's appreciation for democracy as bearing witness to its demolition."
> Jill Lepore, "The Last Time Democracy Almost Died"

WE MUST NOW acknowledge with great urgency that a contagion is infecting the Canadian polity. We failed to see a second pandemic coming through Omicron's fog. This pandemic is testing not our hospitals but our political institutions, our democratic resilience, and our belief that Canada is worth fighting for. This pandemic of disinformation and dishonesty, the Sturm und Drang of the global far right, is threatening our national unity and our sovereignty. It exalts not in nature but in artifice. And through the conduit of the Alberta separatist movement, it will continue to infect our polity. Political techniques will aim first at dividing our peaceable society and then at our dissolution as a sovereign democracy. To defend ourselves we must understand where to draw the line of tolerance. Because on the other side is treason. Recognizing this must inspire a countermovement in defence of Canadian democracy.

The Alberta separatist movement and its enablers in the quasi-separatist UCP were, as we've seen, born of fraud and the COVID-19 pandemic, and they are engaged in treason against the Canadian people. They wear the obscuring masks of grievance, but behind those masks are the menacing faces of traitors. This book has revealed those faces. It has exposed the plot against us. Criminals and conmen and hucksters and conspiracists and collaborators are leading this separatist movement. They are dangerous, illiberal actors whose delinquency in the face of and complete disregard for the standards and regulations of their chosen professions and our electoral and criminal laws have been demonstrated. They have wrested control of the democratic levers of Alberta and are using the seemingly innocuous vehicle of a provincial plebiscite in a way that invites the foreign interference operations of their global far-right brethren.

Direct democracy, as we have also seen, carries tremendous risk, especially when a nation's future is on the ballot. The risk only increases if that nation fails to recognize and brace against the threat posed by algorithms, artificial intelligence, and military-grade psychological warfare. It terrifies me to write this, but I think we are woefully unprepared for what is coming for us. Our misguided belief that Canada is somehow immune from the dangers that confront the rest of the world renders us inert at a time when we must be most engaged.

We need to wake up to the reality that it is our actual intelligence, and not the artificial kind foisted upon us by technology's billionaires and their monstrous data centres, that we must come again to respect. It's the key to our survival. Intelligence backed by human courage and love is the only antidote. "When that intelligence is snuffed out," Albert Camus wrote in 1945, "the black night of dictatorship begins."[1] Inoculation against disinformation and against foreign interference is within our control. The cure for disinformation is the pursuit of good and sound information that is based in rigorously discerned fact. The cure for disinformation is based in knowledge derived from the application of the scientific method. It is based in the humility of learning and the acquisition of understanding and wisdom through concerted and prolonged human effort.

There have always been hucksters, conmen, and megalomaniacal politicians who feel that the rules, laws, norms, values and traditions built up over centuries of human flourishing do not apply to them. Recognizing their designs and examining their stratagems and techniques is necessary to bring about a countermovement to their corrosive efforts. Doing so is not, of course, sufficient in and of itself. A vigilant, and indeed militant, defense of Canada and Canadian democracy is essential. It must come from all of us, though foremost and immediately from our political leaders. We must demand that they find the courage defend us against these dark forces.

This referendum on whether to hold a referendum on Alberta's future in Confederation is a big lie. This lie is foisted upon the nation and intended to reshape perceptions of Confederation. Canada is a representative, constitutional democracy. Not more than a single percentage of the Alberta electorate voted for one of the fringe, separatist candidates in the general election in 2023. And twice over the last year, the courts have ruled that a secession referendum would be unconstitutional and a violation of the treaties. To nonetheless move forward with the referendum is an act of treason. It is a form of psychological warfare conducted against us in alliance with the Trump administration's continual and escalating efforts to have us question our right to exist as a sovereign nation. It needs to be understood as being of a pair with these attacks on our country.

We had better wake up to this reality fast. Because when big lies are allowed to circulate uncontained for too long, horrendous things begin to happen. Executive power is maximalized and consolidated; the judiciary, law enforcement, and intelligence services are weaponized against dissent; corruption and kleptocracy run rampant; minorities are persecuted; immigrants are rounded up by masked gunmen and sent to cages to await deportation; the free press becomes propaganda; the education system is perverted; and—this is the most terrifying of all to me—we lose our grasp on truth. We see it happening to the south of us, but we should in no way be smug about this. It is already happening here. It can develop quickly, before institutions and individuals can find their bearings.

The big lie is a far-right, fascist political technique, a form of mass psychological warfare. Deploying the tactic is actually fairly simple, although it requires a great deal of nerve and perseverance. Our adversaries have both in abundance. Once you tell a colossal untruth, you have to really commit, and they have committed. It will take an equal commitment to turn them aside. The following examples illustrate what I mean.

Donald Trump continues to claim—erroneously, baselessly, and ludicrously—that the 2020 presidential election was stolen from him. He used it as a pretext for an insurrection on the US Capitol on January 6, 2021, that killed seven people and sought to hang Vice-President Mike Pence for fulfilling his role in the peaceful transfer of executive power to the incoming president. To quote the *Final Report of the Select Committee to Investigate the January 6th Attack on the United States Capitol*: "That mob showed up. They were armed. They believed the 'Big Lie' that the election had been stolen. And when Donald Trump pointed them toward the Capitol and told them to 'fight like hell,' that's exactly what they did."[2] America came frighteningly close to losing its democracy that day, and yet it failed to stop the contagion. Four years later, Trump returned to the White House to finish the job. He continues to draw on this big lie as he spreads another wave of disinformation about the integrity of America's electoral processes in advance of the November mid-terms. In a thirty-minute prime-time speech on July 16 that CNN, NBC, and ABC chose not to air, Trump described the American electoral system as "so broken and so vulnerable that no one can possibly defend it."[3] To justify this absurd claim, he cobbled together a collage of conspiracy theories about Chinese interference in the 2020 election that have never been assessed by the US intelligence community, let alone substantiated. Julia Curlee, a former intelligence officer who provided Trump's daily intelligence briefings throughout his first term, told *The Atlantic* that she has "never seen raw, unverified reporting pushed out this way: harvested for the pieces that fit, fashioned into a weapon against American elections."[4] Trump will stop at nothing to ensure his Republican Party retains control of the House and the Senate as he continues to wreak havoc. He has committed to this big lie and with it inflicts profound damage to American democracy, the American people, and America's status in the world.

Vladimir Putin's big lie is just as colossal. It too has led to catastrophe. He has repeatedly claimed that Ukraine is not a real country, that it is naturally part of Mother Russia, and that it requires liberating from neo-Nazis committing genocide against Russian-speaking Ukrainians in the Donbas. Nonsense, of course, but a pretext for war nonetheless. Putin launched his full-scale illegal invasion of Ukraine in February 2022, but as we have seen, the scheme began much earlier with a long-term disinformation campaign resulting, among other things, in phoney secession votes in Crimea, Donetsk, and Luhantz. The war has come at a staggering cost to Ukrainians, though the cost to the Russian people is also severe. New data from the Center for Strategic and International Studies, a US think-tank, estimates Russian battlefield deaths as high as 450,000 and casualties at 1.4 million.[5] As the secession referendums in the Donbas played out, Ukrainians failed to recognize what would befall them. "They had not prepared. They did not expect this," political scientist Maria Popova said of Ukraine's inability to identify the looming danger.[6] The Ukrainians failed to believe that their neighbour could turn on them so suddenly and so violently.

THEY HAD NOT *prepared. They did not expect this.* Big lies come at a tremendous cost if we cannot defend against them early enough and vigorously enough.

On its face, Danielle Smith's big lie that Albertans are aggrieved enough with Ottawa to justify a vote on whether to start down the road to becoming an independent nation may seem relatively innocuous. What's wrong with a little exercise in direct democracy, goes the thinking. Let's just test the temperature and let the separatists blow off a bit of steam. But Smith's big lie is equally malign, anti-democratic, and unconstitutional. Her experiment with direct democracy by executive order is designed to subvert representative democracy. The referendum questions are detached entirely from the UCP's constitution and from the campaign platform on which it was elected. Smith's big lie is an opening to her colleagues within the global far right: her friends at PragerU and Breitbart and the American tech billionaires to whom she's selling the province's agricultural land to build their hyperscale data centres. Her referendum is a trojan horse built and placed within our country via an executive order signed by her alone. She's simply following through on the vision she outlined before becoming premier. Through these acts she is committing treason.

This book has documented her well-established alignment with the Trump administration and the MAGA movement more broadly. But she has also more than once made observations that would please Vladimir Putin. "I've read that two regions of Ukraine feel more affinity to Russia," she wrote on the website Locals.com—a paid-subscriber platform for the far right—on February 24, 2022, eight months before becoming premier. "Should nations be allowed to break away and govern themselves independently? If that's truly what people want, then I think so," she said, echoing Putin's "creative destruction" speech in Sochi.[7] In April of that year, as she was beginning to position herself to take over the UCP leadership, Smith appeared on an ask-me-anything style online chat. Again she was asked about Ukraine and the ongoing Russian invasion. "I think the only answer for Ukraine is neutrality," she replied. "There have been thriving nations who have managed with neutrality; Switzerland being the most obvious example."[8] Journalist Justin Ling unearthed these comments after Smith became premier. His article generated calls for an apology from Smith to Alberta's Ukrainian community, which she initially resisted.[9] She claimed her knowledge and opinion had "drastically evolved" and that she now stood with "Ukraine and the Ukrainian people."[10]

While Smith's perspective on Ukraine may have evolved, the same can't be said for her position on Alberta sovereignty. "People keep asking me about Alberta sovereignty," she wrote before becoming premier. "My view is we need to stop complaining and start doing. There's no turning back. The fight lies ahead."[11] Her big lie follows a similar dark reasoning as she duplicitously takes the fight for Alberta sovereignty forward while wearing a federalist mask. The reality is that the majority of Albertans are far more likely to be frustrated and angry with Smith's own far-right government and its continued assault on the rule of law, provincial health care and education systems, human rights, and even certain books the government has tried to ban from the province's libraries.[12]

Indeed, as I finish writing this book at the end of July, polls suggest an overwhelming majority of Albertans will vote against initiating the process of separation. The weighted polling average indicates that nearly 75 percent of decided voters will vote to remain part of Canada. Polls are not perfect predictors of political outcomes. This is especially the case when the outcomes they are trying to predict contradict the democratic traditions of the polity and are entirely experimental and unprecedented in the democratic world. Moreover, and more practically, a ten-question referendum—which will require ten ballots to be printed for every elector in the province; read and decided upon by every elector who chooses to show up on October 19; and counted by hand because the UCP did away with vote tabulators[13]—has never been attempted before and will likely present the severely encumbered Elections Alberta with a logistical quagmire.

And while it is certainly true that some Albertans feel an antipathy to Ottawa—a form of Western alienation—this is likely secondary to more immediate concerns about the apparent corruption (and attempts to cover up the apparent corruption) that saw $600 million in provincial health care procurement contracts issued to a businessman with little experience in the sector but with close ties to senior officials in the UCP government.[14] To put this figure into context, the Gomery Commission on the notorious "sponsorship scandal" in the late 1990s found that the federal Liberals awarded $2 million in contracts without proper bidding and oversight. The government contracts awarded to Sam Mraiche's companies for things like Turkish Tylenol (which was never used) and substandard medical masks, and the UCP's efforts to cover this up, is by far the biggest procurement and corruption scandal in Canadian history.[15] Very few people seem to have even registered this, however, in part because Smith's big lie is a perfect deflection, a distraction, an attempt at division designed to soak up headlines and attention in order to further consolidate her power. And it is working. She holds the country hostage and is undermining our ability to defend ourselves in a united fashion against Trump's hybrid war.

Our instinct for tolerance shields Smith's big lie from our detection. We accept the grievance narrative out of both an abundance of tolerance and a reticence to engage in a debate that requires calling out conspiracy, prejudice, and bigotry. Over a dozen campaigns in favour of Alberta remaining in Canada have already emerged, each through its participation in this arbitrary process inadvertently validating Smith's lie.[16] Only the First Nations have seen through Smith's chimera clearly enough to mount successful judicial challenges, putting themselves on the front lines of the resistance and winning two landmark decisions in front of Justice Feasby and Justice Leonard. These battles came at significant financial cost, which the First Nations bore on behalf of the rest of Canada. As a result, according to Piikani Nation chief Troy Knowlton, the separatist movement that Danielle Smith and the UCP have enabled has targeted them with increased racism and threats of violence.[17]

Much like Donald Trump's Make America Great Again fabrication, Smith's big lie began with a slogan to encapsulate her vision: "A sovereign Alberta, within a united Canada." She continues to repeat this bogus phrase at every opportunity, and with each unchecked repetition it inches closer to becoming accepted reality. But you do not need to be a scholar of international public law to understand that if Alberta is sovereign, then Canada cannot be united. And if Canada is united, then Alberta, as a province of Canada, cannot be sovereign. No assertion to the contrary should be allowed to stand without swift retort from the highest levels of the federal government. You cannot have your sovereignty both ways. Canada is a nation state, not a trade union.

This is how Smith's big lie continues: "We had ten years of a hostile federal government attacking our industry, trying to shut us in, continuing to over-equalize the rest of the country, and also make laws that went against our foundational values," she said in a Global News interview that is a fair representation of many similar ones. "And so when that looked like it was going to continue with another election of the Liberal government, there's a lot of people who lost hope that Canada could be fixed."[18] Except Canada is far from broken, and blithely asserting that it is does not make it so. Over the ten years Danielle Smith claims Alberta faced a hostile federal government, Alberta's oil and gas production doubled, and the federal government invested $34.2 billion in the TMX pipeline from Edmonton to tidewater in Burnaby, BC. Since 2020, the federal government has provided at least $85.2 billion to the fossil fuels industry.[19] The election of a fourth Liberal government might have been a disappointment to some in Alberta, but Prime Minister Carney now has higher approval ratings in the province than Premier Smith, with 48 percent of respondents to a recent Angus Reid poll approving Carney's leadership and 46 percent strongly disapproving of Smith's performance.[20] Now that a referendum is actually a real proposition and not some theoretical shin kick to Ottawa, support for separatism is softening. Only 18 percent of Albertans would now vote to separate in a binding referendum, according to an Ipsos poll conducted in early June.[21]

The tolerance of Smith's big lie is almost as remarkable as the lie itself. She's been met not with resistance from the federal government but with appeasement and promises to do better. A memorandum of understanding, a promise to subsidize another pipeline for an already heavily subsidized oil and gas industry, and the abandonment of many elements of the federal government's climate policy are acts of appeasement. And yet the premier pushes forward with the referendum.[22]

The ten referendum questions that the premier has set are part of the pageantry supporting her big lie. The ten questions were put on the ballot not by grassroots citizen movements leveraging the newly amended Citizen Initiative Act but via executive order of the UCP cabinet.[23] This shows how little Smith truly values direct democracy and exposes her use of the referendum as a way to mainstream her treasonous agenda outside the legislature. As a citizen of the province, I'm deeply reluctant to even justify the premier's referendum with my vote. I do not recognize any of the questions as legitimate and find their underlying xenophobia and anti-Canadianism abhorrent. Not one moves us forward as a country. On the contrary, they set us back.

Smith is planning on using Albertans as props in a spectacle that may cost as much as a $130 million.[24] But the referendums themselves are a particularly insidious feature of the big lie because they seek to subvert representative democracy and dilute it with easily manipulable plebiscites. We can see the hypocrisy of Smith's approach to direct democracy when she ignores the results of a previous provincial plebiscite and legislates in direct contradiction of its result.[25] The UCP government plans to end the practice of rolling the clocks back an hour in the fall and forward an hour in the spring despite the outcome of a 2021 vote that rejected such a change.[26] So much for the "ultimate" form of democracy! Another recent example involves a petition to ban coal mining on the eastern slopes of the Rocky Mountains. On June 10 the country singer Corb Lund submitted a petition with over two hundred thousand signatures in support of adding his "Water Not Coal" question to the October ballot. He was told shortly thereafter that he'd missed a deadline he is adamant no one informed him of and that an

Elections Alberta verification process estimated the petition fell roughly five thousand signatures short of the minimum threshold for approval. Lund was blunt in his assessment. "It's bullshit," he said. "This whole process is clearly designed to give the government cover to do what they want."[27] It would certainly appear that way.

Smith's referendum would be a laughable if exorbitantly expensive stunt were it not so demonstrably reckless. As we've seen, Chief Desmond Bull of the Louis Bull First Nation is so concerned with the potential threat of foreign interference in the referendum campaign that he championed a resolution calling for the RCMP and Canada's auditor general to investigate whether Smith and the UCP have treasonously violated First Nations' treaty rights. When the Assembly of Treaty Chiefs met in Calgary in June, Bull's resolution unanimously carried.

I spoke with Chief Bull in July. There was an urgency voice, an intensity that seemed to burn through the speaker of my iPhone. He does not see the First Nation resolution as metaphorical or symbolic, nor the threat of foreign interference and influence as theoretical. I asked him where he saw the situation in our province heading. "For me, I'd love to see the RCMP move forward in regards to an investigation. That would satisfy my needs. That would not only satisfy my needs, but more importantly it would hold that no one is above the law. It doesn't matter if you are a premier or a prime minister or anyone that has authoritative power. If you break the law, you are accountable to the law," he told me. "So I would love to see the RCMP follow through on some sort of investigation and hold her [Premier Smith] accountable. Because if we allow her to get away with this, what's stopping every other region or premier from wanting to create that type of noise and say, yes, we as a province or a region want to separate also? If we don't stop it history will repeat itself."[28]

Perhaps those who have been colonized have a more intuitive appreciation of the types of threats before us. Perhaps also the experiences of Chief Big Bear and fourteen of his band in Regina in 1885, and Chief Poundmaker before them, factor in the thinking of the chiefs who unanimously supported the treason resolution. After trials lasting not more than a few minutes, their ancestors were convicted of treason and sentenced to three years in the Manitoba Penitentiary (now Stony Mountain Institution) near Winnipeg. Chief Bull explained that this was for nothing more than "upholding their way of life and trying to hold the government accountable for honouring the treaties."

His view is that the premier has betrayed Canada and the treaties that he understands as the core and foundation of the country. For him that betrayal amounts to treason. In working with the separatists to stage this vote, and in so doing inviting foreign powers to meddle in our domestic affairs while separatist entities breached the Alberta voters' list and compromised voters' personal data, Danielle Smith is victimizing all treaty people. And we are all treaty people, according to Chief Bull, and all of our human rights are in peril as a result of the UCP's treasonous actions.

TO REITERATE: BIG lies are contagions, and the infection can forever alter the politics of a society. Big lies are an assault on truth, of course, but also on reason and rationality. As such they have an unmooring effect, just as an act of betrayal can unmoor a marriage. Alberta separatism is a big lie that prejudiced, feckless, misinformed, conspiracy theorists are perpetrating against the Canadian people. Like all big lies, at its core is a grain of truth just large enough to cause concerned citizens to second-guess themselves. Western alienation is a real feature of our political culture, and we would do well to recognize it and understand its origins. But Alberta separatists have co-opted Western alienation and blown it up into a concocted national unity crisis. The vast majority of Albertans have no desire to separate from Canada, and to assert otherwise is absurd.

None of this is by accident. A 2021 document, *Free Alberta Strategy*, is the etiology of the political disease infecting Alberta.[29] It was authored by Barry Cooper, the University of Calgary political scientist; Rob Anderson, who has become the chief of staff to Premier Smith; and Derek From, a constitutional lawyer. Given the course the Smith's government has taken, this document can be understood as the equivalent of the Heritage Foundation's Project 2025, inarguably the blueprint of Trump's second term and the intellectual driver of his transformation of America into an autocracy. *Free Alberta Strategy* contains an analogous set of recommendations to destabilize Canadian federalism through various legislative initiatives that the Smith government has pursued with a radical fervour. This began, as we've seen, with the unconstitutional Sovereignty Act in 2025. Later that year the government passed the International Agreements Act, which, counter to all norms of statecraft, seeks to put the province on an equal plane with the federal government in terms of managing international relations, asserting that Alberta is not bound by any international agreement signed by the federal government. A move to establish its own police force followed thereafter, as did a demand for reforms to the judicial appointments process that would politicize the judiciary and undermine its independence.[30]

This shakedown approach to federalism amounts to a "do what we say, or we're done" extortion play. "In the event that Ottawa refuses to recognize Alberta's provincial rights of sovereignty, and instead continues its strategy of economic tyranny, co-opted management of our resource sector, and the marginalization of our citizens, it may leave our province with no other recourse but to leave Confederation entirely," the authors of *Free Alberta Strategy* write.[31] Their strategy is rooted in a conspiratorial sense of grievance that is dangerously detached from discernable reality. For his part, Barry Cooper is acutely aware of the treasonous dimension of his intellectual creation. "Of course it is treason," he has said. "Of course we're going to need help from abroad." As we've seen, they've worked hard over the last couple of years to solicit this help from the Trump administration.

Premier Smith stood defiant in the face of the treaty chiefs' resolution requesting an RCMP investigation into her government for treason. "I think it's disgraceful. I think it is disgraceful that any government that wants to be taken seriously would level charges that serious against another government," she said in mid-June at Calgary's Heritage Park while standing in front of a row of vintage gasoline pumps. "Look, I've had my differences with the federal government, but I have never used language like that. I would ask the treaty chiefs to check themselves."[32] Perhaps Smith forgot that in 2024 she told Tucker Carlson to put the federal environment minister, Steven Guilbeault, in his "crosshairs" and previously accused Guilbeault of "continued treachery" against Albertans for his climate policies.

She has intimated that she would not hesitate to check the First Nations if they resort to civil disobedience measures in the face of the referendum's continued harm to them. The Treaty 8 grand chief, Trevor Mercredi, has demanded the immediate cancellation of the referendum because the government has not sought First Nations consent to move forward with the discussion of secession, and consent has not been given. The continued pursuit of the referendum has put First Nations in the province under duress, even as they have won multiple court battles to recognize their treaty rights in this absurd process. Chief Mercredi has reserved the right to take the fight against the referendum to the highways. Referencing the Critical Infrastructure Defence Act, which the Kenney government passed in response to blockades of CN rail lines by Indigenous opponents of the Coastal GasLink through Wet'suwet'en hereditary lands in 2020, Smith said, "I think you saw how serious we are about enforcing that law as we have many times over previous years."[33]

Before Smith became premier, she seemed far more supportive of acts of civil disobedience. In February 2022, she weighed in during a Western Standard livestream discussion of the Freedom Convoy's ongoing blockade at Coutts and expressed her desire to see the blockade's proponents win. "This whole phrase of 'peace, order and good government,' I think it's become a shorthand to: the federal government can do whatever the heck it wants, and we just need to be peaceful and orderly about it. And that's not, in my view, what it should mean." Rob Anderson was also on the segment. "I think it's a beautiful thing," he said. "I just think the whole Freedom Convoy—and that would include what's going on at Coutts and in capitals around the country and now around the world as people are copying Canada, of all things—is one of the most important events, certainly in recent Canadian history."[34]

When it's their friends on the far right being civilly disobedient, civil disobedience is a beautiful thing. But when it's the First Nations exercising their treaty rights, it's criminal. That kind of double standard is at the crux of the Smith government's move to throw off, as it would have us believe, the yoke of the Liberal federal government. None of the fundamental concepts of Canadian democracy seem to matter to these United Conservatives. In fact, they are all under direct attack. Cooperative federalism is replaced with shakedown federalism; representative democracy is replaced with direct democracy; the rule of law is replaced with the arbitrary rule of one; peace, order, and good government is replaced with conflict, chaos, and tyranny; and the treaties, the constitution, and the thousands of acts of accommodation that mark our 159-year history are held in contempt. Alberta has moved into the realm of illiberalism and as a result it is difficult to know if the bonds of Confederation can be upheld and sustained.

As summer fades to fall, the referendum in October will consume much of the country's political oxygen. This manufactured event carries with it the guarantee of continued, concentrated, and multi-faceted foreign interference and influence operations. And while the threats from Russia and China may manifest in clandestine ways—through targeted slopaganda channels and the seeding of our information ecosystem with disinformation amplified by the far right—I am also deeply concerned about the more overt forms of interference that we have seen and will continue to see as a result of the Trump administration's erratic and ominous foreign policy. We now have an adversary on our doorstep. Russia, China, and the United States will laser-point their psychological warfare on this hopelessly and intentionally exposed provincial political process. This is the biggest test the federal security and intelligence community have ever faced, but they will hesitate to step in to protect us, even if it were within their capability to do so. The fate of our country is in the balance, and it seems as though few have acknowledged the threat.

Doubly troubling, the vote also brings with it the possibility for a public order emergency. After all, the leaders of the separatist movement are mostly the same who led the Freedom Convoy. Is it improbable to imagine that if the separatists don't like the result of the vote, they might get back in their trucks and head to the highways or the provincial legislature or even Ottawa, again demanding their "freedom"? Is it beyond our capacity to foresee claims of a rigged vote, furthering the intentional division of our society and further undermining democratic trust? And how are we to understand the continued violations of the rights of First Nations as the treaties are treated as less than an afterthought in this fraudulent process?

The nightmare scenario of course is that the biggest liar of them all seizes on the referendum as an opportunity to turn Alberta into the Donbas of the Prairies. Trump announced in late July that he would use section 338 of the 1930 Smoot-Hawley Tariff Act to impose a 50 percent tariff on roughly $20 billion worth of Canadian products, to take effect on August 19. The legality of this move is highly questionable, but in justification of it, Trump claimed: "Canada has been very, very tough on us over the years, for many years, and no other president's done anything about it. In all fairness to them, they need us to survive. Without us, there's no way they can survive."[35]

His treasury secretary, Scott Bessent, who plays a critical role in Trump's escalating trade war against us, earlier in the year called Alberta "a natural partner for the US." Bessent told far-right commentator Jack Posobiec: "Alberta has a wealth of natural resources, but [the Canadian government] won't let them build a pipeline to the Pacific. Rumour is they may have a referendum on whether they want to stay in Canada or not. I think we should let them come down into the US . . . They have great resources. The Albertans are a very independent people."[36]

Bessent said this shortly after Rath and his gaggle of separatists met with State Department officials for the third time in Washington. Bessent sits atop the bureaucratic hierarchy in the United States. His Treasury Department plays a central coordinating role in the US national security community. He may look like a retired banker, but he is about the last person in the US government we should want eyeing Alberta as a potential acquisition in support of the Trump administration's aims of resource imperialism in the western hemisphere. A statement like this—a soft offer of annexation, if you will—coming from the second-in-command of the US government is radically out of sync with the history of Canada-US cooperation and interdependence that has defined our relationship over the last 150 years. It speaks to the nature of a very different sort of neighbour; one we never imagined we would have, and one with whom we have allowed ourselves to be far too comfortable.

Inviting this contagion into our polity, as the Smith government has done, is treason.

We can tolerate the continued assault on Canada from those who owe us a duty of loyalty for only so long before that tolerance leads to our destruction. Citizenship comes with responsibilities, and the most basic and fundamental of these is loyalty. When Smith became premier of the province of Alberta, she swore an oath of allegiance to the Crown. If we tolerate the assault on the rule of law, then the rule of law will collapse. If we tolerate the subversion of representative democracy with direct democracy, our elections will mean nothing. If we tolerate a betrayal of Canada that will erode our capacity to remain self-determining—if we tolerate treason, in other words—then the concept of Canada will hang by the loosening threads of the thousand acts of accommodation that once held us together.

Canada will only continue to survive as a democracy in a revolutionary age if its component provincial and territorial parts continue to function democratically and adhere to the rule of law, the constitution, and the treaties. We have seen how authoritarians have used plebiscites to divide their populations and consolidate their power. That is happening at this moment in Alberta, and yet we seem oddly resigned to this referendum even as it threatens our future in fundamental ways. Accepting the reality of our current predicament requires shaking off the blinders of denial. It requires a militant and sustained focus on what is happening. It requires us to stop pretending everything will work out in the end if we just muddle through and apply status quo lenses to revolutionary problems.

Canada is one of the great countries in modern human history. We stand as a beacon of freedom in an increasingly illiberal world. Our country is worth defending with everything we have within us. Our greatness is found in our openness, our transparency, our equality, our multiculturalism and diversity, our research and cultural institutions, our free press and public education, our two official languages, and our efforts to expose the truth of our colonial history and to reconcile that truth with First Nations and to move forward as one treaty people. Canada is worth defending militantly, urgently, and with the same level of intensity with which it is being attacked and betrayed.

The alternative is division. It is annexation. It is populist authoritarianism. It is the end of Canada as we know and understand it. If we fail now to defend our country, we may be pulled into the far-right vortex engulfing the United States. We cannot allow that to happen because we're reticent to look the traitors in the eye and call out their treason. We must find the strength and courage to defend ourselves against actions that are leading us down a path fraught with danger. A thousand acts of accommodation once defined our nation. Now, with a thousand acts in defence of Canada, we must fight for our survival.

PL

May–July, 2026

Acknowledgements

FIRST THANKS GO to my wife and family for bearing with me over these last three months. I'm grateful for your unwavering love and patience. I must also thank all the people who gave generously of their time and spoke insightfully to me about various aspects of this book. I could not have pulled this together without you all. The First Nations of Treaty 6, 7, and 8 have shown the way and were among the inspirations for this work in defence of Canada. I was humbled to follow their lead and add my voice to the fight. Finally, I must give special thanks to Dan Wells and the team at Biblioasis for taking a chance on this project, for providing it with the sage and steady editorial hand it needed, and for moving mountains to get it swiftly into the hands of readers. From Edmonton to Windsor, we wove a thread.

Notes

PART 1: INTRODUCTION

1: THE PARADOX OF TOLERANCE

1 See Kenneth Waltz, *Theory of International Politics* (Reading, MA: Addison-Wesley, 1979).

2 See Beatrice Catena, Ondrej Ditych, and Nad'a Kovalčiková, "Smoke and Mirrors: Building EU Resilience Against Manipulation Through Cognitive Security," European Union Institute for Security Studies, Oct. 7, 2025, https://www.iss.europa.eu/publications/briefs/smoke-and-mirrors-building-eu-resilience-against-manipulation-through-cognitive.

3 See Sarah Oates, "The Easy Weaponization of Social Media: Why Profit has Trumped Security for U.S. Companies," *Digital War*, May 11, 2020, 117–22, https://doi.org/10.1057/s42984-020-00012-.

4 Uday Rana, "Separatism promises a 'dangerous bluff,' Carney says on Alberta referendum," Global News, May 25, 2026, https://globalnews.ca/news/11862970/alberta-separatism-mark-carney-brexit/.

5 John Ibbitson, "Why is Canada the most tolerant country in the world? Luck," *Globe and Mail*, July 2, 2026, https://www.theglobeandmail.com/news/politics/why-is-canada-the-most-tolerant-country-in-the-world-luck/article19427921/.

6 Loleen Berdahl, *The Persistence of Western Alienation*, essay no. 9, Institute for Research on Public Policy (2021), 2, https://centre.irpp.org/wp-content/uploads/sites/3/2021/05/The-Persistence-of-Western-Alienation.pdf.

7 Wesley Wark, "Alberta's government is being obtuse about the risk of foreign interference," *Globe and Mail*, June 12, 2026), https://www.theglobeandmail.com/opinion/article-alberta-government-referendum-foreign-interference-risk/.

8 See the submission by Nigel Banks on International Law and Secession included in the Submission of Athabasca Chipewyan First Nation to Cabinet Regarding the Prospect of an Alberta Independence Referendum, May 13, 2026, 485–96, https://acfn.com/submission-of-athabasca-chipewyan-first-nation-to-cabinet-regarding-the-prospect-of-an-alberta-independence-referendum/.

9 See the affidavit of Lily Polenchuk in the Athabasca Chipewyan submission: 524. Polenchuk's affidavit is based on recorded statements made by Jeffrey Rath and Dennis Modry at public events Polenchuk attended in her study of the separatist movement.

10 Marcello Di Cintio, "Among the Separatists," *Tyee*, Apr. 1, 2026, https://thetyee.ca/Analysis/2026/04/01/Among_Separatists/.

11 Matthew Black, "Smith declines to 'demonize' separatists despite Eby's 'treason' remarks," *Edmonton Journal*, Jan. 29, 2026), https://edmontonjournal.com/news/politics/treason-b-c-s-eby-calls-out-alberta-separatists-seeking-u-s-assistance.
12 Karl Popper, *The Open Society and Its Enemies* (London: Routledge, 2002), 660–62.
13 Goebbels quoted in András Sajó, "From Militant Democracy to the Preventive State?" *Cardozo Law Review* 27, no. 5 (2006): 2262, https://larc.cardozo.yu.edu/cgi/viewcontent.cgi?article=3221&context=clr.
14 Karl Loewenstein, "Militant Democracy and Fundamental Rights," *American Political Science Review* 31, no. 3 (June 1937): 423.
15 See Freedom House, *Freedom in the World 2024: The Mounting Damage of Flawed Elections and Armed Conflict*, Feb. 2024, https://freedomhouse.org/sites/default/files/2024-02/FIW_2024_DigitalBooklet.pdf.
16 See Anthony E. Raubitschek, "The Origin of Ostracism," *American Journal of Archaeology* 55, no. 3 (July 1951): 221–29. Raubitschek notes four instances of the law being applied against those guilty of treason, which he has surmised from Thucydides's account of the Peloponnesian War.
17 Loewenstein, "Militant Democracy," 427.
18 Loewenstein, "Militant Democracy," 423.

2: REFERENCES AND REFERENDUMS IN A REVOLUTIONARY AGE

1 Supreme Court of Canada, Reference re Secession of Quebec, [1998] 2. S.C.R. 217 25506, https://decisions.scc-csc.ca/scc-csc/scc-csc/en/item/1643/index.do.
2 The SCC decided to leave political actors the role of determining what would constitute a clear majority and a clear question in the case of a secession referendum and its eventual outcome. This was addressed in the Clarity Act, which provides the House of Commons three criteria when determining whether a clear majority of voters has elected to secede. First, the size of the majority voting in favour of the secession option. Second, the percentage of eligible voters voting in the referendum. And finally, any other matters or circumstances the House of Commons considers relevant can also be taken into consideration when determining whether a majority is a clear one. The Clarity Act also provides for the House of Commons to consider the clarity of the question put to voters. The main criterion here is whether the question would result in the clear expression of the will of the population. Reference re Secession of Quebec, https://decisions.scc-csc.ca/scc-csc/scc-csc/en/item/1643/index.do; And An Act to give effect to the requirement for clarity as set out in the opinion of the Supreme Court of Canada in the Quebec Secession Reference S.C. 2002, c. 26, https://laws-lois.justice.gc.ca/eng/acts/c-31.8/fulltext.html.
3 Reference re Secession of Quebec.
4 Author interview with Margaret Moore, May 26, 2026.
5 Reference re Secession of Quebec, [1998] 2 S.C.R. 217 https://decisions.scc-csc.ca/scc-csc/scc-csc/en/item/1643/index.do, 96.
6 Roy J. Romanow, "A House Half Built," *Walrus*, June 2006, https://thewalrus.ca/2006-06-national-affairs/.
7 Reference re Secession of Quebec, [1998] 2 S.C.R. 217 https://decisions.scc-csc.ca/scc-csc/scc-csc/en/item/1643/index.do, 3.
8 Reference re Secession of Quebec, [1998] 2 S.C.R. 217 https://decisions.scc-csc.ca/scc-csc/scc-csc/en/item/1643/index.do 3.
9 Francis Fukuyama, *The End of History and the Last Man* (New York: Free Press, 2006).

10 Bob Rae, "The Fight for Humanity's Future: Now Comes the Hard Part," *Policy*, Feb. 2026, https://www.policymagazine.ca/the-fight-for-humanitys-future-now-comes-the-hard-part/.

11 Public Inquiry Into Foreign Interference in Federal Electoral Processes and Democratic Institutions, vol. 1: Report Summary, Jan. 2025: 6, https://foreign-interferencecommission.ca/fileadmin/report_volume_1.pdf.

12 Statement from the Chief Justices, Court of King's Bench of Alberta, Jan. 27, 2026, https://albertacourts.ca/kb/resources/announcements/statement-from-the-chief-justices-2026.

13 Dale Smith, "Chief justice commends colleagues for speaking out against judicial attacks," CBA/ABC National, June 9, 2026, https://nationalmagazine.ca/en-ca/articles/courts/2026/chief-justice-commends-colleagues-for-speaking-out-against-judicial-attacks. Chief Justice Wagner's full press conference is available on YouTube, https://www.youtube.com/watch?v=DNeHWu4rkgc.

14 Patrick Lennox, "Shakedown Federalism," *Alberta Views*, June 1, 2026, https://albertaviews.ca/shakedown-federalism/.

15 Bianca Kratt and Christopher Samuel, "Statement on Judicial appointments to Alberta's superior courts and the Supreme Court of Canada," CBA Alberta, Feb. 5, 2026, https://cba-alberta.org/our-impact/submissions/statement-on-judicial-appointments-to-alberta-s-superior-courts-and-the-supreme-court-of-canada/.

16 Clarity Act S.C. 2000, c. 26 An Act to give effect to the requirement for clarity as set out in the opinion of the Supreme Court of Canada in the Quebec Secession Reference, preamble. https://laws-lois.justice.gc.ca/PDF/C-31.8.pdf.

17 Clarity Act preamble.

18 Ricardo Acuna, "Western Separatism: An age-old story entering a new chapter," Canadian Centre for Policy Alternatives, Oct. 1, 2025, https://www.policyalternatives.ca/news-research/western-separatism-an-age-old-story-entering-a-new-chapter/.

19 See Patrick Lennox, "Canada is Already at War With the US—We Just Don't Know it Yet," *Walrus*, Mar. 2026, https://thewalrus.ca/canada-is-already-at-war-with-the-us-we-just-dont-know-it-yet/.

20 Danielle Smith, interview by David Akin, *The West Block*, Global News, May 10, 2026, 6:15, https://www.youtube.com/watch?v=50VxRqymDsw.

21 Danielle Smith, interview by Vassy Kapelos, *Question Period*, CTV News, May 24, 2026, 4:57, https://www.youtube.com/watch?v=Fjs2cw1JcYU.

22 See Bruce Anderson, "New Spark Poll: 15% of Albertans Want to Separate; 21% Would Vote for Referendum" *Policy*, June 12, 2026, https://www.policymagazine.ca/new-spark-poll-15-of-albertans-want-to-separate-21-would-vote-for-referendum. It is worth noting that according to Anderson, separatist sentiment is not gaining momentum. A strong repudiation of the idea is anticipated in the October vote at this stage in the campaign.

23 David Altman, *Direct Democracy Worldwide* (Cambridge: Cambridge University Press, 2010), 91.

24 Liubomir Topaloff, "The Rise of Referendums: Elite Strategy or Populist Weapon?" *Journal of Democracy* 28, no. 3 (July 2017): 129. See also Carl Schmitt, *Constitutional Theory*, trans. and ed. Jeffrey Seitzer (Durham: Duke University Press, 2008).

25 Stephen Tierney, *Constitutional Referendums: The Theory and Practice of Republican Deliberation* (Oxford: Oxford University Press, 2012), 98.

26 Chantal Hébert with Jean Lapierre, *The Morning After: The 1995 Quebec Referendum and the Day that Almost Was* (Toronto: Knopf Canada, 2014), xx.

27 See Margaret Moore's contribution to "Can Alberta Still Separate? Experts Clash over the Landmark Court Decision," *Walrus*, May 20, 2026, https://thewalrus.ca/alberta-separation-decision-experts/#MargaretMoore. I am grateful to Professor Moore for providing me with an interview for this chapter. Her insights and recommendations were invaluable contributions to my understanding of the deficiencies of referendums as democratic instruments.
28 J.P. Alegre, "Alberta's October Referendum Could Cost $100 million," *Deep Dive*, June 9, 2026, https://thedeepdive.ca/albertas-october-referendum-could-cost-100-million/.; Timm Bruch, "Alberta's October referendum could cost taxpayers up to $130M: expert" CTV News, June 17, 2026, https://www.ctvnews.ca/calgary/article/albertas-october-referendum-could-cost-taxpayers-up-to-130m-expert/
29 Alberta Referendum 2026 Questions, https://albertareferendum2026.ca/separation-question/.
30 See Adrian Furnham and Hua Chu Boo, "A Literature Review of the Anchoring Effect," *Journal of Socio-Economics* 40, no. 1 (Feb. 2011): 35–42. Anchoring bias is agreed in the literature to be quite a robust phenomenon, meaning it has been proven to have a significant cognitive effect across a range of studies.
31 "Limited and Declining Support for Separation in Alberta," Ipsos, June 5, 2026, https://www.ipsos.com/en-ca/limited-and-declining-support-separation-alberta.
32 Census of Population–Immigration/Alberta, Statistics Canada, https://www12.statcan.gc.ca/census-recensement/2021/as-sa/fogs-spg/page.cfm?lang=E&topic=9&dguid=2021A000248.
33 Topaloff, "The Rise of Referendums,"134.
34 "Alberta Govt Announces Launch of Fall Referendum Website," Apr. 23, 2026, CPAC, https://www.cpac.ca/headline-politics/episode/alberta-govt-announces-launch-of-fall-referendum-website--april-23-2026?id=cd9a54a9-97bc-452e-8608-9cf41109735a.
35 See Stephen Tierney, "Popular Constitutional Amendment: Referendums and Constitutional Change in Canada and the United Kingdom," *Queen's Law Journal*, 41, no. 1 (2015): 43.
36 See Topaloff, "The Rise of Referendums."

3: TRESOUN | TRĀDITIŌ | TRAÏSON | TREASON

1 Carol Off, *At a Loss for Words: Conversations in an Age of Rage* (Toronto: Vintage, 2025), 1–2.
2 Off, *At a Loss for Words*, 4.
3 See George Orwell, *1984* (Toronto: Penguin Random House, 2008).
4 "Assembly of Treaty Chiefs Demands Premier and UCP Treason Investigation," June 17, 2026, https://www.treatysix.org/post/assembly-of-treaty-chiefs-demands-premier-and-ucp-treason-investigation.
5 Jack Farrell, "'Tyranny of the minority': Court hears injunction bid on Alberta separation petition," *Times Colonist*, Apr. 7, 2026), https://www.timescolonist.com/national-news/tyranny-of-the-minority-court-hears-injunction-bid-on-alberta-separation-petition-12107033.
6 Jack Farrell, "Smith tells First Nations chiefs to 'check themselves' after treason accusation over separation question," CBC News, June 18, 2026, https://www.cbc.ca/news/canada/edmonton/alberta-smith-first-nations-chiefs-separation-9.7240147.
7 Lisa Johnson, "Alberta premier says law will be enforced if separation vote spurs civil disobedience," CBC News, June 5, 2026), https://www.cbc.ca/news/canada/calgary/alberta-law-civil-disobedience-separation-9.7225524.

8 Bmorinstories on Instagram, June 23, 2026, https://www.instagram.com/reel/DZ8DUcbPBi1/.
9 Jason Kenney post, Mar. 6, 2025, https://x.com/jkenney/status/1897792103482376416.
10 Courtney Theriault post, Mar. 6, 2025, https://x.com/cspotweet/status/1897698486814228733?ref_src=twsrc%5Etfw%7Ctwcamp%5Etweetembed%7Ctwterm%5E1897792103482376416%7Ctwgr%5E85f5415144f90941ea3f06e36972c0ac0c81a319%7Ctwcon%5Es3_&ref_url=https%3A%2F%2Fwww.westernstandard.news%2Fnews%2Fkenny-calls-rath-treasonous-kook-as-he-advocates-for-alberta-as-51st-state%2F62860.
11 Rahim Mohamed, "Is it 'treason' for Alberta separatists to manoeuvre with foreign officials? Ottawa says no," *National Post*, Dec. 30, 2026), https://nationalpost.com/news/canada/alberta-separatists-treason.
12 Exchange quoted in "Eye On Alberta," *Alberta Views*, June 2026, 19.
13 "Eby calls out group of Alberta separatists over meeting with White House officials," CTV News, Jan. 29, 2026, https://www.youtube.com/watch?v=oPH-WYrAD68.
14 "B.C. premier again calls separatists seeking U.S. support 'treason'," CBC News, Feb. 3, 2026, https://www.youtube.com/shorts/m6KxaVpS130.
15 Rath quoted in Jessica Murphy and Nadine Yousif, "'Respect Canadian Sovereignty,' Carney tells US officials after they meet Alberta separatists," BBC News, Jan. 29, 2026, https://www.bbc.com/news/articles/cr57j78opgmo.
16 Jeffrey Rath, interview by Vassy Kapelos, CTV News, Feb. 1, 2026, https://www.youtube.com/watch?v=LiHzFnRPDM8&t=198s.
17 Patrick Lennox, "When does a separatist movement become a threat to Canada's national security" January 8, 2026, https://plennox.substack.com/p/when-does-a-separatist-movement-become; it was republished later as "Alberta's Separatist Movement Is a National Security Threat" *Walrus*, February 2, 2026, https://thewalrus.ca/albertas-separatist-movement-is-a-national-security-threat/
18 The Treason Act, https://www.nationalarchives.gov.uk/explore-the-collection/stories/the-treason-act/.
19 Criminal Code (R.S.C. 1985, c. C-46) High Treason.
20 *Report of the Royal Commission on Security* (June 1969), 8, https://publications.gc.ca/collections/collection_2014/bcp-pco/Z1-1966-5-eng.pdf.
21 Report, 5.
22 Report, 109.
23 "'Just the way he is': Here's what some Americans think of Trump's new threats," CBC News, Jan 8. 2025), https://www.cbc.ca/news/canada/trump-annex-canada-reaction-1.7425803.
24 Niall McGee, "Trudeau's comments that Trump wants critical minerals highlight U.S. reliance on Canadian resources," *Globe and Mail*, Feb. 7, 2025, (7 February 2025), https://www.theglobeandmail.com/business/article-trudeaus-critical-minerals-comment-highlights-us-reliance-on-canadian/.
25 Luca Caruso-Moro, "Trump is open to using 'economic force' to acquire Canada; Trudeau responds," CTV News, Jan. 7, 2025, https://www.ctvnews.ca/politics/article/trump-is-open-to-using-economic-force-to-acquire-canada-trudeau-responds/.
26 Tim Shufelt and Dexter McMillan, "How much does Trump hate Canada?" *Globe and Mail*, Apr. 17, 2026), https://www.theglobeandmail.com/investing/article-canada-trump-tariff-threats-social-media-charts/.

27 For a structural theory of the Canada-US relationship that examines the concept of the continental hierarchy within the anarchic international system, see my first book, *At Home and Abroad: The Canada-US Relationship and Canada's Place in the World* (Vancouver: UBC Press, 2009).
28 George Orwell, "Visions of a Totalitarian Future," in *Fascism and Democracy* (New York: Penguin, 2020), 30–35.
29 See remarks on hybrid war by McGill University professor Maria Popova in Evan Dyer, "U.S. interest in Alberta separatism raises red flags over what might come next," CBC News, Feb. 5, 2026, https://www.cbc.ca/news/politics/alberta-separatism-trump-administration-9.7068999.
30 See Robert Kagan "America vs. The World," *Atlantic*, March 2026, https://www.theatlantic.com/magazine/2026/03/trump-national-security-greenland-spheres-of-interest/685673/.
31 Lazaro Gamio, Carol Rosenberg, and Charlie Savage, "Tracking U.S. Military Killings in Boat Attacks," *New York Times*, June 3, 2026), https://www.nytimes.com/interactive/2025/10/29/us/us-caribbean-pacific-boat-strikes.html.
32 For an exploration of the moral implications of this war for the future of Canada-US defence interoperability, see Patrick Lennox, "Canada Can't Pretend America is Still the Good Guy," *Walrus*, Apr. 16, 2026), https://thewalrus.ca/the-us-torpedoed-an-unarmed-ship-who-are-the-good-guys-again/.
33 Jean-Michel Hauteville, "In Cuba, an unprecedented health crisis is deepening under US oil blockade," *Le Monde* May 25, 2026), https://www.lemonde.fr/en/international/article/2026/05/25/in-cuba-an-unprecedented-health-crisis-is-deepening-under-us-oil-blockade_6753797_4.html.
34 See Mandy Taheri, "ICE Budget Compared to World's Militaries as Government Shutdown Looms," *Newsweek*, Jan. 28, 2026), https://www.newsweek.com/ice-budget-compared-to-worlds-militaries-as-government-shutdown-looms-11432447. For Canada's defence budget, 2024–25, seehttps://www.canada.ca/en/department-national-defence/corporate/reports-publications/proactive-disclosure/nddn-main-estimates-2024-2025/overview.html.
35 Tiffany Wertheimer, "Who was Renee Nicole Good, the woman killed by ICE?" BBC News, Jan. 13, 2026, https://www.bbc.com/news/articles/c1jepdjy2560.
36 J. David McSwane, "Two CBP Agents Identified in Alex Pretti Shooting," ProPublica, Feb. 1, 2026), https://www.propublica.org/article/alex-pretti-shooting-cbp-agents-identified-jesus-ochoa-raymundo-gutierrez.
37 *National Security Strategy of the United States of America*, Nov. 2025, 16, https://www.whitehouse.gov/wp-content/uploads/2025/12/2025-National-Security-Strategy.pdf.
38 "Canada's New Defence Strategy is Bold and Unprecedented. Will it Work?" *Walrus*, Feb. 18, 2026, https://thewalrus.ca/defence-industrial-strategy-experts/.
39 "Davos 2026: Special Address by Mark Carney, Prime Minister of Canada," (speech, World Economic Forum, Davos, Switzerland, Jan. 20, 206), https://www.weforum.org/stories/2026/01/davos-2026-special-address-by-mark-carney-prime-minister-of-canada/.
40 Peter Zimonjic, "Carney's Davos speech draws reaction from around the world," CBC News, Jan. 22, 2026, https://www.cbc.ca/news/politics/world-leaders-react-carney-speech-9.7056702.
41 "Davos 2026: Special Address by Donald J Trump, President of the United States of America," speech, World Economic Forum, Davos, Switzerland, Jan. 21, 2026, https://www.weforum.org/stories/2026/01/davos-2026-special-address-donald-trump-president-united-states-america/.

42 Larissa Tracy cites the definition of *tradition* in *Shorter Oxford English Dictionary*, 5th ed. (Oxford: Oxford University Press, 2002).
43 Larissa Tracy, "The Shameful Business of Betrayal and Treason," in *Treason: Medieval and Early Modern Adultery, Betrayal and Shame*, ed. Larissa Tracy. Explorations in Medieval Culture Series 10, no. 1, 21.
44 Ruairí Maguire, "Treason, secession and wars of independence," *European Journal of Political Theory* 25, no. 2 (Apr. 2026): 223–46.
45 Maguire relies upon Cécile Fabre's contention that social membership is a "necessary condition for a relationship to count as Treason-qualifying." See "The Morality of Treason," *Law and Philosophy* (2020) 39, no. 4 (2020): 435.
46 Fabre, 225.
47 2021 Census of Canada Racialized Groups of Albertans (Jan. 2025), 3, https://open.alberta.ca/dataset/04545424-2b43-48f4-9ce9-e26ac408f637/resource/25d9df2d-3e38-4639-b3ab-d0bf94a8af07/download/tbf-osi-2021-census-of-canada-racialized-groups-of-albertans-2025.pdf.
48 Census Profile, 2021 Census of Population–Alberta, https://www12.statcan.gc.ca/census-recensement/2021/dp-pd/prof/details/page.cfm?Lang=E&SearchText=Alberta&DGUIDlist=2021A000248&GENDERlist=1,2,3&STATISTIClist=1,4&HEADERlist=0; See also Nigel Banks, "International Law and Secession," Submission of Athabasca Chipewyan First Nation to Cabinet Regarding the Prospect of an Alberta Independence Referendum, May 1, 2026, 6, https://acfn.com/submission-of-athabasca-chipewyan-first-nation-to-cabinet-regarding-the-prospect-of-an-alberta-independence-referendum/.

PART II: EVIDENCE

4: TRIAL RUN

1 See "Timeline of Events," *Project Natterjack: National After-Action Review into the RCMP's Response to the 2022 Freedom Convoy* (Ottawa: RCMP, 2024), https://rcmp.ca/en/corporate-information/publications-and-manuals/project-natterjack-national-after-action-review#s6.
2 See "Requirements for truckers entering Canada in effect as of January 15, 2022," Public Health Agency, Jan. 13, 2022, https://www.canada.ca/en/public-health/news/2022/01/requirements-for-truckers-entering-canada-in-effect-as-of-january-15-2022.html; https://publicorderemergencycommission.ca/files/overview-reports/COM.OR.00000004.pdf?t=1715017603.
3 Kim Richard Nossal, *Canada Alone: Navigating the Post American World* (Toronto: Dundurn, 2023), 139–40.
4 *Overview Report: Timeline of Certain Key Events*, Public Order Emergency Commission, n.d., https://publicorderemergencycommission.ca/files/overview-reports/COM.OR.00000004.pdf?t=1715017603
5 Kayla Butler, "Nazi, Confederate flags being flown in two Alberta tows," CityNews, May 11, 2021, https://calgary.citynews.ca/2021/05/11/nazi-confederate-flags-being-flown-in-two-alberta-towns/.
6 Alex Boutilier, "Domestic extremism 'here to stay' in Canada, Trudeau's security advisor says," Global News, Mar. 10 2026, https://globalnews.ca/news/8673217/domestic-extremism-here-to-stay-in-canada-trudeaus-security-advisor-says/.
7 Robert Fife and Steven Chase, "Leaders of truck convoy protests sought to overthrow government, national security advisor says," *Globe and Mail*, Mar. 10, 2022, https://www.theglobeandmail.com/politics/article-leaders-of-truck-convoy-protests-sought-overthrow-of-government/.
8 Jody Thomas, interview with author, June 3, 2026.

9 Tom Yun, "Donald Trump voices support for truckers convoy protest in Ottawa," CTV News, Jan. 29, 2022, https://www.ctvnews.ca/canada/article/donald-trump-voices-support-for-truckers-convoy-protest-in-ottawa/.
10 Paul Wells, for example, is sympathetic to the argument that the government should have engaged in discussions with the protestors. He concludes: "I think the important question is whether we hear one another. Even when we're tired. Even when we're scared." Paul Wells, *An Emergency in Ottawa: The Story of the Convoy Commission* (Toronto: Sutherland House, 2023), 77.
11 Wells, *An Emergency in Ottawa*, 59–60.
12 "Memorandum of Understanding," https://commissionsurletatdurgence.ca/files/exhibits/JBA00000064.pdf?t=1668228493.
13 Laura Osman and David Fraser, "Freedom, politics, control and money—the many motivations of the 'Freedom Convoy'," CBC News, Nov. 3,2022, https://www.cbc.ca/news/politics/emergencies-act-divisions-1.6639778.
14 Carrie Tait, "RCMP used undercover operatives, emergency wiretaps to target border blockades in Coutts, Alta.: court docs," *Globe and Mail*, Sept. 7, 2026, https://www.theglobeandmail.com/canada/alberta/article-rcmp-emergency-wiretaps-coutts-blockade/.
15 Tait, "RCMP used undercover operatives," https://www.theglobeandmail.com/canada/alberta/article-rcmp-emergency-wiretaps-coutts-blockade/.
16 Bill Graveland, "Undercover officer testifies at murder-conspiracy trial around Coutts blockade," CBC News, June 11, 2024, https://www.cbc.ca/news/canada/calgary/coutts-trial-blockade-resumes-1.7231137.
17 Meghan Grant, "No bail for man accused of plotting to murder RCMP at Coutts border blockade," CBC News Mar. 2, 2022, https://www.cbc.ca/news/canada/calgary/christopher-lysak-conspiracy-murder-rcmp-coutts-protest-blockade-1.6370031.
18 Caley Gibson, "RCMP arrest 13 people, seize weapons and ammunition near Coutts border blockade," Global News, Feb. 14, 2022, https://globalnews.ca/news/8618494/alberta-coutts-border-protest-weapons-ammunition-seized/.
19 Grant, "No bail for man accused of plotting to murder RCMP," https://www.cbc.ca/news/canada/calgary/christopher-lysak-conspiracy-murder-rcmp-coutts-protest-blockade-1.6370031.
20 Alanna Smith, "Accused in Coutts border blockade trial said he was part of a 'revolution' undercover officer testifies," *Globe and Mail*, June 11, 2024, https://www.theglobeandmail.com/canada/alberta/article-accused-in-coutts-border-blockade-trial-said-he-was-part-of-a/.
21 "RCMP interrogation of Coutts protester Anthony Olienick," Rebel News, July 9, 2024, https://www.youtube.com/watch?v=721qZ6GXWdc.
22 Corey Robinson and Scott D. Watson, "Conspiracy theory, anti-globalism, and the Freedom Convoy: The Great Reset and Conspiracist Delegitimation," *Review of International Studies* 52, no. 2 (2026): 387.
23 "What is the Great Reset—and how did it get hijacked by conspiracy theories?" BBC News, June 23, 2021, https://www.bbc.com/news/blogs-trending-57532368.
24 Adrian Humphreys, "What the mixed verdict in the Coutts Freedom Convoy blockade trial really means," *National Post*, Aug. 19, 2024, https://nationalpost.com/news/canada/what-the-mixed-verdict-in-the-coutts-freedom-convoy-blockade-trial-really-means.
25 "Diagolon Participation in the Freedom Convoy 2022 and Beyond," Canadian Security Intelligence Service, Feb. 21, 2022, https://publicorderemergencycommission.ca/files/exhibits/SSM.NSC.CAN.00001575_REL.0001.pdf?t=1667946237.

26 Darren Bernhardt, "'A perfect solution': Manitoba border blockade ends as RCMP escort protesters away," CBC News, Feb. 16, 2022, https://www.cbc.ca/news/canada/manitoba/emerson-border-blockade-protest-manitoba-rcmp-update-1.6353568.
27 Laura Osman and David Fraser, "Winter 'Freedom Convoy' blockades cost billions to Canada's economy, inquiry hears," CP24, Nov. 16, 2022, https://www.cp24.com/news/2022/11/16/winter-freedom-convoy-blockades-cost-billions-to-canadas-economy-inquiry-hears/.
28 Catharine Tunney, "Death threats against Trudeau sent to CBSA during convoy protests, Emergencies Act inquiry hears," CBC News, Nov. 16, 2022, https://www.cbc.ca/news/politics/cbsa-blockade-threat-1.6652530.
29 Wesley Wark, "How the Freedom Convoy Broke the Emergencies Act," *Walrus*, Mar. 9, 2026, https://thewalrus.ca/after-the-freedom-convoy-what-is-the-emergencies-act-actually-for/.
30 Darren Major, "Federal government appeals Emergencies Act use during convoy protest to Supreme Court," CBC News, Mar. 17, 2026, https://www.cbc.ca/news/politics/government-appealing-emergencies-act-use-supreme-court-9.7132438.
31 *The Disinformation Dozen: Why Platforms Must Act on Twelve Leading Online Anti-Vaxxers*, Center for Countering Digital Hate, Mar. 24, 2021, 6, https://counterhate.com/research/the-disinformation-dozen/.
32 Jack Goodman and Flora Carmichael, "Coronavirous: Bill Gates 'microchip' conspiracy theory and other vaccine claims fact-checked," BBC News, May 29, 2020, https://www.bbc.com/news/52847648.
33 Jeremy Appel, "Conspiracy Theorist Danielle Smith Is Leading in Alberta's Conservative Party Race," *Jacobin*, Sept. 12, 2022, https://jacobin.com/2022/09/conspiracy-theorist-danielle-smith-alberta-canada-conservative-party. See also Sarah Rieger, "Alberta talk radio host deletes tweet with false claim that there's a 100% cure for coronavirus," CBC News, Mar. 22, 2020, https://www.cbc.ca/news/canada/calgary/coronavirus-cure-claim-1.5506187; and Jason Markusoff, "From COVID care to cancer, there's a pattern to Danielle Smith's 'alternative' medical thoughts," CBC News, July 25, 2022, https://www.cbc.ca/news/canada/calgary/danielle-smith-ucp-leadership-cancer-controllable-dubious-1.6531883.
34 Dean Bennett, "'Warped stance on COVID': Fired Alberta Health Services border member calls out Smith," Global News, Nov. 18, 2022, https://globalnews.ca/news/9290333/alberta-premier-danielle-smith-bleak-role-model-fired-health-leader/.
35 Micah Lee, "Oath Keepers, Anti-Democracy Activists, and Others on the Far Right are Funding Canada's 'Freedom Convoy'," *Intercept*,Feb. 17, 2022, https://theintercept.com/2022/02/17/freedom-convoy-givesendgo-canada-oath-keepers-funding/.
36 The Honourable Paul S. Rouleau, *Report of the Public Inquiry into the 2022 Public Order Emergency, Volume 1*, Feb. 2023, 16.1, 96. https://publicorderemergencycommission.ca/files/documents/Final-Report/Vol-1-Report-of-the-Public-Inquiry-into-the-2022-Public-Order-Emergency.pdf.
37 *Overview Report: Fundraising in Support of Protestors*, Public Order Emergency Commission, n.d., 7 https://publicorderemergencycommission.ca/files/overview-reports/COM.OR.00000005.pdf?t=1667488145.
38 Corporate records reveal the Alberta Prosperity Society was founded on Jan. 31, 2022.
39 Wells, *An Emergency in Ottawa*, 56–57.
40 https://rathandcompany.com/covid-19-vaccine-class-action-lawsuit/.

41 Jared Wesley, *Alberta Separatism and the Freedom Convoy: A New Brand of Western Alienation*, Social Cleavages Series, Aug. 2022, 1, 13, https://publicorderemergencycommission.ca/files/documents/Policy-Papers/Social-Cleaveges-Alberta-Separatism-and-the-Freedom-Convoy-Wesley.pdf.
42 *Report of the Public Inquiry into the 2022 Public Order Emergency Volume 1: Overview*, 2023, 29, https://publicorderemergencycommission.ca/files/documents/Final-Report/Vol-1-Report-of-the-Public-Inquiry-into-the-2022-Public-Order-Emergency.pdf.
43 *Report of the Public Inquiry* Rouleau, 30, https://publicorderemergencycommission.ca/files/documents/Final-Report/Vol-1-Report-of-the-Public-Inquiry-into-the-2022-Public-Order-Emergency.pdf.

5: ORIGINS OF A QUASI-SEPARATIST PARTY

1 Emily Laxer and Jacob McLean, "The 'People's Chamber'? Populism and Social Movement Politics in Alberta's Sovereignty Debate," *Journal of Canadian Studies* 60, no. 1 (March 2026): 142.
2 Daniel Drache and Marc D. Froese, *Has Populism Won? The War on Liberal Democracy* (Toronto: ECW Press, 2022), 12.
3 Jared Wesley, "Populism, Sovereignty, and Democracy in Alberta—Address to the McGill Institute for the Study of Canada," Jan. 19, 2026, https://substack.com/@drjaredwesley/p-184653742.
4 Drache and Froese, 11.
5 Marc D. Froese, interview with author, June 6, 2026. The Social Credit Party in Alberta was, for example, openly anti-Semitic but had to purge the anti-Semites from the party after the war.
6 Charles Rusnell, Jennie Russell, and Allison Dempster, "Kenney, Callaway campaigns collaborated to attack Brian Jean during UCP leadership race leaked documents show," CBC News, Mar. 16, 2019, https://www.cbc.ca/news/canada/edmonton/kenney-callaway-campaigns-collaborated-against-brian-jean-1.5059899.
7 Jen Gerson, "What really happened inside Alberta UCP's 'Kamikaze' campaign," *Maclean's*, Mar. 18, 2019, https://macleans.ca/politics/what-really-happened-inside-the-alberta-ucps-kamikaze-campaign/.
8 Rusnell, Russell, and Dempster, "Kenney, Callaway campaigns collaborated," https://www.cbc.ca/news/canada/edmonton/kenney-callaway-campaigns-collaborated-against-brian-jean-1.5059899.
9 Charles Rusnell, and Jennie Russell, "Unravelling the controversy behind the 2017 UCP leadership race," CBC News, Mar. 28, 2019, https://www.cbc.ca/news/canada/edmonton/kenney-galloway-kamikaze-campaign-1.5073789.
10 Email from Cameron Davies to Matt Wolf, Subject: Week 1 & 2 Comms Draft, Aug. 13, 2017.
11 Gerson, "What really happened,": https://macleans.ca/politics/what-really-happened-inside-the-alberta-ucps-kamikaze-campaign/.
Rusnell, Russell, and Dempster, "Kenney, Callaway campaigns collaborated," https://www.cbc.ca/news/canada/edmonton/kenney-callaway-campaigns-collaborated-against-brian-jean-1.5059899.
12 Tables of the administrative penalties issued by Elections Alberta: https://www.elections.ab.ca/investigations/findings-decisions/administrative-penalties/.
13 Tracy Moran and Rahim Mohamed, "Another Alberta separatist leader is courting U.S. conservatives in Washington and Mar-a-Lago," *National Post*, Nov. 12, 2025, (12 November 2025), https://nationalpost.com/news/another-alberta-separatist-leader-is-courting-u-s-conservatives-in-washington-and-mar-a-lago.

14 Justin Giovanetti, "Kenney's elimination of the elections commissioner a step back from 'evolutionary' system," *Globe and Mail*, Nov. 25, 2019, https://www.theglobeandmail.com/canada/alberta/article-kenneys-elimination-of-election-commissioner-a-step-back-from/.
15 "No charges as RCMP conclude probe into Alberta's 2017 UCP leadership race," CBC News, Mar. 8, 2024, https://www.cbc.ca/news/canada/edmonton/alberta-rcmp-ucp-leadership-fraud-investigation-1.7137976.
16 "No charges as RCMP conclude probe," https://www.cbc.ca/news/canada/edmonton/alberta-rcmp-ucp-leadership-fraud-investigation-1.7137976.
17 Alex Ballinger, "Lance Armstrong could have won without the drugs, says Phil Liggett," *Cycling Weekly*, Mar. 1, 2021, https://www.cyclingweekly.com/news/racing/lance-armstrong-could-have-won-without-the-drugs-says-phil-liggett-492110.
18 C.B. Macpherson, *Democracy in Alberta: Social Credit and the Party System* (Toronto: University of Toronto Press, 1953), 263.
19 Daniel Drache and Arthur Kroker, "C.B. Macpherson, 1911-1987," *Canadian Journal of Political and Social Theory* XI, no. 3 (1987): 99.
20 Loewenstein, *Militant Democracy*, 422.
21 Stephen Maguisiak, "Who Is 'Take Back Alberta' and What Do They Really Want?" *Press Progress*, Apr. 11, 2023, https://pressprogress.ca/who-is-take-back-alberta-and-what-do-they-really-want/.
22 Charles Rusnell, "The Bully Who Haunts Alberta's Election," *Tyee* May 17, 2023, https://thetyee.ca/News/2023/05/17/Bully-Haunting-Alberta-Election/.
23 Rusnell, "The Bully."
24 Bill Graveland, "Alberta Court of Appeal upholds four-month jail term for organizer of Coutts blockade," CBC News, Mar 9, 2026, https://www.cbc.ca/news/canada/calgary/alberta-appeal-coutts-denied-9.7121369.
25 Jacob Maclean, Emily Laxer, and Efe Peker, "Taking Alberta Back: Faith, Fuel and Freedom on the Canadian Far Right," *Religions* 15, no. 1250 (2024): 16.
26 Jason Markusoff, "'We need to control the party': a look inside Take Back Alberta's UCP insurgency," CBC News May 9, 2023, https://www.cbc.ca/news/canada/calgary/take-back-alberta-david-parker-control-party-board-ucp-1.6834387.
27 Gary Mason, "Alberta's own Tea Party movement is a deeply troubling development" *Globe and Mail*, May 11, 2023, https://www.theglobeandmail.com/opinion/article-albertas-own-tea-party-movement-is-a-deeply-troubling-development/.
28 "'The lunatics are trying to take over the asylum': Keney quotes to remember," Global News, Oct. 2, 2022, https://globalnews.ca/news/9170529/jason-kenney-quotes/.
29 Decision re: Aitkens, Alberta Securities Commission, Oct. 2, 2019, https://www.asc.ca/-/media/ASC-Documents-part-1/Notices-Decisions-Orders-Rulings/Enforcement/2019/10/AITKENS-Ronald-James-DECISION-2019-10-02-54837281.ashx.
30 Maguisiak, "Who Is 'Take Back Alberta'?" https://pressprogress.ca/who-is-take-back-alberta-and-what-do-they-really-want/.
31 Roy Beyer quoted in McLean, Laxer, and Peker, "Taking Alberta Back," 15.
32 Jacob McLean, "Carbon Convoys: Extractive Populism and the Canadian Far Right" (PhD diss., York University, 2025), 170.
33 Jacob McLean, interview with author, June 4, 2026.
34 For an extraordinary exposition of this cover-up see, Geoff Dembicki, *The Petroleum Papers: Inside the Far-Right Conspiracy to Cover Up Climate Change* (Vancouver: Greystone Books, 2022).
35 McLean, Laxer, and Peker, "Taking Alberta Back," 3.

36 Elizabeth Hames, "Don't dismiss them as 'crackpot': Who are Canada's yellow vest protesters?" CBC News, Jan. 11, 2019, https://www.cbc.ca/news/canada/edmonton/yellow-vests-canada-alberta-1.4974721. See also Hamdi Issawi and Omar Mosley, "The yellow vests drove across Canada and back to Alberta. Now what?" *Toronto Star*, Mar. 5, 2019, https://www.thestar.com/edmonton/the-yellow-vests-drove-across-canada-and-back-to-alberta-now-what/article_5c2b8942-2563-50e4-b6fc-e262860b76b1.html.

37 Tyler Dawson, "Credibility of Canada's fledgling yellow vest movement threatened by extremists, fringe groups" *National Post*, Jan. 21, 2019, https://nationalpost.com/news/canada/canadas-fledgling-yellow-vest-movement-struggles-to-distance-itself-from-extremists-fringe-groups.

38 Tadzio Richards, "Our Lobbyist Premier" *Alberta Views*, Oct. 26, 2024, https://albertaviews.ca/our-lobbyist-premier/

39 "Danielle Smith, "Alberta Prosperity Project is the 'or else' if Ottawa refuses to negotiate," Alberta Prosperity Project, Oct. 14, 2022, https://www.youtube.com/watch?v=ZqbS4gLL9k4.

40 "Jason Kenney slams UCP candidate Danielle Smith's Alberta Sovereignty Act' plan," CTV News, Sept. 22, 2022, https://www.youtube.com/watch?v=rXWTvflu1w.

41 Smith managed to secure the win in the UCP leadership contest over Travis Toews, 53.77 percent to 46.23 percent. Damien Wood and Michael Franklin, "Danielle Smith wins Alberta UCP leadership, named premier-designate," CTV News, Oct. 6, 2022, https://www.ctvnews.ca/calgary/article/danielle-smith-wins-alberta-ucp-leadership-named-premier-designate/.

42 Aaron Wherry, "The Alberta Sovereignty Act plays a dangerous game—for political reasons," CBC News, Dec. 1, 2022, https://www.cbc.ca/news/politics/alberta-sovereignty-act-analysis-wherry-1.6671036. See also Lennox, "Shakedown Federalism," https://albertaviews.ca/shakedown-federalism/.

43 Darren Major, "Trudeau says he's 'not looking for a fight' over Alberta Sovereignty Act," CBC News, Nov. 30, 2022, https://www.cbc.ca/news/politics/trudeau-reacts-to-alberta-sovereignty-act-1.6669555. Trudeau's remarks transcribed from the video link included in the online article.

44 Barry Cooper, "The Alberta sovereignty act is unconstitutional on purpose," *National Post*, June 21, 2022, https://nationalpost.com/opinion/barry-cooper-the-alberta-sovereignty-act-is-unconstitutional-on-purpose.

45 *Hansard*, Dec. 7, 2022, 255, https://docs.assembly.ab.ca/LADDAR_files/docs/hansards/han/legislature_30/session_4/20221207_1930_01_han.pdf.

46 *Hansard*, Dec. 7, 2022, 256, https://docs.assembly.ab.ca/LADDAR_files/docs/hansards/han/legislature_30/session_4/20221207_1930_01_han.pdf.

47 Jason Proctor, "Northern Gateway pipeline approval overturned," CBC News, June 30, 2016, https://www.cbc.ca/news/canada/british-columbia/northern-gateway-pipeline-federal-court-of-appeal-1.3659561.

48 Pete Evans, "TransCanada pulls plug on Energy East pipeline," CBC News, Oct. 5, 2017, https://www.cbc.ca/news/business/transcanada-energy-east-1.4338227.

49 Jeffrey Jones, "Koch blames Alberta's climate policies for cancellation of oil sands project," *Globe and Mail*, Dec. 19, 2016, https://www.theglobeandmail.com/report-on-business/industry-news/energy-and-resources/koch-blames-albertas-climate-policies-for-cancellation-of-oil-sands-project/article33376554/.

50 Dembecki, *Petroleum Papers*, 51.

51 Christopher Leonard, "David Koch was the Ultimate Climate Change Denier," *New York Times*, Aug. 23, 2019, https://www.nytimes.com/2019/08/23/opinion/sunday/david-koch-climate-change.html.

52 Barry Cooper, interview by Stuart McNish, *Conversations that Matter*, June 23, 2020, 9:23, https://www.youtube.com/watch?v=cFyIgMds6YY&t=316s.
53 I spoke with Barry Cooper on Feb. 18, 2026, for my article, "Shakedown Federalism," https://albertaviews.ca/shakedown-federalism/.
54 Lisa Johnson, "Third-party advertiser Take Back Alberta fined more than $100K by Elections Alberta," Canadian Press, Feb. 4, 2026, https://www.thecanadianpressnews.ca/politics/third-party-advertiser-take-back-alberta-fined-more-than-100k-by-elections-alberta/article_77d3fffd-bd51-5d02-bd57-84adb6831d63.html.
55 Matthew Black, "Take Back Alberta and David Parker fighting 2023 Elections Alberta fines over alleged Charter breaches," *Edmonton Journal*, May 14, 2026, https://edmontonjournal.com/news/politics/take-back-alberta-david-parker-elections-alberta-fines-charter-breaches.
56 Karen Bartko, "Take Back Alberta founder plans to fight $112K in fines levied by Elections Alberta," Global News, Feb. 5, 2025, https://globalnews.ca/news/11006037/take-back-alberta-david-parker-election-fines/.
57 Marc Froese, interview with author, June 6, 2026.
58 Stephen Magusiak, "Take Back Alberta Leaders are Training 'Scrutineers' to Infiltrate Campaigns and Act as 'Security' on Voting Day," *Press Progress*, May 16, 2023, https://pressprogress.ca/take-back-alberta-leaders-are-training-scrutineers-to-infiltrate-campaigns-and-act-as-security-on-voting-day/.
59 One exception is David Climenhaga, who raised the possibility in 2025 after the Elections Alberta fines were made public. The long-time Alberta journalist and former staff writer for the *Globe and Mail* and *Calgary Herald* assessed the result to be close enough in some key ridings that Take Back Alberta's illegal campaign expenditures might have had an impact on the outcome. Climenhaga fruitlessly called for an inquiry. See David Climenhaga, "Did Take Back Alberta steel the 2023 Alberta provincial election for the United Conservative Party?" AlbertaPolitics.ca Feb. 6, 2025, https://albertapolitics.ca/2025/02/did-take-back-alberta-steal-the-2023-alberta-provincial-election-for-the-united-conservative-party/.
60 Joel Dryden, "Support for Alberta separatism flat, struggling high earners more likely supporters: poll," CBC News Apr. 28, 2026, https://www.cbc.ca/news/canada/calgary/alberta-separatism-janet-brown-mitch-sylvestre-9.7178496. It should be noted that Ipsos has found three types of separatists in Alberta. The committed ones make up 56 percent of those who would vote to separate and would accordingly follow through to establish an independent country. The conditional (25 percent) and symbolic (19 percent) want to use the vote as "leverage" and "send a message to Ottawa." "Support for Independence in Alberta Reaches Levels Similar to Quebec," Ipsos, Jan. 23, 2026, https://www.ipsos.com/en-ca/support-independence-alberta-reaches-levels-similar-quebec.

6: THE BETRAYAL OF CANADA

1 Nicholas Frew, "'Offensive and false': Alberta premier's office denies Smith urged US to interfere in federal election," CBC News, Mar. 23, 2025, https://www.cbc.ca/news/canada/edmonton/alberta-premier-smith-u-s-canada-election-interference-breitbart-1.7491318.
2 Steven Chase and Ian Bailey, "Alberta refuses to sign joint statement on Trump tariffs from first ministers' meeting," *Globe and Mail*, Jan. 15, 2025, https://www.theglobeandmail.com/politics/article-alberta-refuses-to-sign-joint-statement-on-trump-tariffs-from-first/.
3 Noah Kirsch, "'Masquerading as a university': inside the brazen right wing plan to conquer American schools," *Guardian*, Apr. 8, 2026, https://www.theguardian.com/education/ng-interactive/2026/apr/08/prageru-university-conservatism.

4 Geoff Dembicki, "Danielle Smith and Ben Shapiro Discuss Canada Electing 'Solid Allies' to Trump at Florida Event," DeSmog, Mar. 27, 2026, https://www.desmog.com/2025/03/27/danielle-smith-and-ben-shapiro-discuss-canada-electing-solid-allies-to-trump-at-florida-event/.

5 Jeremy Appel, "Premier's Office spent nearly $20K on PragerU fundraiser gala," *Progress Report*, Aug. 6, 2025, https://www.theprogressreport.ca/premier-prageru-fundraiser.

6 Kelly Geraldine Malone, "Trump says Poilievre 'not a MAGA guy,' calls Freeland a 'whack'," Global News, Feb. 28, 2025, https://globalnews.ca/news/11055372/donald-trump-pierre-poilievre-chrystia-freeland-comments-tariff-threat/.

7 "First Ministers' statement on the Canada-United States relationship," Jan. 15, 2025, https://www.pm.gc.ca/en/news/statements/2025/01/15/first-ministers-statement-on-the-canada-united-states-relationship.

8 Danielle Smith, https://x.com/ABDanielleSmith/status/1879640059256914037.

9 Alanna Smith and Ian Bailey, "Smith Distances herself from Take Back Alberta leader after Poilievre Comments," *Globe and Mail*, Feb. 27, 2026, https://www.theglobeandmail.com/canada/alberta/article-danielle-smith-distancing-herself-from-tba-leader-after-comments-on/.

10 Donna Kennedy-Glans, "Former backroom political staffer takes centre stage in Take Back Alberta movement," *National Post*, Nov. 27, 2024, https://nationalpost.com/news/politics/david-parker-takes-centre-stage-in-take-back-alberta.

11 Christian Lamour, "A brave old world: The Nuanced Combination of State-National Retrotopia and Transnational Populism by an Assembled Radical-right Family," *Futures* 156 (2024), 2.

12 See James Deaville and Jamie Meyers-Riczu, "How AI-Generated Music Anthems are Supporting Alberta Separatism," *Conversation*, May 21, 2026, https://theconversation.com/how-ai-generated-music-anthems-are-supporting-alberta-separatism-280419.

13 Jen Gerson, "Who Gave the Alberta Prosperity Society $1million?" *Line*, Mar. 17, 2026, https://www.readtheline.ca/p/jen-gerson-who-gave-the-alberta-prosperity.

14 Emily Mertz, "NDP received more donations than UCP in 2022: Elections Alberta reports," Jan. 31, 2023, https://globalnews.ca/news/9450268/alberta-ndp-ucp-political-donations-fundraising/.

15 Alberta Law Society report on the conduct of Jefferey Rath, May 8, 2025, https://documents.lawsociety.ab.ca/wp-content/uploads/2024/07/29093605/Rath-Jeffrey-HE20240189-HCR-Public.pdf.

16 Jonny Wakefield, "Alberta separatist lawyer facing hearing over allegations of 'abusive, offensive' communication in legal case," *Edmonton Journal*, May 28, 2026, https://edmontonjournal.com/news/politics/alberta-separatist-lawyer-jeffrey-rath-law-society-hearing-abusive-offensive-communication-allegations.

17 Zena Olijnyk, "Alberta judge overturns $11.5M contingency fee award for Indigenous benefits settlement," *Canadian Lawyer*, Dec. 10, 2020, https://www.canadianlawyermag.com/practice-areas/litigation/alberta-judge-overturns-115m-contingency-fee-award-for-indigenous-benefits-settlement/336156.

18 "Canada Settles Agricultural Benefits specific claims with nine First Nations under Treaties 5,6 and 10," media release, Oct. 18, 2024, https://www.canada.ca/en/crown-indigenous-relations-northern-affairs/news/2024/10/canada-settles-agricultural-benefits-specific-claims-with-nine-first-nations-under-treaties-5-6-and-10.html.

19 "Court of Appeal finds agreement resulting in $28 million lawyer's fee unenforceable," Sturgeon Lake Cree Nation statement, Feb. 27, 2025, https://www.facebook.com/photo/?fbid=1164208515712029&set=a.740700841396134

20 Jeffrey Rath, interview by Elie Cantin-Nantel, Mar. 28, 2026, 5:19, https://www.youtube.com/watch?v=IosZoZU_SFo&t=420s.
21 Ilya Gridneff and Myles McCormick, "Trump officials met group pushing Alberta independence from Canada," *Financial Times*, Jan 29, 2026, https://www.ft.com/content/11dc2140-6a5d-4536-b766-52c920affcc7?syn-25a6b1a6=1.
22 Jeffrey Rath, interview by Vassy Kapelos, CTV News, Feb. 1, 2026, https://www.youtube.com/watch?v=LiHzFnRPDM8.
23 By "the three of us" Rath meant his APP partners Dennis Modry and Mitch Sylvestre.
24 Charles Rusnell, "Alberta Health Services criticized for 'unlawful' suspension of surgeon," CBC News, Feb. 25, 2015, https://www.cbc.ca/news/canada/edmonton/alberta-health-services-criticized-for-unlawful-suspension-of-surgeon-1.2971785.
25 Holmes v. Modry 2025 BCSC 430, Mar. 12, 2025, https://www.canlii.org/en/bc/bcsc/doc/2025/2025bcsc430/2025bcsc430.html?resultId=8d9fdd64e4b04f42b4f48c48dc88088f&searchId=2026-02-19T14:01:38:135/6ad98fe520a94260acdceof130ff6ffb, para 25.
26 Kevin Maimann, "Family seeking $1.3M owed by Alberta separatist leader Dennis Modry after court order," CBC News, Mar. 4, 2026, https://www.cbc.ca/news/canada/dennis-modry-misappropriated-funds-9.7105913.
27 "Open letter from a doctor to Jason Kenney," Western Standard, Dec. 11, 2020, https://www.westernstandard.news/opinion/must-read-open-letter-from-a-doctor-to-jason-kenney/article_38f6a560-f8fb-5e0a-86b9-ee5ffa8449d5.html.
28 Jason Kenney, https://x.com/jkenney/status/1371631509426171909.
29 Clarification of information penned by formerly registered physician Dr Modry, media release, College of Physicians and Surgeons of Alberta, Dec. 17, 2020, https://cpsa.ca/news/clarification-of-information-penned-by-formerly-registered-physician-dr-modry/.
30 Allan Smith and Abigail Williams, "Canadian separatists optimistic after meetings with Trump officials," NBC News Feb. 12, 2026, https://www.nbcnews.com/politics/trump-administration/canadian-separatists-alberta-meetings-trump-officials-rcna258230.
31 Rachel Parker, "Trump's INSANE PLAN for Alberta Independence," Dec. 24, 2025, https://www.youtube.com/watch?v=voRmBN-JF2k&t=1194s.
32 Parker, "Trump's INSANE PLAN," 21:00, https://www.youtube.com/watch?v=voRmBN-JF2k.
33 "Ottawa 'steals' $50 BILLION per year from Alberta: Jeffrey Rath," Rebel News, Nov. 27, 2025, 2:02, https://www.youtube.com/watch?v=oZO5K7O1lZs&t=1s.
34 Parker, "Trump's INSANE PLAN," 20:31, https://www.youtube.com/watch?v=voRmBN-JF2k.
35 Alberta Prosperity Project, *The Value of Freedom: A Draft Fully Costed Fiscal Plan for an Independent Alberta* (2025), https://albertaprosperityproject.com/wp-content/uploads/2025/11/Value_of_Freedom-DraftFiscal-Plan-10July2025.pdf.
36 Jeffrey Rath, interview by Elie Cantin-Nantel, Mar. 28, 2026, 7:00, https://www.youtube.com/watch?v=IosZoZU_SFo.
37 Tyler Dawson, *The Republic of Alberta* (Toronto: Sutherland House, 2026), 78.
38 APP, *The Value of Freedom*, 29. This racist dog whistle plays on the trope that immigrants are poor drivers.
39 Marc Froese, interview with author, June 6, 2026.
40 Julia Carrie Wong, "Pete Hegseth's holy war: The militant Christian theology animating the US attack on Iran," *Guardian*, Apr. 10, 2026, https://www.theguardian.com/us-news/ng-interactive/2026/apr/10/pete-hegseth-christianity-iran-war-crusade.

41 Homily of Pope Leo XIV, Mar. 29, 2026, https://www.vatican.va/content/leo-xiv/en/homilies/2026/documents/20260329-palme.html.

42 These include Iran, Iraq, Nigeria, Somalia, Syria, Venezuela, and Yemen. See Aaron Blake "Trump's 'blow 'em up' threat to Oman means he's now attacked or threatened 1 out of every 13 countries," CNN, May 27, 2026, https://www.cnn.com/2026/05/27/politics/oman-trump-threat-attack-countries.

43 Thomas Homer-Dixon and Adam Gordon, "We need to prepare for the possibility that the US uses military coercion against Canada," *Globe and Mail*, Jan. 5, 2026, https://www.theglobeandmail.com/opinion/article-we-need-to-prepare-for-the-possibility-that-the-us-uses-military/.

7: CONSTITUTIONAL CRASH OUT

1 Author interview with Chief Desmond Bull, 6 July 2026.

2 Richard Warnica, "I went home to the heartland of Alberta independence. Even after covering Donald Trump for 10 years, I was still terrified by what I found," *Toronto Star*, July 27, 2026, https://www.thestar.com/opinion/star-columnists/im-an-albertan-whos-been-covering-donald-trump-for-10-years-i-went-home-to-write-about-the-independence-movement-i-was-terrified-by-what-i-saw/article_2a003f93-2769-4509-97bd-5b03e841c966.html. See also: Andrew Coyne, "Canada is one of history's most successful countries. Here's a look at who's trying to destroy it and why," *Globe and Mail*, May 15, 2026, https://www.theglobeandmail.com/opinion/article-canada-is-one-of-historys-most-successful-countries-heres-a-look-at/

3 Richard Warnica, "I went home to the heartland of Alberta independence," *Toronto Star*, May 8, 2026, https://www.thestar.com/opinion/star-columnists/im-an-albertan-whos-been-covering-donald-trump-for-10-years-i-went-home-to-write-about-the-independence-movement-i-was-terrified-by-what-i-saw/article_2a003f93-2769-4509-97bd-5b03e841c966.html.

4 Chief Desmond Bull, interview with author, July 6, 2026..

5 Letter to Premier Danielle Smith, Apr. 30, 2025, https://www.sturgeonlake.ca/wp-content/uploads/2020/07/Cease-Desist-Premier-Smith_1.pdf.

6 Janice Makokis, Doreen Cardinal-Somers, and Orlagh O'Kelly, "Oh Canada: Alberta is on native land," *Globe and Mail*, May 8, 2025, https://www.theglobeandmail.com/opinion/article-oh-canada-alberta-is-on-native-land/.

7 Letter to Prime Minister Mark Carney, Apr. 30, 2025, https://mikisewcree.ca/letter-to-prime-minister-carney-request-to-uphold-treaties.

8 "Blackfoot Confederacy Chiefs Denounce Bill 54 and Affirm Blackfoot Treaty Sovereignty," media release, May 1, 2025, https://blackfootconfederacy.ca/blackfoot-confederacy-chiefs-denounce-bill-54-and-affirm-blackfoot-treaty-sovereignty/.

9 "Joint Media Statement Regarding Alberta's Place in Confederation," media release, May 2, 2025, https://tsuutina.com/wp-content/uploads/2025/05/G4-Nations-Statement-on-Separation.pdf.

10 "Potential for Alberta Separation," Pikani Nation.com, May 2, 2025, https://piikanination.com/posts/2025-05-02_potential-for-alberta-separation.

11 The Constitution Acts 1867 to 1982 91 (24), https://laws-lois.justice.gc.ca/eng/const/page-3.html.

12 Robert Hamilton, "'Get the province of Alberta in line': Treaty Promises, Provincial Power, and the Role of Indigenous Nations in Discussions on Alberta Secession," ABLawg.ca, May 30, 2025: https://ablawg.ca/2025/05/30/get-the-province-of-alberta-in-line-treaty-promises-provincial-power-and-the-role-of-indigenous-nations-in-discussions-on-alberta-secession/.

13 "Smith makes demands of Ottawa and separation talk," *Alberta Views*, May 5, 2025, https://albertaviews.ca/may5-9/.
14 https://albertarepublicans.com/actionhub/mla-independence-scorecard/. See also: Sean Amato, "Is your MLA an Alberta Separatist? The Republican list draws controversy." City News, Feb. 6, 2026, https://calgary.citynews.ca/2026/02/06/alberta-ucp-mla-separatists/.
15 "MLAs Supporting Independence," Republican Party of Alberta, https://albertarepublicans.com/actionhub/mla-independence-scorecard/.
16 "MLAs Supporting Independence," Republican Party of Alberta. MLA RJ Sigurdson and MLA Rajan Sawhney requested their names be removed from Cameron Davies' Seperatist Scorecard, which he obliged. Davies has said he is happy to remove any names of MLAs at their request.
17 The Alberta Washington Office is co-located within the Canadian Embassy at 501 Pennsylvania Ave N.W., Washington, D.C. See both: Dan Singleton, "Longtime Olds-Didsbury MLA to step down and head to Washington," *The Albertan*, May 7, 2025, https://www.thealbertan.com/olds-news/longtime-olds-didsbury-mla-to-step-down-and-head-to-washington-10629126; and Donna Kennedy-Glans, "The complicated, high-risk task ahead for Alberta's new man in D.C.," *National Post*, June 22, 2025, https://nationalpost.com/news/albertas-new-man-in-dc-nathan-cooper.
18 https://www.linkedin.com/in/nathan-m-cooper-16abb612/details/experience/; https://cooper4carstairs.wordpress.com/about/.
19 See Sunshine list stats for James Ragoitte, 2021, $250, 506.12, https://www.sunshineliststats.com/alberta/employers/jobs-economy-and-innovation/james-rajotte/.
20 Donna Kennedy-Glans, "The complicated, high-risk task ahead for Alberta's new man in DC," *National Post* (June 22, 2025, https://nationalpost.com/news/albertas-new-man-in-dc-nathan-cooper.
21 Timothy Snyder, *On Tyranny: Twenty Lessons from the Twentieth Century* (New York: Crown, 2017), 38.
22 Letter to Justice Colin Feasby, Dec. 4, 2025.
23 Adam M. Dodek, "Lawyering at the Intersection of Public Law and Legal Ethics: Government Lawyers as Custodians of the Rule of Law," *Dalhousie Law Journal* 33, no. 1 (2010): 1.
24 Wirring v. Law Society of Alberta, 2025 ABCA 413 (CanlII), https://canlii.ca/t/kh2qt.
25 Court of King's Bench of Alberta. Chief Electoral Officer of Alberta and Mitch Sylvestre and Minister of Justice of Alberta. Reasons for decision of the Honourable Justice Colin C.J. Feasby 2025-12-05, https://www.canlii.org/en/ab/abkb/doc/2025/2025abkb712/2025abkb712.html, paras 250–254.
26 Court of King's Bench of Alberta. Reasons for decision, para 252.
27 Court of King's Bench of Alberta. Reasons for decision, paras 250–254.
28 Court of King's Bench of Alberta. Reasons for decision, Appendix.
29 https://www.cbc.ca/news/canada/calgary/alberta-premier-danielle-smith-says-courts-should-not-be-gatekeepers-on-independence-questions-9.7006383.
30 Court of King's Bench of Alberta. Statement from the Chief Justices, Jan. 27, 2026, https://albertacourts.ca/kb/resources/announcements/statement-from-the-chief-justices-2026.

8: THE CENTURION PLUNDER

1 Charles Rusnell, "The Wild Claims of Jeff Rath, Separatist Firebrand," *Tyee*, Jan. 26, 2026, https://thetyee.ca/News/2026/01/26/Wild-Claims-Jeff-Rath-Separatist-Firebrand/.

2 Jeffrey Rath, interview with Matt Skube, CTV News, Feb. 2, 2026, 2:50, https://www.youtube.com/watch?v=wCZSC1kGwWM.
3 Jeffrey Rath, interview with Elie Cantin-Nantel, Mar. 28, 2026, https://www.youtube.com/watch?v=IosZoZU_SFo&t=402s.
4 Jeffrey Rath, interview with Matt Skube, CTV News, Feb. 2, 2026, https://www.youtube.com/watch?v=wCZSC1kGwWM.
5 Carlos Hernández, "If you are reading this it is because I'm dead: here's what I want to tell you about how to live," *Guardian*, Feb. 6, 2026, https://www.theguardian.com/commentisfree/2026/feb/06/reading-this-i-am-dead-how-to-live.
6 Jeffrey Rath, interview with Matt Skube, CTV News, Feb. 2, 2026, https://www.youtube.com/watch?v=wCZSC1kGwWM.
7 Canada's Equalization Formula, https://lop.parl.ca/sites/PublicWebsite/default/en_CA/ResearchPublications/200820E.
8 Tegan Hill and Trevor Tombe, "Is Equalization Unfair to Alberta? A Dialogue," *Alberta Views*, Dec. 1, 2025, https://albertaviews.ca/equalization-payment-unfair-alberta/.
9 Michelle Bellefontaine, "Albert judge extends order freezing separatist lawyer's assets in legal dispute with First Nation," CBC News, July 15, 2026, https://www.cbc.ca/news/canada/edmonton/rath-mareva-order-extended-alberta-first-nation-9.7271969.
10 In the Court of King's Bench of Alberta, Rupert Meneen and Jeffrey R.W. Rath Professional Corporation, carrying on business as Rath & Company, in its capacity as Trustee of Jeffrey R.W. Rath, July 15, 2026, Decision, 17.
11 Ashleigh Stewart, "'Pattern of Behaviour': Rath faces mounting questions over First Nations trusts," Global News, July 15, 2026, https://globalnews.ca/news/11967739/jeff-rath-first-nations-trusts/.
12 Court file 2601-11367, Court of King's Bench Alberta, July 15, 2026. Jeffrey R.W. Rath Professional Corporation. Receivership Order.
13 See "Marty Up North" on the Western Standard website, hosted by Marty Belanger, an openly racist separatist who has posted videos of himself abusing elderly women while collecting petition signatures at the side of an Alberta highway.
14 Charles Rusnell, Bluesky, July 3, 2026, https://bsky.app/profile/charlesrusnell.bsky.social/post/3mpp2ph53jc2b. I emailed Rusnell to inquire about an image included in his post. Rusnell found the item on the government of Alberta's sole-source contracting website, which provides disclosure of contracts that were not competitively let.
15 David J. Climenhaga, "Is the Alberta Prosperity Project having trouble getting signatures for separation petition," *Rabble*, Mar. 10, 2026, https://rabble.ca/politics/canadian-politics/is-the-alberta-prosperity-project-having-trouble-getting-signatures-for-separation-petition/.
16 Jesse Snyder, "Alberta's separatists are running into an administrative snag as they look to collect 177,000 signatures," *National Post*, Mar. 27, 2026, https://nationalpost.com/news/canada/alberta-separatists-petition.
17 Lauren Heintz, "Organizers of Alberta separatism petition say signature goal has been reached one month ahead of deadline," CityNews, Mar. 31, 2026, https://calgary.citynews.ca/2026/03/31/alberta-separatism-petition-signatures/.
18 Jen Gerson, "Elections Alberta's massive failure could have put people in danger. I tried to warn them," *The Line*, Apr. 30, 2026, https://open.substack.com/pub/theline/p/scoop-jen-gerson-elections-albertas?r=19io5h&utm.

19 Lisa Johnson, "Alberta's chief electoral officer warns proposals in Bill 54 will hurt investigations," CBC News, May 10, 2025, https://www.cbc.ca/news/canada/edmonton/alberta-electoral-officer-bill-54-voting-referendum-1.7532070.
20 "Message to Albertans Re: Unauthorized Use of List of Electors," May 1, 2026, https://www.elections.ab.ca/resources/media/news-releases/message-to-albertans-re-unauthorized-use-of-list-of-electors/.
21 Carrie Tait, Chen Wang, and Matthew Scace, "RCMP probing allegations that Alberta separatist organization accessed, distributed electors list," *Globe and Mail*, Apr. 30, 2026, https://www.theglobeandmail.com/canada/alberta/article-elections-alberta-confirms-potential-data-breach/.
22 https://www.freedomcalendar.net.
23 "The Centurion Project: Engaging Citizens in the Political Process," The Critical Compass, May 1, 2026, https://www.youtube.com/watch?v=kyHBHfNT2Hk&t=769s. Also see reporting from Jeremy Appel, who broke the story of the Elections Alberta raid on the Centurion Event he attended: "Elections Alberta investigating separatist for accessing the voters list," The Orchard, Apr. 30, 2026, (30 April 2026), https://www.youtube.com/watch?v=kyHBHfNT2Hk&t=769s.
24 See Timothy Caulfield, "Lies, Damn Lies, and Tucker Carlson," *Walrus*, Jan. 25, 2026, https://thewalrus.ca/tucker-carlson-alberta/.
25 Sam Forster, "An Interview with Alberta separatist leader Cameron Davies," *Canadian Affairs*, June 22, 2025, https://www.canadianaffairs.news/2025/06/22/republican-party-of-alberta-leader-interview/.
26 "Alleged Inappropriate Distribution of List of Electors," Elections Alberta media release, Apr. 30, 2026, https://www.elections.ab.ca/resources/media/news-releases/alleged-inappropriate-distribution-of-list-of-electors/.
27 Luke LeBrun, "Alberta Separatist Group's Controversial Voter ID App Has Links to US Ambassador, MAGA Influencers and Wealthy Michigan Republicans," *Press Progress*, May 18, 2026, https://pressprogress.ca/alberta-separatist-groups-controversial-voter-id-app-has-links-to-us-ambassador-maga-influencers-and-wealthy-michigan-republicans/.
28 Rory White, "Alberta Voter data found on website of US company linked to Centurion Project," *Canada's National Observer*, May 20, 2026, https://www.nationalobserver.com/2026/05/20/investigations/alberta-voter-data-10x-votes-centurion-project.
29 Patrick Lennox, "How Did and Alberta Separatist Group Get Its Hands on the Voter List?" *Walrus*, May 4, 2026, https://thewalrus.ca/how-did-an-alberta-separatist-group-get-its-hands-on-the-voter-list/.
30 Luke LeBrun, "Alberta Separatist Group's Controversial Voter ID App," https://pressprogress.ca/alberta-separatist-groups-controversial-voter-id-app-has-links-to-us-ambassador-maga-influencers-and-wealthy-michigan-republicans/.
31 Excerpt of Tucker Carlson speech, 10xVotes, Sept. 23, 2024, 1:40, https://www.youtube.com/watch?v=mpe7ZSmxNqs&t=148s.
32 Luke LeBrun, "Alberta Separatist Group's Controversial Voter ID App," https://pressprogress.ca/alberta-separatist-groups-controversial-voter-id-app-has-links-to-us-ambassador-maga-influencers-and-wealthy-michigan-republicans/.https://pressprogress.ca/alberta-separatist-groups-controversial-voter-id-app-has-links-to-us-ambassador-maga-influencers-and-wealthy-michigan-republicans/.
33 Angela Amato, "Alberta NDP claims 2 UCP members attended virtual Centurion Project meeting," CTV News, May 5, 2026, https://www.ctvnews.ca/edmonton/article/2-ucp-members-attended-virtual-centurion-project-meeting-ndp-shows/.

34 Jack Farrell and Lisa Johnson, "Danielle Smith says NDP should have warned her of Alberta Voter list privacy leak," Global News, May 6, 2026, https://globalnews.ca/news/11838074/alberta-separatism-centurion-project-voter-list-politician-accusations/. Nenshi had the legal responsibility to protect the list, which is covered in section 19 of the Elections Act.

35 UCP statement quoted in Dan Singleton, "'Flat out lie': Olds-area man not in separatist meeting linked to voters list breach," *The Albertan*, May 6, 2026, https://www.thealbertan.com/mountain-view-county-news/flat-out-lie-olds-area-man-not-in-separatist-meeting-linked-to-voters-list-breach-12243987.

36 Angela Amato, "Alberta NDP claims 2 UCP members attended virtual Centurion Project meeting," CTV News, May 5, 2026, https://www.ctvnews.ca/edmonton/article/2-ucp-members-attended-virtual-centurion-project-meeting-ndp-shows/.

37 Jared Wesley, "A call for an independent public inquiry into the management and use of Alberta's voter list," *Canada's National Observer*, May 7, 2026, https://www.nationalobserver.com/2026/05/07/opinion/call-independent-public-inquiry-management-use-albertas-voters-list.

38 Marcus Kolga, Jennie Phillips, Brian McQuinn, and Bartel Ven de Walle, *Decision Making and National Unity Under Threat: Foreign Interference, Cognitive Sovereignty, and the Alberta Referendum*, May 6, 2026, https://disinfowatch.org/wp-content/uploads/2026/05/Alberta-and-Foreign-Interference-Report-Final-052026-web.pdf.

39 Marcus Kolga, interview with author, July 10, 2026.

40 Pjotr Sauer and Shaun Walker, "Revealed: Russia's top secret spy school teaching hacking and election meddling," *Guardian*, May 7, 2026), https://www.theguardian.com/world/2026/may/07/revealed-russia-top-secret-spy-school-hacking-western-electoral-interference.

41 "Citizen Initiative Petition Verification Begins," media release, Elections Alberta, July 6, 2026, https://www.elections.ab.ca/resources/media/news-releases/ci-petition-verification-begins-sylvestre/.

42 https://www.elections.ab.ca/recall-initiative/initiative/current-initiative-petitions/

43 "Elections Alberta verifies signatures for petition calling for independence reference," CBC News, July 25, 2026, https://www.cbc.ca/news/canada/edmonton/elections-alberta-separation-petition-verified-9.7283199.

44 "'Anti-Democratic': Danielle Smith Slams Judge For Tossing Alberta Referendum," CTV Your Morning, May 14, 2026, https://www.youtube.com/watch?v=jjaWqPfbWO4.

45 Jackie Carmichael, "Alberta Premier Danielle Smith defends decision to appeal court ruling on separatism petition," *Edmonton Journal*, May 16, 2026, https://edmontonjournal.com/news/politics/alberta-premier-danielle-smith-defends-appeal-separatism-petition.

46 Letter to Prime Minister Mark Carney, May 15, 2026, signed by Chief Sheldon Sunshine and Chief Billy-Joe Tuccaro of Sturgeon Lake Cree Nation and Mikisew Cree First Nation, https://www.facebook.com/story.php?story_fbid=1526061842882567&id=100064362986855&mibextid=wwXIfr&rdid=H9Mf3eMEjmZQuOVp.

47 Karen Bartko, "Alberta referendum committee meeting implodes when UCP prematurely releases statement," Global News, May 20, 2026, https://globalnews.ca/news/11858047/alberta-select-special-citizen-initiative-proposal-review-committee-meeting-chaos/.

48 Premier's Address to the Province, May 21, 2026, https://www.alberta.ca/premiers-address-to-the-province.
49 Constitutional Referendum Amendment Act, 1992.
50 Joel Dryden, "Nate Horner, Matt Jones stepping down as Alberta cabinet ministers," CBC News, May 20, 2026, https://www.cbc.ca/news/canada/calgary/nate-horner-alberta-finance-minister-matt-jones-9.7206189.

PART III: COMING TO JUDGMENT

9: THE DONBAS OF THE PRAIRIES

1 "Understanding Foreign Interference," see in particular "Why Canada is a Target," Public Safety Canada, https://www.publicsafety.gc.ca/cnt/ntnl-scrt/frgn-ntrfrnc/ndrstndng-frgn-ntrfrnc-en.aspx.
2 *Global State of Democracy 2022: Forging Social Contracts in a Time of Discontent*, Global State of Democracy Initiative, https://www.idea.int/democracytracker/gsod-report-2022.
3 "Hundreds of scholars say U.S. is swiftly heading toward authoritarianism," NPR, Apr. 22, 2025, https://www.npr.org/2025/04/22/nx-s1-5340753/trump-democracy-authoritarianism-competive-survey-political-scientist.
4 "Erosion of the rule of law in Trump's second term," Bright Line Watch, 2026, https://brightlinewatch.org/erosion-of-the-rule-of-law-in-trumps-second-term/.
5 Steven Levitsky and Lucan Way, "The New Competitive Authoritarianism," *Journal of Democracy* 31, no. 1 (2020): 51–65.
6 Frank Langfitt, "Is the U.S. slipping into 'Competitive Authoritarianism?'" NPR, May 16, 2026, https://www.npr.org/2026/05/13/nx-s1-5816313/word-of-week-competitive-authoritarianism.
7 "President Trump Discusses the Capture of Nicolás Maduro in Venezuela," Senate Democrats, Jan. 3, 2026, https://www.democrats.senate.gov/newsroom/trump-transcripts/transcript-president-trump-discusses-the-capture-of-nicolas-maduro-in-venezuela-10326.
8 Kerry Buck, "Trump's National Security Strategy is hostile to Canada—and the democratic world," *Globe and Mail*, Dec. 8, 2025, https://www.theglobeandmail.com/opinion/article-trumps-national-security-strategy-is-hostile-to-canada-and-the/.
9 Timothy Snyder, *The Road to Unfreedom* (New York: Crown, 2018), 105.
10 "Russia meddled in Scottish independence referendum to aid SNP, claims security expert," *Express*, Jan. 15, 2017, https://www.express.co.uk/news/uk/754332/russia-spies-scotland-independence-referendum-aid-snp-claims-security-expert.
11 Severin Carrell, "Russian cyber-activists 'tried to discredit Scottish independence vote,'" *Guardian*, Dec. 13, 2017, https://www.theguardian.com/politics/2017/dec/13/russian-cyber-activists-tried-to-discredit-scottish-independence-vote-says-analyst.
12 Snyder, *Road to Unfreedom*, 105.
13 National Centre for Social Research, "Scottish Social Attitudes survey marks 25 years tracking Scotland's changing views," Oct. 9, 2025, https://natcen.ac.uk/news/scottish-social-attitudes-survey-marks-25-years-tracking-scotlands-changing-views.
14 Adrian Chen, "The Agency," *New York Times Magazine*, June 2, 2015.
15 Emily Ebbott, Morgan Saletta, and Richard Stearne, *Understanding Mass Influence: A Case Study of the Internet Research Agency as a Contemporary Mass Influence Operation*, 2021, 5, https://www.unsw.edu.au/content/dam/pdfs/unsw-canberra/dri/2023-02-research/2023-02-Understanding-Mass-Influence---A-case-study-of-the-Internet-Research-Agency.pdf.

16 Dan Sabbagh, Luke Harding, and Andrew Roth, "Russia report reveals UK government failed to investigate Kremlin interference," *Guardian*, July 21, 2020), https://www.theguardian.com/world/2020/jul/21/russia-report-reveals-uk-government-failed-to-address-kremlin-interference-scottish-referendum-brexit.
17 *"UK government 'did not want to know' about Russian interference in EU referendum,"* Guardian News, July 21, 2020, https://www.youtube.com/watch?v=VOPkVopQP7k
18 See Carole Cadwalladr, "The Great British Brexit robbery: how our democracy was hijacked," *Guardian*, May 7, 2017, https://www.theguardian.com/technology/2017/may/07/the-great-british-brexit-robbery-hijacked-democracy. See also Carole Cadwalladr, "AggregateIQ: the obscure Canadian tech firm and the Brexit data riddle," *Guardian*, Mar. 31, 2018, https://www.theguardian.com/uk-news/2018/mar/31/aggregateiq-canadian-tech-brexit-data-riddle-cambridge-analytica and Peter Geoghegan, *Democracy For Sale: Dark Money and Dirty Politics* (London: Head of Zeus, 2021).
19 The Cambridge Analytica Files, March 17, 2018, https://www.theguardian.com/news/2018/mar/17/cambridge-analytica-facebook-influence-us-election.
20 Idrees Kahloon, "How Britain Became as Poor as Mississippi," *Atlantic* (July 2026), https://www.theatlantic.com/magazine/2026/07/uk-productivity-economy-reform-party/687303/.
21 Nicolas Bloom, Philip Bunn, Paul Mizen, Pawel Smietanka, and Gregory Thwaites, "The Economic Impact of Brexit," National Bureau of Economic Research, working paper 34459 (2025), https://www.nber.org/papers/w34459.
22 Nicole Perlroth, *This is How They Tell Me the World Ends: The Cyber Weapons Arms Race* (New York: Bloomsbury, 2023), 314–16.
23 Michael S. Schmidt. "Trump Invited the Russians to Hack Clinton. Were they Listening?" *New York Times*, July 13, 2018, https://www.nytimes.com/2018/07/13/us/politics/trump-russia-clinton-emails.html.
24 Stephanie Murray, "Putin: I wanted Trump to win the election," *Politico*, July 16, 2018, https://www.politico.com/story/2018/07/16/putin-trump-win-election-2016-722486.
25 "Assessing Russian Activities and Intentions in Recent US Elections," Office of the Director of National Intelligence, Jan. 6, 2017, ii, https://www.govinfo.gov/app/details/GOVPUB-PREX28-PURL-gpo76345.
26 Robert S. Mueller, *Report on the Investigation Into Russian Interference in the 2016 Election*, Vol. I, 1–5 (Washington: US Department of Justice, 2019).
27 *Mueller report*, 1–4; 14–35.
28 *Mueller report*, 1–5, 36–50.
29 Mueller report, 50–51.
30 Olga Lautman, "Catalonia: Where There's Trouble There's Russia," Centre for European Policy Analysis, Sept. 27, 2021, https://cepa.org/article/catalonia-where-theres-trouble-theres-russia/.
31 Vasco Cotovio and Emanuella Grinberg, "Spain: 'Misinformation' on Catalonia referendum came from Russia," CNN, Nov. 13, 2017, https://edition.cnn.com/2017/11/13/europe/catalonia-russia-connection-referendum.
32 David E. Alandete, *Russian Interference in the Catalan Independence Crisis (2014–2022)*, European People's Party Group (2022), 16, https://octuvre.cat/wp-content/uploads/2024/01/Russian_interference_in_the_Catalan_inde.pdf?utm.
33 "Russian National Charged with Conspiring to Have U.S. Citizens Act as Illegal Agents of the U.S. Government," media release, US Department of Justice, July 29, 2022, https://www.justice.gov/archives/opa/pr/russian-national-charged-conspiring-have-us-citizens-act-illegal-agents-russian-government.

34 "Alexander Ionov case: US charges Russian with interfering in US politics," BBC News, July 30, 2022, https://www.bbc.com/news/world-us-canada-62359884.

35 Antonio Baquero, Kevin Hall, Alina Tsogoeva, Jesús G. Albalat, Christo Grozev, Lorenzo Bagnoli, and Stefano Vergine, *Fueling Secession, Promising Bitcoins: How a Russian Operator Urged Catalonian Leaders to Break with Madrid*, Organized Crime and Corruption Reporting Project, May 8, 2022, https://www.occrp.org/en/investigation/fueling-secession-promising-bitcoins-how-a-russian-operator-urged-catalonian-leaders-to-break-with-madrid. See also Christina Gallardo, "Russian group offered Catalan separatist leaders 10,000 soldiers, judge says," *Politico*, Oct. 28, 2020, https://www.politico.eu/article/russian-group-offered-catalan-separatist-leaders-10000-soldiers-according-to-judge/.

36 "How 'separatists' are prosecuted in Russia—Independence lawyers on one of Russia's most controversial statutes," *Meduza*, Sept. 21, 2016, https://meduza.io/en/feature/2016/09/21/how-separatists-are-prosecuted-in-russia.

37 "Meeting of the Valdai International Discussion Club," President of Russia English website, Oct. 19, 2017, http://en.kremlin.ru/events/president/news/55882.

38 Serhiy Kudelia, *Seize the City, Undo the State: The Inception of Russia's War on Ukraine* (Oxford: Oxford University Press, 2025), 74.

39 Kudelia, *Seize the City*, 83.

40 Allan Smith and Abigail Williams, "Canadian separatists optimistic after meetings with Trump officials," NBC News, Feb. 12, 2026, https://www.nbcnews.com/politics/trump-administration/canadian-separatists-alberta-meetings-trump-officials-rcna258230. See also Stephanie Ha, "'High level': Alberta separatist group won't confirm which members of Trump's administration it met with," CTV News, Feb. 1, 2026, https://www.ctvnews.ca/politics/article/high-level-alberta-separatist-group-wont-confirm-which-members-of-trumps-administration-it-met-with/ and Jeffrey Rath, interview with Rachel Parker, 16:36–16:42, https://www.youtube.com/watch?v=voRmBN-JF2k&t=1195s.

41 Jeffrey Rath, interview with Rachel Parker, 15:55–16:18, https://www.youtube.com/watch?v=voRmBN-JF2k&t=1195s.

42 Marcus Kolga et al., *Decision Making and National Unity Under Threat*, 13, https://disinfowatch.org/wp-content/uploads/2026/05/Alberta-and-Foreign-Interference-Report-Final-052026-web.pdf.

43 Stephanie Baker and Priyanjana Bengani, "The Most Potent Weapon in Russia's Disinformation War," Bloomberg, Apr. 27, 2026, https://www.bloomberg.com/graphics/2026-russia-disinformation-storm-1516-videos/?embedded-checkout=true. See also Nadiya Balovsiak, "Storm-1516 and rise of Russia's disinformation networks," Ukrainian Week, June 14, 2026, https://ukrainianweek.com/storm-1516-russian-disinformation/. Storm-1516 is thought to be a continuation of the Internet Research Agency, which was shut down after Putin and Prigozhin had a falling out. Soon afterwards, Prigozhin died in a plane crash.

44 "Analysis of the Russian information manipulation set Storm-1516," Secrétariat general de la défense et de la sécurité national (May 2025), https://www.sgdsn.gouv.fr/files/files/Publications/20250507_TLP-CLEAR_NP_SGDSN_VIGINUM_Technical%20report_Storm-1516.pdf.

45 Chris Kremidas-Courtney, "Storm-1516: A wake-up call for Europe's cognitive defence," European Policy Centre, May 13, 2025, https://www.epc.eu/publication/Storm-1516-A-wake-up-call-for-Europes-cognitive-defence-650d24/.

46 In an interview with Rise of Alberta on May 9, 2025, Jeffrey Rath argued that the US and other countries would recognize Alberta as an independent country on the day it declared itself to be such, drawing parallels to Kosovo, https://www.instagram.com/reels/DJcbYMxyQEt/.

47 Keith Wilson, "The US Will Recognize Alberta's Independence," Dec. 26, 2025, https://www.youtube.com/watch?v=8CoLUYPoxs8.
48 Balovsiak, "Storm-1516." https://ukrainianweek.com/storm-1516-russian-disinformation/.
49 See Chris Ross, Ben Steel, Zeynep Pehlivan, Mika Desblancs-Patel, and Aengus Bridgman, "Slopaganda: The Inauthentic YouTube Network Selling Secession to Albertans," Apr. 21, 2026, https://www.cdmrn.ca/slopaganda-the-inauthentic-youtube-network-selling-secession-to-albertans. See also Eric Szeto, Ivan Angelovski, Christian Paas-Lang, Jordan Pearson, Jeff Yates, and Nicholas De Rosa, "Dutch YouTube creators behind Alberta separatist videos getting millions of views," CBC News, Apr. 23, 2026, https://www.cbc.ca/news/canada/alberta-separatist-youtube-channels-netherlands-9.7174719.
50 See Chris Ross et al., "Slopaganda," 1.
51 Eric Szeto et al, "Dutch YouTube creators," https://www.cbc.ca/news/canada/alberta-separatist-youtube-channels-netherlands-9.7174719.
52 See my comments in Charles Rusnell, "The Dishonest Online Campaign to Support Alberta Separatism," *Tyee*, Apr. 21, 2026, https://thetyee.ca/News/2026/04/21/Dishonest-Online-Campaign-Support-Alberta-Separatism/.
53 "Steve Bannon on Trump's Threat to Canada," Jan. 19, 2026, https://www.youtube.com/watch?v=U3SrW56kbVo.
54 "Steve Bannon Explains Why Canada Should Consider Trump's Game Changing Proposal," JV News Nation, Feb. 6, 2025.
55 "Bannon: Canada Hostile to the United States," DisinfoWatch, Jan. 18, 2026, https://www.youtube.com/watch?v=nBWzkbWOWIE.
56 Emma Graney and Matthew Scace, "Experts worry Elections Alberta lacks the resources to deal with foreign interference," *Globe and Mail*, Jan. 24, 2026, https://www.theglobeandmail.com/business/article-experts-worry-elections-alberta-lacks-resources-to-deal-with-foreign/.
57 Daniel Rogers, interview with David Cochrane, *Power and Politics*, Nov. 13, 2025, 9:04, https://www.youtube.com/watch?v=GX1PCJsTuco.
58 *RCMP Federal Policing: Annual Report 2022*, 10, https://rcmp.ca/sites/default/files/doc/rcmp-federal-policing-annual-report-2022.pdf.
59 Foreign Interference and Security of Information Act, https://laws-lois.justice.gc.ca/eng/acts/o-5/page-3.html#h-385110.
60 Steven Chase, "Canada's foreign influence registry to come into force in early August," *Globe and Mail*, July 2, 2026, https://www.theglobeandmail.com/politics/article-canadas-foreign-influence-registry-expected-to-launch-in-early-august/.
61 Elizabeth Thompson, "Foreign influence commissioner could monitor and Alberta referendum on separation," CBC News, Feb. 26, 2026, https://www.cbc.ca/news/politics/foreign-influence-alberta-independence-9.7107301.
62 Marie Lamensch, "As Foreign Interference Takes Hold, Ottawa Looks Away," *Walrus*, Aug. 19, 2025, https://thewalrus.ca/as-foreign-interference-takes-hold-ottawa-looks-away/.

10: SURVIVING THE BIG LIE

1 Albert Camus, "Defence of Intelligence" in *Resistance, Rebellion, and Death*, trans. Justin O'Brien (New York: Vintage, 1960), 64.
2 *Final Report of the Select Committee to Investigate the January 6th Attack on the United States Capitol* (Washington: US House of Representatives, 2022), 12, https://www.govinfo.gov/content/pkg/GPO-J6-REPORT/pdf/GPO-J6-REPORT.pdf.

3 Trump's speech quoted in Jamil Smith, "Trump is invoking foreign election interference to justify his own," *Guardian*, July 19, 2026, https://www.theguardian.com/commentisfree/2026/jul/19/trump-foreign-election-interference.
4 Shane Harris, Michael Scherer, Sarah Fitzpatrick, and Yvonne Wingett Sanchez, "Trump Still Hasn't Found What He's Looking For," *Atlantic*, July 17, 2026, https://www.theatlantic.com/politics/2026/07/trump-election-fraud-speech/687950/.
5 Seth G. Jones and Riley McCabe, "Russian Blood and Treasure: The Ballooning Costs of Putin's War," Center for Strategic and International Studies (2026), https://www.csis.org/analysis/russian-blood-and-treasure-ballooning-costs-putins-war.
6 Evan Dyer, "U.S. interest in Alberta separatism raises red flags over what might come next," CBC News, Feb. 5, 2026, https://www.cbc.ca/news/politics/alberta-separatism-trump-administration-9.7068999.
7 Dylan Short, "Danielle Smith under fire for past online comments on Ukraine invasion," *Calgary Herald*, Oct. 15, 2022, https://calgaryherald.com/news/politics/online-posts-show-premier-danielle-smith-questioned-who-was-at-fault-in-russia-ukraine-conflict.
8 Justin Ling, "Danielle Smith's Magical Mystery Media," Bug-Eyed and Shameless, Oct. 18, 2022, https://www.bugeyedandshameless.com/p/danielle-smiths-magical-mystery-media?utm_source=publication-search. For video of the comment, see Justin Ling, "Danielle Smith on denuclearizing Ukraine," Oct. 18, 2022, https://www.youtube.com/watch?v=qtPuiCT8ztM. For reaction from the federal government, see Ian Bailey, "Defence minister taken aback by comments from Alberta premier about Russia's war in Ukraine," *Globe and Mail*, Oct.18, 2022, https://www.theglobeandmail.com/politics/article-politics-briefing-defence-minister-taken-aback-by-comments-from/.
9 Paula Tran, "Alberta Premier Danielle Smith not apologizing for comments over Ukraine-Russia war," Global News, Oct. 17, 2022, https://globalnews.ca/news/9204341/alberta-premier-danielle-smith-ukraine-war-comments/. See also Alex Boyd, "Danielle Smith apologizes for 'ill informed' remarks on Ukraine," *Toronto Star*, Oct. 18, 2022, https://www.thestar.com/news/canada/danielle-smith-apologizes-for-ill-informed-remarks-on-ukraine/article_5d298950-82e2-59c4-9ca8-e4ff0712a496.html.
10 Omar Sherif, "Alberta Premier Smith apologizes for past comments on Russian invasion of Ukraine," CBC News, Oct. 18, 2022, https://www.cbc.ca/news/canada/calgary/danielle-smith-apology-ukraine-remarks-1.6621165.
11 Justin Ling, "Danielle Smith spent years promising a 'sovereign' Alberta utopia. It was a mirage," *Toronto Star*, May 27, 2026, https://www.thestar.com/opinion/star-columnists/danielle-smith-claims-to-want-canadian-unity-her-past-comments-suggest-otherwise/article_55c14616-ec1b-4a2f-b83e-e819bb5 5789c.html.
12 See "Majority of Albertans Disapprove of the Danielle Smith's Performance," Ipsos, June 5, 2026, https://www.ipsos.com/en-ca/majority-albertans-disapprove-danielle-smiths-performance. See also "Premiers' Performance: Eby, Smith, and Ford each tumble to new lows approval," Angus Reid, June 11, 2026, https://angusreid.org/premiers-performance-june-2026/.
13 Michelle Bellefontaine, "Alberta overhauls election laws to allow corporate donations, change referendum thresholds," CBC News, Apr. 29, 2026, https://www.cbc.ca/news/canada/edmonton/alberta-overhauls-election-laws-to-allow-corporate-donations-change-referendum-thresholds-1.7522144.

14 Carrie Tait, "Alberta premier, ministers accepted NHL playoff tickets after voting to loosen ethics rules," *Globe and Mail*, July 18, 2024, https://www.theglobeandmail.com/canada/alberta/article-alberta-premier-minister-accepted-tickets-to-playoff-hockey-games/. See also Carrie Tait and Alanna Smith, "Board of Alberta Health Services fired on same day that investigation report was due," *Globe and Mail*, Mar. 21, 2025, https://www.theglobeandmail.com/canada/alberta/article-board-of-alberta-health-services-fired-on-same-day-that-investigation/ and Carrie Tait, Jana G. Pruden, and Tom Cardoso, "Police search offices of Sam Mraiche-owned firm as part of Alberta procurement probe," *Globe and Mail*, Mar. 18, 2026, https://www.theglobeandmail.com/canada/alberta/article-police-search-sam-mraiche-firms-hq-in-alberta-procurement-probe/.

15 The $600 million in government contracts to Sam Mraiche, if proven, are approximately twelve times as large as the previous two large-scale government corruption scandals in Canadian history. The McGill Hospital bribery case from 2014 and the SNC Lavalin bribery case that involved the federal government concerned amounts less than $50 million.

16 Dave Cournoyer, "Tracking who's who in the Alberta separation referendum debate," Daveberta, July 14, 2026, https://substack.com/home/post/p-201402418.

17 Brandi Morin, "'They hate us more now': Treaty Chiefs rally against Alberta separatism," *Ricochet Media*, June 16, 2026, https://ricochet.media/indigenous/they-hate-us-more-now-treaty-chiefs-rally-against-alberta-separatism/.

18 Danielle Smith, interview with David Akin, *The West Block*, May 10, 2026, 2:07, https://www.youtube.com/watch?v=50VxRqymDsw.

19 *Climate Promises, Industry Handouts: Canada's Fossil Fuel Funding in 2025–Media Backgrounder*, Environmental Defence (May 2026), 3, https://environmentaldefence.ca/wp-content/uploads/2026/05/Environmental_Defence_2025_FFS_Report-1.pdf-1.pdf.

20 "Premiers' Performance: Eby, Smith, and Ford each tumble to new lows approval," Angus Reid, June 11, 2026, https://angusreid.org/premiers-performance-june-2026/. See also Matthew Renfrew, "Mark Carney is more popular in Alberta than Danielle Smith and Pierre Poilievre," *Cult MTL*, July 14, 2026, https://cultmtl.com/2026/07/mark-carney-is-more-popular-in-alberta-than-danielle-smith-and-pierre-poilievre/.

21 "Limited and Declining Support for Separation in Alberta," Ipsos, June 5, 2026, https://www.ipsos.com/en-ca/limited-and-declining-support-separation-alberta. See also Tyler Dawson, "Despite what separatists think, Albertans actually aren't that mad," *Globe and Mail*, July 20, 2026, https://www.theglobeandmail.com/opinion/article-alberta-referendum-secession-vote-2019-polls/.

22 Benjamin Shingler, "Canada is still backing the fossil fuel industry with billions, report finds," CBC News, Mar. 27, 2024, https://www.cbc.ca/news/canada/fossil-fuels-canada-subsidies-1.7156152. See also Arno Kopecky, "No Matter Which Way You Look At It, Carney Has Abandoned Climate," *Walrus*, Dec. 22, 2025, https://thewalrus.ca/no-matter-which-way-you-look-at-it-carney-has-abandoned-climate/.

23 Alberta Referendum 2026, https://albertareferendum2026.ca

24 Timm Bruch, "Alberta's October referendum could cost taxpayers up to $130M: expert," CTV News, June 17, 2026, https://www.ctvnews.ca/calgary/article/albertas-october-referendum-could-cost-taxpayers-up-to-130m-expert/.

25 The result of the referendum on daylight saving time was close: 48.8% of electors favoured ending the practice and 50.2 voted to preserve it. See Referendum Results, Oct. 18, 2021, https://www.elections.ab.ca/elections/referendum/referendum-results/.

26 Jack Farrell, "'Alberta Time': Bill tabled to ditch clock changes, keep daylight time all year," CityNews, Apr. 23, 2026, https://calgary.citynews.ca/2026/04/23/alberta-daylight-time/.
27 David Berry, "Corb Lund Calls Bullshit on Alberta's Rigged Referendum Rules," *Forward Weekly*, July 5, 2026, https://forwardweekly.ca/corb-lund-referendum.
28 Desmond Bull, interview with author, July 6, 2026.
29 Rob Anderson, Barry Coooper, and Derek From, *Free Alberta Strategy: A Strong, Free and Sovereign Alberta Within Canada* (2021), https://d3n8a8pro7vhmx.cloudfront.net/albertainstitute/pages/337/attachments/original/1637104983/Free_Alberta_Strategy_-_Web_Version.pdf?1637104983https://www.freealbertastrategy.com.
30 Patrick Lennox, "Shakedown Federalism," *Alberta Views*, June 1, 2026, 40–42.
31 Rob Anderson et al., *Free Alberta Strategy*, 37, https://d3n8a8pro7vhmx.cloudfront.net/albertainstitute/pages/337/attachments/original/1637104983/Free_Alberta_Strategy_-_Web_Version.pdf?1637104983.
32 "Alberta's Danielle Smith tells First Nations Chiefs to 'check themselves' over treason accusations," Global News, June 18, 2026, https://www.youtube.com/watch?v=oA6CwXkxdAo.
33 Lisa Johnson, "Alberta premier says law will be enforced if separation vote spurs civil disobedience," CBC News, June 5, 2026, https://www.cbc.ca/news/canada/calgary/alberta-law-civil-disobedience-separation-9.7225524.
34 Luke LeBrun, "'We Want to See It Win in Coutts': Video Shows Danielle Smith Endorsing Illegal Convoy Blockade," *Press Progress*, May 2, 2023, https://pressprogress.ca/we-want-to-see-it-win-in-coutts-video-shows-danielle-smith-endorsing-illegal-convoy-blockade/.
35 Adrian Morrow, "Section 338 of the Tariff Act give Trump an easy—but untested—way to impost levies," *Globe and Mail*, July 21, 2026, https://www.theglobeandmail.com/world/us-politics/article-section-338-smoothawley-tariff-act-trump/. See also Shrai Popat, "Trump defends 50 % tariffs on Canada, saying 'they need us to survive'," *Guardian*, July 21, 2026), https://www.theguardian.com/us-news/2026/jul/21/trump-defends-tariff-canada.
36 Jessica Murphy, "'A natural partner': US treasury secretary weighs in on Alberta separatism," BBC News, Jan. 23, 2026, https://www.bbc.com/news/articles/cy8ylqxozw4o.

PATRICK LENNOX is a Canadian writer based in Edmonton, Alberta. For over a decade he worked with Canada's security and intelligence community in both Ottawa and in Edmonton to counter foreign interference. He first started writing about Canada-US relations twenty years ago, and has a PhD in political science from the University of Toronto. His previous works include *At Home and Abroad: The Canada-US Relationship and Canada's Place in the World*, and *An Independent Foreign Policy for Canada? Challenges and Choices for the Future*, co-edited with Brian Bow.

